HORACE DARWIN'S SHOP

A History of
The Cambridge Scientific Instrument Company
1878 to 1968

Horace Darwin in middle age (c. 1897).

*'You design something
for a purpose,
and you make it well,
and it ends up
being beautiful'*

ANON

HORACE DARWIN'S SHOP

A History of
The Cambridge Scientific Instrument Company
1878 to 1968

M J G CATTERMOLE
BSc, CEng, MIEE, CPhys, MInstP, MInstMC

A F WOLFE
FCIS, FCCA

Adam Hilger, Bristol & Boston

British Library Cataloguing in Publication Data

Cattermole, M. J. G.
    Horace Darwin's shop: a history of the Cambridge Scientific
    Company
    1.Cambridge Scientific Instrument Company—History
    I. Title   II. Wolfe, A. F.
    338.7′68175′0942659   HD9706.6.G74C

ISBN 0-85274-569-9

Published under the Adam Hilger imprint by IOP Publishing Limited
Techno House, Redcliffe Way, Bristol BS1 6NX, England
PO Box 230, Accord, MA 02018, USA

Typeset by Bath Typesetting Ltd, Bath
Printed in Great Britain by J W Arrowsmith Ltd, Bristol

PREFACE

THE scarcity of really skilled instrument-makers in the English provinces during the middle years of the nineteenth century is indicated by the small number of firms outside London exhibiting at the Great Exhibition of 1851 —a meagre eight entries. Furthermore, those eight manufacturers were concentrated in only four cities: Birmingham, Bristol, Liverpool and Sheffield.

During the 1870s the rapidly-developing new Departments of Physiology and Experimental Physics at Cambridge University provided the stimulus for the establishment of an instrument-making firm in what must surely have been potentially one of the prime locations in Europe. However, neither of the founders of this company—Albert Dew-Smith and Robert Fulcher—possessed sufficient knowledge of engineering to enable it to expand far beyond its initial aim of satisfying the instrument-making demands of the University. If the second partnership between Dew-Smith and Horace Darwin had not been formed in 1881—trading under the new name of The Cambridge Scientific Instrument Company —the original firm would almost certainly have folded within a very few years.

The latter part of the nineteenth century was a time not only of great scientific progress but also of major technological advance, especially in the field of electrical engineering. Indeed, some historians have referred to the period from 1880 to 1915 in British history as the time of the Second Industrial Revolution. In 1891 Darwin assumed sole control of The Cambridge Scientific Instrument Company. He was, by then, in a unique position. He had ready access to the latest work of his friends and peers at the University and a talent for creating simple, elegantly engineered designs. He diversified the products of the Company from the purely scientific to include instruments to satisfy the new and ever-increasing demands of British industry, which was struggling to meet severe competition from Germany and the USA by becoming more efficient. It was this diversification into instruments for industry which later provided the Company with a profit base sufficient to withstand the many lean years of depression during the next three-quarters of a century.

It is hoped that this account of the early years of The Cambridge Scientific Instrument Company, whilst not an analytical business history, will prove informative and useful to students of the history of instrumentation as well as being of interest to those readers who may already know something of the history of the Company and its products. The historical account in Part 1 includes mention of those instruments of particular relevance to the growth of the Company whilst the chapters in Part 2 are devoted to individual instruments or topics which seemed to deserve more detailed attention. Unfortunately many other interesting instruments made at one time or another by the Company have had to be omitted in order to keep the size of this volume within practical bounds.

As an aid to those wishing to undertake further research, comprehensive notes and references have been included for each chapter, although detailed references to all the information obtained from the archive of Cambridge Scientific Instrument Company documents in the Cambridge University Library have not been included. Instead, a copy of the typescript draft of this book, incorporating full references to this material has been deposited in the archive in the Library (C.S.I.Co., Box 37). The authors are grateful to the Library authorities for providing this facility. A short summary of the contents of the archive is included in the introduction to the list of Notes and References.

During the preparation of this book we have received help and advice from a large number of individuals and institutions. We are particularly grateful to Dr E. D. Barlow, grandson of Sir Horace Darwin, a director of the Company for twenty-five years and Chairman from 1963 to 1972 and 1974 to 1975, for his continual encouragement and for permission to research and publish material from the Company's archive in the University Library.

We acknowledge with gratitude the advice and assistance of the staffs of the following bodies:

Birmingham University Physics Department; Cambridge City Council Planning Department; Cambridge and County Folk Museum; Cambridge University Computer Laboratory; Cambridge University Engineering Department; Cambridge University Library; Cambridge University Zoological Department; the Cambridgeshire Collection at the Cambridge City Central Library; Cambridgeshire County Record Office; Cambridgeshire Mental Welfare Association; the Green Howards Regimental Museum; the House of Commons Library; the Imperial War

Museum Department of Printed Books; the Ministry of Defence Adastral Library; the Royal College of Surgeons of England, the Royal Geographical Society Map Room; the Royal Naval College Library; the Royal Society Library; the engineering staff of St Paul's Cathedral; the Science Museum, London; Trinity College Library, Cambridge; the United States Geological Survey Library, the United States Library of Congress, Science and Technology Division; the Wedgwood Museum; the Whipple Museum of the History of Science, Cambridge.

Our thanks are due to the following individuals for information received:

Mrs O. Checkland, Miss M. Croarken, Dr J. Hall (Cambridge University Library), Professor P. B. Moon (Birmingham University Physics Department), Professor C. W. Oatley (Cambridge University Engineering Department), Mr R. Potter (Surveyor to the Fabric at St Paul's Cathedral), Mrs F. Shakespear, Mr P. Titheradge (Custodian of Down House), Mrs V. Tolliday, Mrs E. K. H. Whipple, Professor M. V. Wilkes (Cambridge University Computer Laboratory). Dr M. Williams (London School of Economics Business History Unit).

We thank Mr G. P. Darwin for permission to publish Major Leonard Darwin's biographical note of Sir Horace Darwin's childhood and a number of extracts from the personal correspondence of various members of the Darwin family, and Mrs S. Gurney for permission to quote the extracts from Gwen Raverat's book *Period Piece*. We are grateful to the following bodies for permission to reproduce the illustrations listed: the Cambridge University Library (*Figures 1.1, 1.2, 2.6,* and *6.1*) the Master and Fellows of Trinity College, Cambridge (*Figure 1.4*) and the Trustees of the Wedgwood Museum (*Figure 10.1*).

We are indebted to Mr R. Wilson and Mr G. L. Young for patiently reading the manuscript and making many valuable suggestions, and to our long-suffering wives we owe a special debt of gratitude for their steadfast support throughout the researching and writing of this book.

Finally, we would like to make known our sincere appreciation of the unremitting patient assistance given by the staff of the Manuscript Room in the Cambridge University Library where the archive of The Cambridge Scientific Instrument Company is housed. To Margaret Pamplin and Peter Gautrey we extend our especial thanks, for without their help the work would not have been completed.

In conclusion, we gratefully acknowledge that the research of this book was facilitated by grants from the Twenty-Seven Foundation and the Worshipful Company of Scientific Instrument Makers.

M. J. G. C. and A. F. W.

CONTENTS

Contents

ILLUSTRATIONS

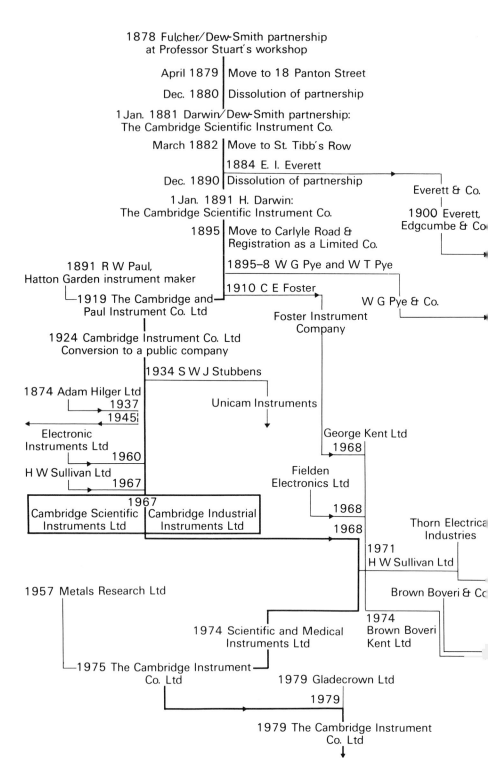

Company tree, tracing the ancestry of The Cambridge Instrument Company to the present day.

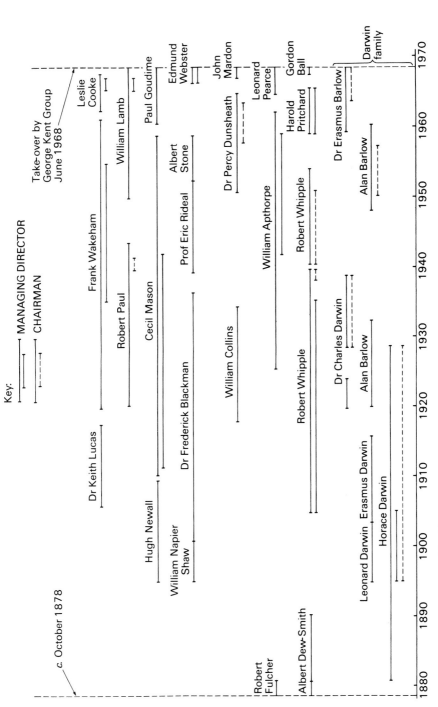

Directors of the Company.

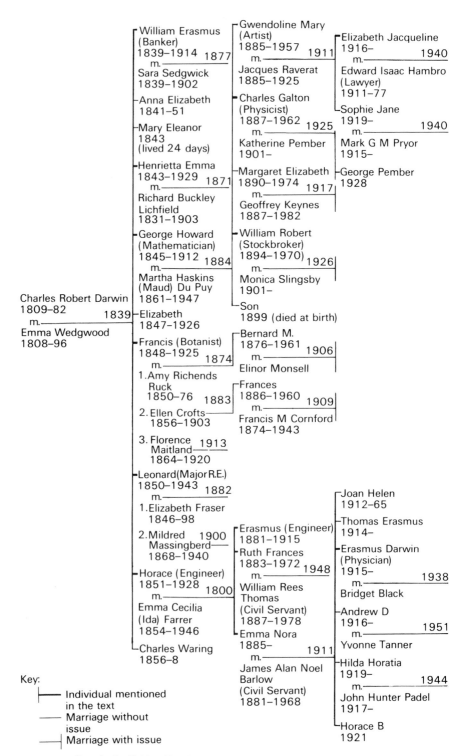

Darwin family tree. For clarity those descendants not pertinent to the text have been omitted.

Part 1

CHAPTER ONE

Horace Darwin—the young engineer

HOW does one define a 'successful man', particularly a 'business man'? An economist would undoubtedly base his answer to this question on monetary values. But surely the answer lies deeper than this. There are other ways of judging a man's standing than by financial achievement. And if the man is also an outstanding engineer and a competent scientist, monetary values become even less significant in the final assessment of that person's contribution to the progress of mankind and the wellbeing of his fellows.

Horace Darwin rarely charged realistic prices for the instruments which he designed and manufactured. His interest lay in finding the most elegant solutions to the engineering problems posed to him as an instrument designer. He ran a business, known in his family as 'Horace's Shop', and to the outside world as The Cambridge Scientific Instrument Company. In terms of the profits made by that business he was not particularly successful, but in terms of the refined simplicity of the designs he created, the quality of the products which he manufactured and the scientific and technological advances made by others using his instruments, he was outstandingly successful.

Darwin came from a famous family. He was the youngest surviving son of Charles Darwin, the eminent biologist, and was born at the family home at Downe in Kent in 1851. The following account of his childhood and adolescence is attributed to his brother, Leonard:[†1]

---

† *The original handwritten manuscript is unsigned but has been endorsed by Robert Whipple: 'Notes by Major Leonard Darwin. 12 June; 1932.' The text was apparently dictated by Leonard Darwin as the handwriting is clearly identifiable as that of Mildred Darwin, Leonard's second wife.*

Horace Darwin

Horace Darwin, the ninth child of Charles Darwin, was born on 13 May 1851 at Down House, which became his actual home or his home centre for the first 30 years of his life. As a boy his health was poor, his troubles being described as 'nervous', though whether that meant more than that the doctors were puzzled, as was the case with most of his ailments later in life, must remain an open question. This early ill health was at its worst when he was about 12 years old, after which it gradually improved, though later in life he had certain definite and serious illnesses, including one operation.†

He cared little for games when young, which no doubt helped to cut him off somewhat from other boys. He was, however, physically strong when well, he was a good high jumper, and very fond of riding. He was indeed a good and bold horseman though his opportunities for proving that this was the case were not very great. The life at Down was very quiet, chiefly because of his father's wretched health. Horace Darwin was 8 years old when the Origin of Species *was published, an epoch-making work which was completed in 13 months of incessant labour, making its author's health even worse than usual for the next three or four years.*

There were, however, five brothers who all pulled well together, and this made the need for outside friendship less felt. Horace Darwin was especially attached to his eldest brother William, the two being perhaps drawn together by similarity of character; for both were quite incapable of doing anything which they felt to be definitely wrong, whether in small things or in great. Before lawn tennis was invented, long country walks were one of the chief forms of amusement of the brotherhood, and they all acquired, perhaps especially Horace, a keen affection for that exceedingly quiet neighbourhood. Those who visit Down House, now the property of the British Association and open to the public as a memorial to Charles Darwin, can still realise how quiet the country then was if they select a view with no bungalows in sight, if they shut their eyes to all golfers and aeroplanes and if they remember that most of the grass fields were then under plough. There were footpaths in many directions, making a delightful variety of walks for those who took no thought of the cakes of mud brought back on their boots.

When Horace Darwin was born was a time of great sadness for all the Down household; for less than a month previously his sister Annie had died at Malvern, necessarily away from her mother's care. Those who wish to realise what feelings could be aroused in the mind of Charles Darwin by his affection for his children should read his pathetic description of the character of this beloved little daughter, written immediately after her death.² But putting this tragedy aside, and leaving out of account the constant strain on the mother of the family due to this cause and to the fairly frequent illnesses of her children, Down House was certainly the centre of an exceptionally happy home life.

During their earlier years the education of both sons and daughters was carried on by governesses, these being chosen, strangely enough, without much regard to their educational qualifications, but with every care in other respects. This was due to the ill health of the father, leading him during many years to leave all such questions largely in the hands of the mother, who seemed to consider that the influence of good home surroundings was of far more importance to a growing family than any mere instruction could be.

When old enough Horace Darwin was sent with a brother a year older than himself, riding on a pony and a donkey, to begin their classical education at the house of a clergyman some four miles away;‡ and here it may well be doubted whether the memory of the character of this high minded and sympathetic instructor was not of more value to him

---

† *An operation in 1893 for appendicitis, the surgeon being Sir Frederick Treves.*

‡ *The brother was Leonard. The clergyman was the Revd George Varenne Reed, rector of Hayes in Kent.*³

than any faint recollections of the elements of Latin grammar which may have remained to him throughout his life. At a later date the schoolroom at Down was turned into a workshop for Horace Darwin's use and here his lathe and other tools certainly gave him some highly valued manual training which he much enjoyed.

That he could think for himself on scientific matters when only 11 years old may be indicated by the following extract from a letter from his father to Lord Avebury. 'See what it is to be well trained. Horace said to me yesterday, "If everyone would kill adders they would come to sting less." I answered, "Of course they would, for there would be fewer." He replied indignantly, "I did not mean that; but the timid adders which run away would be saved, and in time they would never sting at all." Natural selection of cowards!'[4]

When his health had sufficiently recovered, that is, at the age of 13 or so, he was sent to a private school at Clapham, where three of his brothers were being, or had been, educated.[†] There he was neither unhappy nor particularly cheerful, for he was surrounded by an uncongenial set of school fellows and the teaching was both old-fashioned and spiritless, except in mathematics, from which he no doubt benefited considerably. The school was, in fact, rapidly going downhill, a state of things which his father failed to perceive.

During one of the school holidays, when he was just 15 years of age, he and the elder brother above mentioned, were sent alone together for a week for a tour through North Wales, which they much enjoyed; and here the object of the parents probably was to cultivate a spirit of self-confidence in these boys, a cultivation little needed in Horace Darwin's case. That he could look after himself was indicated by the fact that when hardly 17 years of age he advised his father to take him away from school and to send him to a tutor, who would give him more individual attention, an advice which was wisely followed. The result was that he spent the remainder of his time before going to Cambridge at the house of a clergyman at Southwold, where a few other pupils were being similarly trained and this was to him an enjoyable period of his life.

He entered Trinity College, Cambridge, in October 18[71] and after he had passed his 'Little Go', an obstacle not to be despised in the case of one with a broken education and a scant knowledge of classics, he devoted himself to mathematics and other scientific studies.[‡] He took his degree in the mathematical tripos, being placed amongst the [Senior Optime Class].

---

† Clapham Grammar School. William had been sent to Rugby; Charles Darwin following the custom among gentry of that period of sending the eldest son to public school and younger sons to a private school.

‡ Horace's parents were greatly relieved to hear from his brother George that Horace had passed the 'Little Go' and Charles Darwin immediately wrote the following congratulatory letter to his son:[5]

> 6 Queen Anne Street, Friday morning
> 8.30 a.m., December 15th, 1871

My dear Horace,

We are so rejoiced, for we have just had a card from that good George in Cambridge saying that you are all right and safe through the accursed 'Little Go'. I am so glad, and now you can follow the bent of your talents and work as hard at mathematics and science as your health will permit. I have been speculating last night what makes a man a discoverer of undiscovered things; and a most perplexing problem it is. Many men who are very clever—much cleverer than the discoverers —never originate anything. As far as I can conjecture, the art consists in habitually searching for the causes and meaning of everything which occurs. This implies sharp observation, and requires as much knowledge as possible of the object investigated. But why I write all this now I hardly know—except out of the fullness of my heart; for I do rejoice most heartily that you have passed this Charybdis.

> Your affectionate father,
> C. Darwin

*One cannot but suspect that he would have got a higher place in the list if he
had devoted himself more to the technicalities of mathematics, or, in other words, had been
more effectively crammed; for his was certainly an eminently mathematical mind. He did
not make a wide circle of friends at Cambridge, but amongst those who were his intimates
were Walter Leaf (see his autobiography) Frank Balfour, the eminent biologist who met
an early death when climbing in the Alps, and his brother Gerald, now Lord Balfour.
These were the type of men who quickly realised his charm and his true worth.*

*After leaving Cambridge he went as a pupil to Messrs Eastons and Anderson's
engineering works at Erith; and this he held to have been a very valuable part of his
training, more especially because he worked side by side with the regularly employed
workmen in the shops. He used often to bicycle over to Down from Erith for weekends,
probably on that type of machine with a very big wheel in front and a very little
one behind. At all events he remembered very clearly falling forward over the big front
wheel of such a bicycle which he said was a remarkable sensation because of the ample
time given in which to realise that a smash was inevitable. Later on he bought another type
of bicycle now long since forgotten, the wheels of which were made to turn in opposite
directions by the movement of the handlebar, thus enabling it to turn in a very small circle.†
When going down hill this machine had the habit of setting up a violent oscillatory
movement leading to a catastrophe far more alarming than the one just described so he
declared, from actual experience of both. These facts are only worth noting as showing how
keen he was to try all new inventions.*

*After leaving Erith he was employed for a short time at Brighton and elsewhere
in engineering in connection with water supply. But as this part of his life is better known
to others than to me I will leave it to others to place it on record.*

As a young man Horace Darwin's interest in anything scientific
was insatiable. In 1873, whilst he was still an undergraduate he began
keeping a notebook of his ideas for all sorts of mechanical devices.[6] The
contents make fascinating reading. In an early entry dated 10 September
1873 (the time of the boneshaker bicycle) Darwin describes his idea for a
bicycle wheel in which the rim would be supported from the hub by a
series of leaf springs.

A much later entry described a temperature controlled 'hot
closet'. The temperature sensing system consisted of a pair of concentric
cylinders with hot pitch filling the space between them. Whilst the inner
cylinder was rotated at a constant speed by clockwork, a constant
moment device was used to detect variations in the drag on the outer
cylinder.

Darwin took his degree of BA as a Senior Optime in the
Mathematical Tripos at Cambridge in 1874. The apprenticeship with
Messrs Eastons and Anderson of Erith, which followed, lasted for three
years and it was while he was at Erith that he designed his first scientific
instruments. One such was an auxanometer, used to record the growth of
small plants. (A pointer, lightly attached to the growing plant, traced a
record on a sheet of smoked paper wrapped round a slowly rotating
vertical drum.) The wooden drum was constructed with the aid of the
works' pattern maker and Darwin used to speak with affection of this

---

† *The 'Phantom', patented in 1868 by W. F. Reynolds and J. A. Mays.*[7]

man who was unusually kind to him. The instrument was made for his brother Francis and is now preserved in the Whipple Museum in Cambridge.

Another, better known device, was the micrometer system (*Fig.* 1.2) for use with the 'worm stone' at Down House. To enable his father to study the rate at which stones on the surface of the ground were buried by the action of worms beneath them, Darwin devised this arrangement of a large flat stone, 460 mm in diameter, with a hole in the centre. Three metal V-grooves set into the stone radially about the central hole supported a vertical micrometer and the gradual sinking of the stone by the action of worms was registered against metal rods, 2.63 m long, driven into the ground through the central hole. Experiments with the worm stone and micrometer (which may still be seen at Down House) were begun by Charles Darwin in 1877 and continued over a period of 19 years until the stone was accidentally moved in 1896. Horace Darwin reported the results in a paper to the Royal Society in 1901.[8]

Figure 1.1 Down House, the family home of the Darwins. The house was purchased in 1928 by George Buckston Browne, a Fellow of the Royal College of Surgeons, who, in a generous gesture, transferred it to the safekeeping of the British Association for the Advancement of Science, together with an endowment for its maintenance and preservation so that it might become a permanent memorial to Charles Darwin and his family. (Photo: Cambridge University Library.)

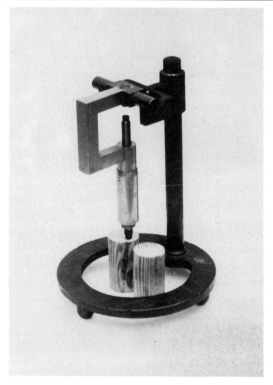

Figure 1.2 Horace Darwin's Worm Stone micrometer c. 1877. The photograph is taken from the set of slides used to illustrate the paper in which Charles Darwin's measurements were presented to the Royal Society in 1901. The wooden cylinders simulate the protruding tops of the long metal stakes which were driven into the ground in the garden of Down House. (Photo: Cambridge University Library.)

Returning to Cambridge in the autumn of 1877, Darwin began to earn a living by acting as a consulting engineer for various friends in connection with drainage and water supply schemes. He also continued to do some work for Messrs Eastons and Anderson as a consultant but, he was, by then, becoming seriously interested in instrument design. In a letter to his mother, written at the end of January, 1878, having first told her of the major investigative project he was about to undertake in Brighton (monitoring the water level of twenty-seven wells and the pressure of the mains 'at all hours of the day and night') he then went on to outline, enthusiastically, his ideas for a self-recording meteorograph:[9]

> '. . . I went to see F. Galton and asked what he thought of a self-recording thermometer I had thought of, and he approves, and says I must try some simple preliminary experiments and then get a grant from the Meteorological Committee

to try it properly, and then it would be an expensive machine and would print the temperature by wet and dry bulb thermometer, the height of the barometer, the direction of the wind, the velocity of the wind, the quantity of rain, every hour during the day and night, and the year, the month, the day of the month, and the hour on which each observations are [sic] taken; it will be jolly if I do get the grant to try all this. It will print them all on one piece of paper in a neat tabular form. Of course I shall try simply a thermometer first and see how that works. I can think of nothing else but thermographs and Waterworks. ....'

Darwin's interest in instrument design had been stimulated on his return to Cambridge by his renewed association with Albert George Dew-Smith, a former close friend from his student days. Dew-Smith, who was born on 27 October, 1848, at Salisbury, had entered Trinity College in 1869, two years before Horace Darwin. Although he did not work very seriously for his degree, he passed the Natural Science Tripos of 1872. For the latter part of his time as an undergraduate Dew-Smith studied under Dr Michael Foster, the newly appointed Trinity Praelector in Physiology, and subsequently Dew-Smith and Michael Foster became close friends. (Michael Foster was the son of Michael Foster FRCS, a surgeon practising in Huntingdon, near Cambridge. Educated at Huntingdon Grammar School, he studied classics at University College and won the classics scholarship on the results of his BA examination. Then, having regard to his father's success in medicine, Foster chose to enter University College Medical School where, having carried off the Gold Medal for Anatomy and Physiology and that for Chemistry, he obtained his MD in 1859.)

After graduating Dew-Smith continued to live in Cambridge. As a result of a legacy in 1870 (when he changed his name from 'Dew') he had become a wealthy man. When rooms in Bishop's Hostel in Trinity College were later allotted to him by the College he adorned the walls with examples of Rossetti, Burne-Jones and other artists of the day. He had a love of beautiful things and he collected rare prints and precious stones. He liked to startle his companions by casually taking a handful of uncut gems from his pocket or a drawer with a remark such as 'What do you think of these Baubles?'[10] Robert Louis Stevenson, who occasionally stayed at Trinity College when visiting Sir Sidney Colvin, is supposed to have modelled his character Attwater in *The Ebb Tide* on Dew-Smith's personality.

Physically, he was a tall man with finely cut features, black silky hair and, like most gentry of that period, a neatly pointed beard. To quote Sir J. J. Thomson:[11] 'He was a man of fine presence and distinguished manners and if he had kept the tobacconist shop in Rupert Street he would have handed a packet of cigarettes over the counter with the air of a monarch presenting the insignia of a Knight of the Garter to one of his subjects.' Although he was soft-spoken he spoke in a deliberate manner and Sir Sidney Colvin wrote of the powerful personality which was covered by the external veneer of blandness. When recounting anything of special interest which had happened to himself Dew-Smith had a habit of avoiding the first person singular, and instead of saying 'I did,' or 'I felt,' would say 'One did,' or 'One felt.' Colvin quotes the occasion when an official at a railway station was offensively rude to Dew-Smith. 'What did you do?' he was asked. Dew-Smith replied, in a deprecating voice, 'Well, you know, one had to put him through the door panels.'[12] It is scarcely surprising that Dew-Smith became a prominent figure in Cambridge society.

For a few years after receiving his BA, Dew-Smith carried out research at the Department of Physiology. He collaborated with Michael Foster in the publication of two major papers which dealt with the effects of electrical currents on the hearts of molluscs and frogs.[13,14] Dew-Smith did not, however, teach physiology at Cambridge and in 1876 he gave up his researches. The Department of Physiology was developing rapidly and much of his time was taken up with helping Foster with the administration and financial work.

Foster was in fact hampered by a chronic shortage of funds. At the time of his appointment as Trinity Praelector in May 1870 he had been given an initial grant of £400 by Trinity College to purchase furniture and essential apparatus for his lecture room-cum-laboratory. When this money was exhausted Foster used his own money—the fees he received from his students—to continue to buy the apparatus which he needed so that the school might keep pace with the work being done elsewhere, particularly in the continental universities. Much of the newest continental equipment was expensive and Dew-Smith frequently provided the cash for these purchases. In 1875, and for some years afterwards, Dew-Smith provided the balance of money needed to pay J. N. Langley's salary as Foster's demonstrator (Trinity College contributed £50 annually towards this expense).

In 1878 Dew-Smith was allocated rooms in Bishop's Hostel in Trinity College although he was not a Fellow. Sharpey-Schafer in his *History of the Physiological Society* (of which both Dew-Smith and Michael Foster were founder members) commented that the rooms 'appertained to Foster' and this may well have been an expression of gratitude on Foster's part for Dew-Smith's financial assistance in building up the Department of Physiology.[15] Dew-Smith was also allowed the privileges of High Table although, not being a Fellow, again he had no claim to them.

By the time Horace Darwin returned to Cambridge in 1877 the Department of Physiology was a thriving concern. Although Darwin was not involved in Dew-Smith's activities in equipping the Physiological Laboratory there is no doubt that his renewed association with Dew-

Smith and Michael Foster (who was an old family friend) did awaken in him an awareness of the dearth of good instruments and instrument designers in Britain at that time. In some university towns instrument makers had established thriving businesses making apparatus for the experimenters at the university. In Glasgow, for example, the optician, James White, was fully occupied making equipment for William Thomson (Lord Kelvin). Cambridge was not so fortunate in this respect—a situation of which William Thomson was obviously aware when he declined the newly founded Chair of Experimental Physics at Cambridge in 1870 (i.e. the establishment of the Cavendish Laboratory) for he gave as one of his reasons 'The great advantages I have here with the new College, the apparatus and the assistance provided, the convenience of Glasgow for getting mechanical work done, give me the means of action which I could not have in any other place.'[16]

In the spring of 1878 Professor Stuart, Professor of Mechanism at Cambridge, began to make equipment for members of the University in the workshop attached to the Department of Mechanism, primarily because he needed the income from this work in order to pay the wages of the two mechanics he employed as instructors in the workshop.

James Stuart was the son of a linen-mill owner at Balgonie in Fifeshire. He was born in 1843 and as a child he showed an aptitude for mathematics. When he was about 12 years old he began to learn the use of tools and machines, joining the mill apprentices for part of each day in the mill workshop. At the age of 16 not only was he accepted as a student at St Andrew's University, but he was also allowed to omit the first year of the course. Thus he obtained his BA degree after only two years of study, winning a Ferguson Scholarship in classics and mathematics, which he could have taken up at any Scottish University. Stuart, however, elected to go to Trinity College, Cambridge, and in 1866 he graduated as a third wrangler with a college fellowship. In 1867 he took up the post of Assistant Tutor at Trinity although he now also had the management of the Balgonie Mill to cope with, his father having died in 1866.

Whilst a tutor at Trinity, Stuart played a leading part in organising a system of inter-collegiate lecture courses and also helped to establish the University's extra-mural courses in various provincial towns. In 1875 his friends persuaded him to apply for the newly vacant Jacksonian Professorship at Cambridge, somewhat against his better judgement, and when it became clear that the University would prefer the Chair to be filled by a chemist he immediately withdrew his application. Fortunately, later in 1875 the new Chair of Professor of Mechanism was established by the University and Stuart promptly made application. He easily beat his two rival challengers in the election and when the results were announced his friends jubilantly collected him from his rooms and escorted him to the Senate House to be installed, whilst the bells of Great

St Mary's Church rang out their traditional greeting to a new professor.

Like Michael Foster, James Stuart had to build up his department from scratch, his only assets being a half-share in the Jacksonian lecture room in the New Museums Building, the use of two small rooms behind it and a collection of models of mechanical contrivances and machines, most of which needed to be repaired. Thus, early in 1876 Stuart brought one of the Balgonie craftsmen, James Lister, to Cambridge to act as his assistant in repairing the collection of models.

By 1877 Stuart had decided that he must have a workshop so that his pupils could learn the use of tools. He made the point to the University authorities in his annual report in April 1877, but apparently did not receive much support for his request. So, during the summer vacation of 1877 he cleared one of the two small rooms behind the lecture-room and fitted it up as an instructional workshop with a lathe and some hand tools.[29] This workshop was later to grow into the Engineering Laboratories of the University.

Initially there were only places for four pupils in his workshop, but by January 1878 the course had proved so popular that three new pupils had to be squeezed in. Stuart found two skilled mechanics (who were frequently employed as instrument-makers in the workshop attached to the Cavendish Laboratory) to act as instructors and, to pay their wages, he began to make apparatus for other departments and members of the University staff.

Almost certainly one of the these mechanics was a man named Robert Fulcher. Fulcher is reported to have been trained at the Royal Arsenal in Woolwich and by midsummer of 1878 Stuart had made him chief mechanic in charge of the workshop.

In June 1878 Professor Stuart persuaded the University authorities to provide him with a wooden hut to serve as a larger workshop for twenty-five students. In return he agreed to furnish and equip it at his own expense and to run it without cost to the University. The hut was erected during the long vacation of 1878 and as the work progressed Stuart grew more and more excited and impatient for the building to be completed so that he could start to equip it. On 3 August, 1878, he wrote to his mother, 'Fulcher, of course, is very pleased with the prospect of a larger workshop' and on 9 August he wrote telling her that he had been to London with Fulcher (to look at machine tools). He added, 'I shall be heartily glad when it is finished and when Fulcher is started to get the inside of it in order, for he is a willing and most praiseworthy worker.' By October the work of fitting out the new workshop was in full swing and on 7 October Stuart's letter to his mother included the comment that Fulcher was 'in ecstasies' over the workshop.[17]

Stuart kept an account book in which he detailed the costs of equipping his new workshop. In this he records purchasing various tools and equipment from Fulcher: 'Stock purchased from Fulcher with his valuation.'[18] The sum paid to Fulcher was fifty guineas. He also lists equipment given to him by various friends and colleagues at the University and amongst these items is a lathe from Horace Darwin worth £15.0s.0d. Unfortunately, the lathe appears not to have been in very good order as later, amongst the list of costs of overhauling some of this equipment is recorded the sum of £4.18s.4d, 'to repair Darwin's lathe'. The account book shows that Stuart continued to buy various tools and materials through Fulcher after the Michaelmas term started on 18 October until 31 December, 1878.

With the increased space and more students, Stuart took on more mechanics in his workshop to teach his students how to use the machines. The following accounts, extracted by Robert Whipple from a cost book which no longer exists, detail the wages they received:[19]

Professor Stuart's Teaching, 18 October to 13 December 1878:

Fulcher	$174\frac{1}{4}$	hours	@ 1/-	Teaching	8.14. 3
Walter[†]	186	hours	@ $11\frac{1}{4}$d	,,	8.14. $4\frac{1}{2}$
Milne	9	hours	@ 9d	,,	6. 9
Taylor	5	hours	@ 9d	,,	3. 9
Frederick	$12\frac{1}{2}$	hours	@ 3d	,,	3. $1\frac{1}{2}$
					£18. 2. 3

Fulcher	$30\frac{1}{2}$	hours	@ 1/-	Work in Shop	1.10. 6
Walter[†]	110	hours	@ $11\frac{1}{4}$d	,,	5. 3. $1\frac{1}{2}$
Milne	8	hours	@ 9d	,,	6. 0
Taylor	49	hours	@ 9d	,,	1.16. 9
Frederick	$41\frac{3}{4}$	hours	@ 3d	,,	10. $5\frac{1}{4}$
Lee	$6\frac{1}{2}$	hours	@ 3d	,,	5.11$\frac{1}{2}$
					£9.12. $9\frac{1}{4}$

The names of the workmen are confirmed by a similar list in Stuart's account book for the period 18 October to 31 December 1878:

Work done in Shop on Tools and Machines:

Fulcher	35 hours
Degordon[†]	141 hours
Milne	9 hours
Taylor	$46\frac{1}{2}$ hours
Frederick	48 hours
Lee	$15\frac{1}{2}$ hours

At some time during 1878, probably when the fitting out of the new workshop was completed in October, Fulcher and Dew-Smith came

---

† *Probably 'Walter Degordon'.*

to an arrangement with Professor Stuart whereby Fulcher was allowed to use the machines in the workshop to make apparatus on a commercial basis. Dew-Smith provided the financial backing. (Earlier that year Dew-Smith had told Michael Foster that he 'thought about getting rid of some of his rubbish.'[20] When Sotheby's advertised the auction of Dew-Smith's 'rubbish' for 29 January, 1878, their description was rather more eloquent: 'A very choice library[†] and a small but rich collection of ancient engravings and modern drawings'. The gross sum raised at the auction was £3080.3s.0d.)

On 10 January, 1879, Fulcher advertised for the first time in the *Journal of Physiology*:[21]

ROBERT FULCHER
Manufacturer of Scientific Instruments
is prepared to supply
apparatus of all kinds used in Physiological Research,
including Recording and Electrical Apparatus.
3 Downing Terrace, Lensfield Road, Cambridge[‡]

The arrangement with Professor Stuart soon turned out to be unsatisfactory and Dew-Smith and Fulcher decided to find their own premises. On 15 March, 1879, Horace Darwin wrote to his brother George: 'Dew and Fulcher have got a new shop and will go into it at Easter.'[22] In April 1879 Fulcher left Stuart's workshop, taking Milne with him and employing two new men, Bailey and Collins. There is a final mention of Fulcher in Stuart's account book in association with a list of equipment 'ascertained to be there on taking it over from Fulcher on 16 April, 1879 (the Wednesday after Easter).

The 'new shop' was a hay-loft at 18 Panton Street, on the north corner of Russell Street, near the Panton Arms. It had a slate roof and brick walls, except for the wall at one end which was wood and abutted on to a slate roof under which the owner, William Wallis, a fly proprietor, kept his carriages. Mr Wallis seems to have been a man of diverse talents as Spaldings Directory of 1881 gives his occupation as 'Aeolian pianoforte maker and tuner'.[23]

Fulcher did not advertise in the May or July issues of the *Journal of Physiology*, but the September issue carried a repeat of his January

---

[†] *The Manuscripts Room of the Cambridge University Library possesses Dew-Smith's catalogue of his library (C.U.L. Ref. Add. 6461) and a glance at its pages reveals just how choice were the contents of Dew-Smith's library. The entries in this handsome volume are in Dew-Smith's handwriting and artistically illustrated in a number of places by small drawings in ink. The catalogue was part of a bequest to the University Library by the Librarian, Francis Jenkinson, who was a Fellow of Trinity and a family friend of the Darwins. He is believed to have been given it by Dew-Smith's wife, Alice, after Dew-Smith's death in 1903.*

[‡] *Now No. 45 Lensfield Road.*

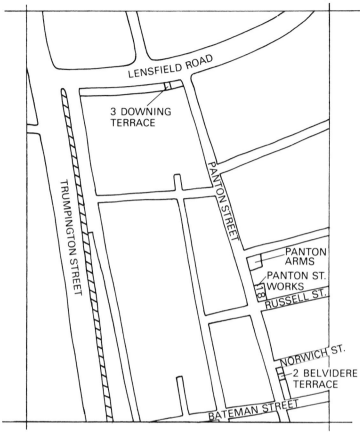

Figure 1.3 Map showing the locations of Fulcher's house in Downing Terrace and his business premises in Panton Street and Belvidere Terrace c. 1880.

advertisement with the address amended: '18 Panton Street (late 3 Downing Terrace, Lensfield Road, Cambridge).'

By this time Horace Darwin had begun to make a name for himself as a mechanical designer. As a close friend of Dew-Smith he was keenly interested in the progress of Dew-Smith's business enterprise with Fulcher and he was also very interested in the growth of the Department of Mechanism under James Stuart. Stuart had already realised Darwin's abilities and, when he heard that Fulcher and Dew-Smith intended moving out of his workshop, to set up on their own, he sought out Darwin and made him a proposition which caused Darwin to think deeply. Darwin summarised these proposals and his own feelings on the matter in a long letter to his brother George on 17 February, 1879, written from London:[24]

> '. . . I have had a great deal of talk with Stuart about
> the shop, and I will give you a short account of the state things
> are in. Dew-Smith and Fulcher are going to leave the shop and
> are going to set up on their own account; they find that they
> cannot make it pay, and generally can't get on with the present
> arrangements. There are 19 pupils working in the shop. Stuart is
> really anxious for me to come up and help him. What he
> proposed is that I should become a partner with him in the shop
> as a commercial concern, dividing the profits both from the pupils
> and the work turned out. There are many objections to this, too
> many to go into, but the first is that I am convinced that the
> profits will be little or more probably nothing. . . . I suggested to
> him that my being made a demonstrator would be far better, but
> then I do not think I should be inclined to stay up in the
> vacations for the £100 or the £150 that the University would
> give me. I gave no definite answer, but said I would consider
> it. . . . You know I should very much like to do anything I could
> to make an Engineering School up there. It is also against it
> having to get new men, as Fulcher of course goes with Dew-
> Smith. . . . I have had a long talk with Father about it, and
> everyone at home. When you come back I shall want to talk it
> over more fully and see what you think. . . .'

Because of his love of engineering Horace Darwin was very tempted by the possibility of joining forces with Stuart in the Department of Mechanism. The problem was that the terms were not right. It was neither one thing nor the other; neither a full-time University appointment nor a full-time commercial arrangement and Darwin could not see how Stuart's proposals could be a profitable or satisfying arrangement. For a while he toyed with the idea of applying for a demonstratorship but his family and friends were against it and Stuart would have no half measures; if he supported Darwin's application, Darwin would have to join him in the commercial operation of the workshop. Darwin came to a decision. He turned it all down, but not without some regrets as his letter to his brother George, written on 15 March, 1879, from Downe, shows:[25]

> '*Dear George,*
>   *I'm just back from Cambridge, and I have busted up
> the demonstratorship; I came to the conclusion that it would not
> do. Father was a good deal against it, and Balfour thought that
> it would be doubtful whether it would do, and in fact was
> against my going in for it, so I talked it over with Stuart, and
> put it all down to Father, and then he said that he would not
> think it worth while to try and make the University make me
> demonstrator unless I was going in for all he wanted vis: to
> become partner in the whole thing commercially, which I was
> dead against so we parted and the whole thing is bitched* [sic]. *I
> suppose it is best, but I do regret not coming up, and I also feel
> I might have done a little to have made the Engineering School a
> success, which as God knows I should have liked very much. . . .*'

Darwin was by now undertaking a considerable amount of instrument design work. He received commissions from Dew-Smith to design a governor and a colour mixer and he also acted as a consultant to other clients, having the instruments made in Fulcher's workshop, but carrying out the final adjustments himself. In July 1878 he had received a £25 grant from the Meteorological Council to make a model of his proposals for a meteorograph. When the design was complete Darwin asked Fulcher to make the model but in the spring of 1879 Fulcher had so much work that on 16 March, 1879, Darwin had to write to R. H. Scott, the Secretary of the Meteorological Office, explaining that the construction of the instrument had been delayed because Fulcher was very busy.

By November 1879 the instrument was completed and Darwin demonstrated it to Professor Stokes and Francis Galton. In many ways the design was similar to the meteorographs designed by Dr Theorell.[26,27] In the self-recording thermometer a platinum wire gradually moved down the tube until it touched the mercury surface, which action closed a circuit. The movement down the tube was linked to a simple counter with embossed figures, the counter thus indicating the temperature as measured by the mercury column and the embossed figures on the counter enabling a print-out of the temperature to be obtained using the ribbon from a typewriter.[28] Unfortunately the demonstration does not seem to have gone too well and in December 1879 Darwin received a polite letter from the Meteorological Office: 'The Council do not think it right to press you to continue your experiments with the view to their being utilized by them.' Whilst Darwin's method of printing the data was novel, the execution of his idea was too clumsy.

Early in 1880 Darwin designed an actinometer (a light meter sensitive to infra-red radiation) for Captain William Abney, of the Royal Engineers, and Professor Henry Roscoe. Horace Darwin would have been introduced to Captain Abney by his brother Leonard who was a Major in the Royal Engineers and, like Captain Abney, was interested in chemistry and photography.[29] Abney was both a practical photographer and a respected expert in experimental photography. At the time that Darwin was commissioned to design the actinometer Abney was working on colour analysis and the development of a photographic emulsion which would be sensitive to red and infra-red light.

Professor Roscoe, too, was experienced in the same field. After obtaining his BA at University College, London, in 1852 he went to Heidelberg and studied for his PhD under R. W. von Bunsen. Roscoe continued to work with Bunsen on the measurement of the chemical action of light until 1857, devising techniques whereby light levels could be compared using standard photographic paper. In 1857 he was elected Professor of Chemistry at Owen's College in Manchester, a post he held until 1885 when he resigned the chair after entering Parliament.

Originally Abney and Roscoe ordered one actinometer but by May 1880 the quantity required had been increased to six and Darwin wrote to Professor Roscoe on 10 May, 1880, to explain that he would now be able to reduce the unit price considerably. His letter ended: 'I shall endeavour to make the instrument as cheap as possible consistently with first-rate workmanship.'[30] The instruments were sold to Professor Roscoe for £40 each, but a later check showed that Darwin had underestimated the cost and in September 1881 he and Dew-Smith quoted a price of £60 each to a potential customer.

Later in 1880 Darwin also designed a photonephometer—a cloud camera—for Captain Abney, who was a member of the Kew Meteorological Committee. An account sent in December 1880 set out the the costs of the work:[31]

                                                          28 December, 1880

Capt. Abney R.E. in account with Horace Darwin
1880   £ s d
Dec. 20th   Paid Mr. Fulcher for work done up
               to this date on Photonephometer   71. 6.1
               One Dallmeyer lens   3.19.2
               Due to me for designing and
               adjusting Photonephometer   11. 9.0

                                                          £86.14.3

For a while Fulcher's workshop flourished. At one time he was employing six men and a boy, and as the business expanded he took over the ground floor of 18 Panton Street, underneath the workshop, to use as an office. He also rented No. 2 Belvidere Terrace from James Hicks a builder of City Road in Cambridge. Belvidere Terrace was a hundred yards farther along Panton Street, between Norwich Street and Belvoir Street. Although the hayloft at 18 Panton Street has long since been demolished (the site has recently been redeveloped as Russell Court) Belvidere Terrace still stands, No. 2 now being known as 71 Panton Street. The first floor of the house in Belvidere Terrace was used to store finished instruments, William Pye living in the rest of the premises from the end of February 1881.[†]

In addition to the instrument-making work the business under-took the publication of the *Journal of Physiology* and a note on the front

---

† *Robert Fulcher is not mentioned in Spalding's street directories and lists of Cambridge residents for that period. However, in 1878 Fulcher was advertising his business address as 3 Downing Terrace (now 45 Lensfield Road) for which the 1878 directory gave the occupant as J. Fulcher, his occupation appearing as 'attendant at the Cavendish Laboratory.' Since William Pullin was the attendant at the Cavendish Laboratory from 1873 to 1880 this was probably a misprint for R. Fulcher, the reference being to his earlier post of instrument maker there. In the next edition of the directory in 1881, 3 Downing Terrace was occupied by the Reverend Robert Wilson Stoddart and William Pye was the occupant of 2 Belvidere Terrace.*

cover of Volume III, No. 1, dated August 1880, stated that the *Journal* had been issued for the proprietors by Robert Fulcher, 18 Panton Street, Cambridge. The *Journal*, which was printed by the Cambridge University Press, was started in 1878, under the editorship of Michael Foster, largely as a result of Dew-Smith's encouragement. For some years it was a decidedly unprofitable exercise and it provides another example of the financial support Dew-Smith gave to the activities of the Department of Physiology.

In the issue of the *Journal* dated 20 December, 1879, a full page advertisement gave details of the types of instruments which Fulcher was prepared to make and similar advertisements continued to appear in the *Journal* throughout 1880. However, only one instrument attributable to Robert Fulcher is known. It is a sliding microtome, made in brass, very similar to those made in hardwood by Rivet about 1870. This instrument is now in the Department of Zoology in Cambridge.

Figure 1.4 Sir Michael Foster, photographed by Dew-Smith. (Photo: By courtesy of the Master and Fellows of Trinity College, Cambridge. Trinity College Library reference 0.17.4/6.)

Fulcher was, in fact, engaged in making relatively simple apparatus, much of it under the guidance of Michael Foster. Neither Fulcher nor Dew-Smith possessed sufficient knowledge of mechanical engineering to satisfy the needs of the Physiological and other laboratories in the University, and therein lay the crunch. In the autumn of 1880 it became clear that if the business was to progress further, changes had to be made. Michael Foster may well have been the key instigator behind these changes. He had first hand knowledge of the work in hand in Fulcher's workshop, including the instruments which Darwin was designing for his own clients and which were being made there. Knowing the apparatus he needed in his own laboratory Foster would have been only too well aware of the limitations of the Dew-Smith/Fulcher arrangement and he may well have intuitively foreseen the advances in instrument design which might be achieved by the business if Horace Darwin's engineering talents could be permanently engaged. W. H. Gaskell summed up this almost instinctive talent of Foster in his obituary in 1908 when he described Foster as a 'discoverer of men rather than of facts.'[32]

During the autumn of 1880 Darwin began working on the design of a cathetometer for Professor Poynting. Since 1878 Poynting, who was a Fellow of Trinity, had been carrying out experiments at the Cavendish Laboratory, to determine the mean density of the earth, but in the autumn of 1880 he was elected to the Chair of Physics at the newly founded Mason College in Birmingham. This was later to become the University of Birmingham and Poynting continued as Professor of Physics until his death in March 1914.

On 28 December, 1880, Darwin wrote to Poynting about the forthcoming changes in Fulcher's Workshop:[33]

> '*Dear Poynting,*
>   *I think that the original arrangement about the Cathetometer was that I should design it and get it made by the firm of Robert Fulcher, but as certain alterations are in progress of being made in this firm which may alter your wishes, it is only fair to you to tell you of them and to ask you for further instructions. After Jan. 1st 1881 the business now known as Robert Fulcher will be carried on, provided no unforeseen circumstances occur, as The Cambridge Scientific Instrument Company under the management of the Proprietors, who will be A. Dew-Smith and myself . . . .*'

Exactly how the changes in the control of the business were brought about is not recorded. It seems very unlikely that Darwin would have even considered joining Fulcher and Dew-Smith as an equal partner had he been offered the opportunity. Almost certainly he would have wanted a greater say in the work to be undertaken by the business. Foster would probably also have discouraged a triumvirate, feeling that Fulcher, who lacked the education of Darwin and Dew-Smith, would have been out of place in such an arrangement. It is more likely that Fulcher was offered the position of Workshop Manager working for a new partnership consisting of Darwin and Dew-Smith. But this is speculation. What is known, from a letter written by Ida Darwin, Horace's wife, to his brother George on 13 February, 1881, is that the eventual break-up of the Fulcher/Dew-Smith partnership was quite acrimonious.[34] The dissolution of the partnership took place on 8 December, 1880, and was formally published in the London Gazette of 10 December. Robert Fulcher left the firm (and took up the teaching of mechanisms) and a draft agreement for a new partnership between Dew-Smith and Horace Darwin was prepared.

Mr W. Hacon, Horace Darwin's solicitor, evidently advised against some of the points in the proposed agreement and this produced a typical Darwin family conference at Down House. In a letter to Dew-Smith, written at Downe on 23 December, 1880, Horace Darwin wrote that he had consulted Mr Farrer (his brother-in-law and later Lord Farrer), his father, and his brother George about the objections which Mr Hacon had raised and they were all agreed that he would be right to act contrary to Mr Hacon's advice on all points except one. The exceptional item concerned Darwin's acceptance of the liabilities and book debts associated with the publication of the *Journal of Physiology*. Darwin, rather apologetically, suggested a compromise clause on this item.

On 26 January, 1881, Dew-Smith wrote to his brother, Charles, who was acting as his solicitor, to say that he was sending by registered post 'a list of Materials, Tools, Book Debts, Instruments in Stock, Furniture and Fittings and instruments in course of construction. The whole amounting to £2074.7*s*.11*d*. Mr Darwin has agreed to purchase the undivided moiety of the whole affair for the sum of One thousand and fifty pounds, £1050. The capital of the business will therefore consist of the sum Two thousand one hundred pounds. Will you be good enough to make out the Deed in accordance with this.'[35] On 27 February, 1881, Darwin wrote to Mr Hacon, confirming his agreement of Dew-Smith's figures, and the deed was finalised.

In January 1881 the usual full-page advertisement appeared in the *Journal of Physiology*, but this time headed by a bold announcement which stated that 'The business hitherto conducted by Mr Robert Fulcher will in future be carried on by The Cambridge Scientific Instrument Company at the same address.'

Thus, The Cambridge Scientific Instrument Company, 'Horace's Shop', came into being on 1 January, 1881.

*   *   *   *   *

CHAPTER TWO

The Partnership between Darwin and Dew-Smith

ROBERT Fulcher having left the business, a skilled man was needed to take charge of the workshop with its five workmen. On 16 December, 1880, a letter was sent to a Mr William T. Pye, who was living in Battersea in London, offering him the position of foreman 'in the workshop that we intend to carry on after January 1st next,' at a salary of £130 per annum with a rent and tax-free house.[1] This salary proved insufficient to attract Pye so on 20 December the offer was increased to £150, which he accepted. The offer to Pye was based on a three-month trial period but after only two months Pye had proved his worth and in a letter dated 24 February, 1881, his position was confirmed and permission given for him to occupy the promised house—No. 2 Belvidere Terrace. Darwin and Dew-Smith did, however, reserve their use of the rooms on the first floor as storage for finished instruments.

Pye was a skilled mechanic who had had considerable experience of experimental work with a variety of London firms, including William Ladd of Beak Street, Richard Chipperfield of Clerkenwell, and Tisley of Brompton Road. He had worked with several of the early physicists at the Royal Institution. Although Pye turned out to be rather a despot in the works, the men under him trusted him. Sir J. J. Thomson, for many years Professor of Experimental Physics at the Cavendish Laboratory at Cambridge, wrote of him:[2]

> *'Pye himself was a bit of a "character" as well as a good workman; he held very decided views about most things, including the merits of those for whom he was making apparatus. He expressed these views quite freely, to the great delight and amusement of his master.'*

Thomson was referring here to Dew-Smith. Evidently there were initially some problems with Pye's status as the new foreman and, unfortunately,

Dew-Smith's gentlemanly manners were the cause of the difficulties. In her letter to George Darwin dated 13 February, 1881, Ida Darwin commented on the situation:

> '*I am glad to say Mr Dew* [sic] *has seen the error of his ways in calling all the workmen 'Mr' and is trying to get out of the way of it so as to give Mr Pye alone a distinctive title.*'[3]

Both Darwin and Dew-Smith came to rely on Pye's judgement and he subsequently rose to the position of Manager. In 1895, when the business became a Limited Company he was appointed Company Secretary. He left the Company in 1898 when he went into partnership with his son, W. G. Pye.

George Meaden was another first-class mechanic. He had been trained as an engineer's fitter and was originally taken on by Fulcher, in May 1879, at 8*d*. per hour. He proved of great value whenever particularly fine work was required. In his spare time he took a leading part in the Co-operative Movement in Cambridge and served as President of the Cambridge Co-operative Society for a total of twenty-five years before his retirement in 1926. He died in January 1944.

Darwin and Dew-Smith found considerable difficulty in recruiting employees who were sufficiently skilled to meet their exacting standards. Instrument makers at that time were expected to make the whole instrument from start to finish, starting from block metal. The standard rate of pay was 8*d*. per hour and the men worked a 54-hour week. Darwin and Dew-Smith would only employ the best mechanics and a letter from Dew-Smith, dated 18 May, 1881, replying to an applicant seeking employment, shows that they knew exactly the type of men that they wanted:[4]

> *Sir,*
>
> *In reply to your letter of yesterday's date, we do not want specially Barometer or Thermometer Makers. What we do want are really first class Instrument Makers used to Lathe, Vice, Finishing and Lacquering. If this is your case you may try the job on your own Terms with prospect of a rise. But please do not come unless you feel you can turn out work of the highest class.*
>
> *No travelling expenses allowed.*
> *Faithfully yours,*
> *A. G. Dew-Smith for the Company*

One of the apprentices in 1884 was E. I. Everett. When he subsequently left the firm he moved to London and, in 1896, he set up in business on his own account, handling all sorts of light engineering work but specialising in high-grade laboratory instruments. A few years later, in 1900, he was joined by Mr Kenelm Edgcumbe (who later became the Earl of Mount Edgcumbe) and the name of the company was changed to

Everett, Edgcumbe & Co. Over the next fifty years their company became well-known as manufacturers of high-quality electrical engineering instruments.

The first clerk-cum-storekeeper at the Company was Alfred H. Reed. He had originally been engaged by Fulcher in 1880. In his early years he recorded issues from the stores on a slate. Later he took on much of the work normally carried out by a Company Secretary and he was formally appointed to that post in 1905, a position he held until he retired in 1932. Reed was an avid reader, particularly of biographies, and his ambition was to become a librarian. At one time he applied for a post in the Cambridge University Library and was greatly disappointed when his application was turned down.

The early press-copy letter-books indicate the way Darwin and Dew-Smith divided the work whilst the Company was becoming established, Dew-Smith corresponding with the customers and Darwin taking charge of the design and manufacture of the instruments. One of the first letters written by Dew-Smith on behalf of the Company, on 10 January, 1881, was to W. H. Caldwell concerning a Zeiss microtome, for which Robert Fulcher and subsequently The Cambridge Scientific Instrument Company were agents. Special care had evidently been taken to make certain that the screw was free from shake on Caldwell's instrument. A letter the next day to another customer advised him that his Roy freezing microtome had been tested by Dr Roy the previous day and found satisfactory and on 4 February another letter to a potential purchaser of a freezing microtome advised: 'They are made here under Dr Roy's supervision and he is good enough to test them all for us when finished. We have several in stock ready for delivery.'[5] On the same day another customer enquiring about this type of microtome was told: 'At the Cambridge Laboratory at this time even a very inexperienced assistant is cutting sections for a large class daily in as few minutes as he formerly took hours to do the work in with the ordinary razor. The sections moreover are uniformly large and thin.'[6] The price quoted, with ether spray producer and two moulds for paraffin blocks, used when freezing was not required, was £6.10s.0d.

Dr Charles Smart Roy, the inventor of this instrument, was an ingenious and prolific designer of instruments for use in experimental physiology so that many instruments bore his name. An Edinburgh graduate, he worked for several years on the Continent before being selected by Michael Foster as the first recipient of the George Henry Lewes studentship in 1881. In 1881 Roy was appointed Professor Superintendent of the Brown Institution (which was founded in 1871 as a part of the University of London) and in 1884 he was elected a Fellow of the Royal Society and appointed as the first Professor of Pathology at Cambridge.

Dr Roy evidently tested all the 'Roy' microtomes before they left the works and in the summer one of the first royalty agreements to be made by the Company was made with him. The terms were set out in a letter dated 27 July, 1881, signed by both Darwin and Dew-Smith:[7]

> *Dear Sir,*
>> *The arrangement we propose to make with you concerning the Instruments of your devising is as follows:*
>> *You shall be charged with our ordinary price for the first example made, which shall become your property. After six others have been sold you shall be credited with the amount of the ordinary selling price of the object, and after every succeeding six have been sold you shall be further credited with the amount of the ordinary selling price of the object at the time.*
>> *This shall relate to all Instruments which you order to be made from your own drawings and which are bona fide modifications of existing Instruments, or are new inventions.*
>> *This arrangement shall be in force from 1 January, 1881 (except in the case of the Freezing Microtome which shall start from 1 June, 1881) and shall last until 31 December, 1881, and shall then be terminated or renewed by agreement of both parties.*
>> *We do not undertake to submit our books for inspection, and our accounts as delivered to you shall be considered as final. This agreement shall be considered as strictly private and confidential between you and ourselves.*

Unfortunately Dr Roy seems to have been rather a trying person to work with and although Darwin and Dew-Smith apparently did their best to give him preferential treatment the letter books show that they were not always successful in satisfying his impatience. During October/November 1881 the Company made Roy a cardiograph to his drawing. On 2 November, no doubt in reply to an enquiry as to its progress Dew-Smith telegraphed that it was nearly half finished, adding that he hoped to see Dr Roy at 'The Savile' the next day. The instrument was speedily finished, for next month Roy was sent an invoice 'For making a Frogheart Cardiograph to drawing, £14.3s.0d.'[8]

However, a few weeks later, on 16 January, 1882, Dew-Smith had to write a firm but polite letter after Dr Roy had complained of the service he was receiving:[9]

> *Dear Sir,*
>> *We regret not having seen you today as you had led us to expect, as we then should have had an opportunity of discussing with you your criticism on our treatment of you and of the work that you are so good as to entrust to us. We think that on the whole we have treated you very fairly indeed and we have no hesitation whatever in saying that your work is always put in hand and has always the preference over any other that we may have in hand at the time. Your elasticity apparatus was in hand during the holidays when, as you may know, no work is done for*

*about 10 days. We pushed on with it as soon as we could and
when we could do so no further we wrote to you asking for
advice in the matter. Your Cardiograph about which you wrote to
us on January 9th is in hand and had you come today you would
have found the greater part of it finished. In this instance we
admit that we have to reproach ourselves for not having replied to
your letter as it was written to us and not merely as a private
letter to one of us. In this matter we will not fail in the future.
With reference to the drawings which you are good enough to
send us and which you call 'painfully detailed', we can only say
that we are accustomed to working drawings and have no difficulty in understanding them, but we cannot admit your criticism
that our queries and answers upon them are so wide of the mark
as to lead you to believe that we had either 'not read' your letters
or had 'intentionally misunderstood them'. We indeed fail to
recollect an instance in which such a criticism could be justified. . . .*

Although, as happened with Dr Roy, some customers would
provide a drawing or sketch of their requirements, Darwin would, if
necessary, design a complete piece of apparatus to meet a customer's
needs. If a piece of experimental equipment proved successful it might
become standard apparatus in the laboratory. Such was the case with
Roy's Tonometer and Gaskell's modification of Roy's Tonometer. Both
were used in experiments with frogs' hearts and included in the Company's Price List No. 2, dated September 1882—the earliest printed list
known to have survived.

For the business to be successful it was of course also essential
that the customers should be satisfied with the instruments which they
received. Since the Company was a continuation of the Fulcher/Dew-
Smith partnership this included instruments made during that period
and a brave face had to be presented to the costs of ensuring this satisfaction. Thus, in reply to an American Professor of Physiology at Harvard
Medical School, who was having problems with a kymograph made by
Fulcher, Dew-Smith wrote on 15 August, 1881: 'If you will send the
instrument back to us we will do all we can to return it to you in a good
condition for working. We may add that we should very much prefer to
pay all expenses of transit etc., and to return to you free of all cost to
you.'[10]

Most of the early instruments made by the Company were for
use in physiological laboratories for the simple reason that this was where
the demand lay. To begin with, many of the designs were based on
continental instruments although Darwin, with advice from Michael
Foster, frequently effected improvements. In a letter to a potential
customer on 29 November, 1881, Darwin wrote: 'We think we make more
numerous and more varied kinds of Physiological Instruments than any
other makers and we shall be glad to give you detailed information, and in
some cases Photographs of our instruments if you will be so good as to

indicate to us such as you may consider most appropriate for the purpose in question.'[11]

One of the earliest pieces of physiological equipment designed by Darwin was an artificial respiration apparatus, used to keep an animal alive but anaesthetised on the operating table. An air-chloroform mixture was pumped in and out of the animal's lungs by a two-cylinder pump. In a letter to an American professor on 21 January, 1881, he states: 'It is worked by simply attaching it to the ordinary watertap. One that we made has been working in the Cambridge Laboratory for the past four months and has given great satisfaction. It is very economical in its use of water. It delivers and exhausts any required quantity of air, suitable to the smallest rabbit or the largest dog and will work at any velocity required.'[12] At that time this was a significant advance in the design of artificial respiration apparatus and the equipment was supplied to a large number of physiological laboratories.

From its inception the Company was associated with the work of prominent figures within the University at Cambridge. In March 1881 bills were sent to Lord Rayleigh for repair work on the British Association Standard Coil Apparatus, and also for making a commutator 'by direction of Mr J. J. Thomson.'[13] In 1883 the Company made the Rayleigh electric motor used by Lord Rayleigh in his researches on the 'Absolute Value of the British Association Unit'. This was a synchronous motor, operated by a tuning fork, and was widely used subsequently as a timing motor.

The colour mixer, which Darwin had designed for Dew-Smith in 1879, was another item to be included in the Company's Price List No. 2 of September 1882: 'This is supplied either for rotating a single disc at ordinary velocities, or furnished with a special arrangement by means of which two discs may be rotated at very high and unequal velocities.' Coloured discs of cardboard were supplied with the instrument, the object being to mix the light from the different colours in varying proportions. Somewhat surprisingly the auxanometer, originally designed by Darwin for his brother Francis whilst Darwin was at Erith, was not included in the Price List until December 1883.

During his service in the Royal Engineers, Leonard Darwin was based for a time at Chatham (with Lord Kitchener). The School of Military Engineering at Chatham wished to be able to photograph explosions and during the autumn of 1880 Leonard Darwin asked his brother Horace to design a system of cameras which could be triggered at known intervals. In Darwin's design each camera was fitted with a shutter operated by an electromagnet. The electromagnets were triggered from a timing device consisting of a flywheel rolling down an inclined plane on its axle, the protruding ends of the axle knocking over vertical wires to make the electrical connections at the required intervals (*Fig.* 2.1). In the

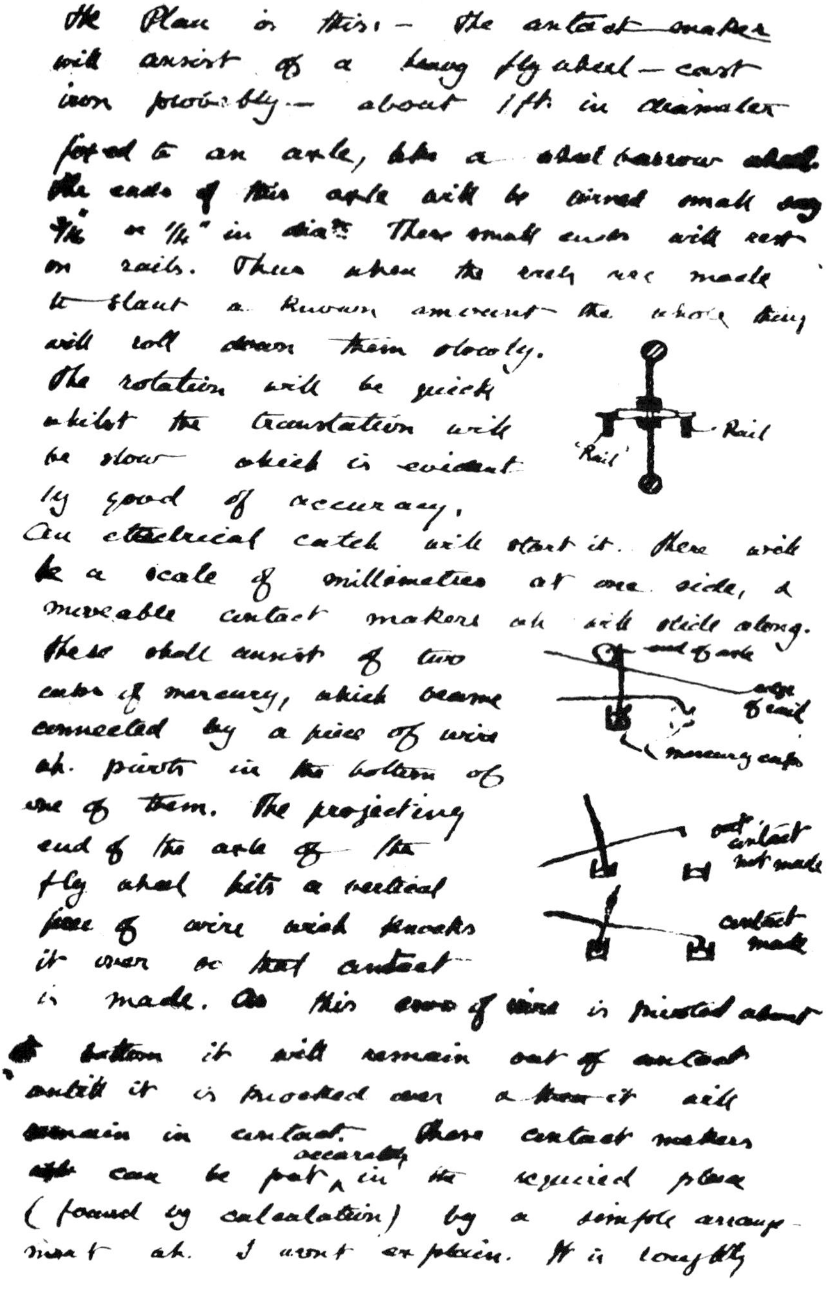

the Plan is this — the contact maker
will consist of a heavy fly wheel — cast
iron probably — about 1ft in diameter
fixed to an axle, like a wheel barrow wheel.
The ends of this axle will be turned small say
1/16" or 1/8" in dia'r. These small ends will rest
on rails. Then when the ends are made
to slant a known amount the whole thing
will roll down them slowly.
The rotation will be quick
whilst the translation will
be slow — which is evident
ly good of accuracy,

An electrical catch will start it. There will
be a scale of millimetres at one side, &
moveable contact makers which will slide along.
These shall consist of two
cups of mercury, which became
connected by a piece of wire
ah. placed in the bottom of
one of them. The projecting
end of the axle of the
fly wheel hits a vertical
piece of wire which knocks
it over so that contact
is made. As this piece of wire is pivoted about
its bottom it will remain out of contact
until it is knocked over a then it will
remain in contact. These contact makers
can be put accurately in the required place
(found by calculation) by a simple arrangement ah. I wont explain. It is roughly

Figure 2.1 Extract from the letter to Leonard Darwin (25 December, 1880) in which Horace Darwin set out his ideas for the design of the 'Photobustoscope'. (Photo: C.S.I.Co., Box 1, Letter-book pp. 8–11.)

Darwin family correspondence the equipment was invariably referred to as the 'Photobustoscope'! On 25 December, 1880, Horace Darwin wrote to Leonard suggesting he should place a formal enquiry with the Company and by the middle of February 1881 the manufacture of the apparatus was well advanced. As Ida Darwin remarked in a letter to George Darwin on 13 February: 'It is almost done and sometimes works very satisfactorily, . . .'[14] However, since the equipment did not appear in the Company's Price List until December 1883 perhaps at other times it did not work quite so satisfactorily.

Darwin had similar difficulties with the exposing system when he came to make a second cloud camera for use with the photonepho-meter which he had originally designed for Captain Abney in 1880. The two cameras were set up at Kew Observatory in order to determine the height and speed of clouds by simultaneous photography, Captain Abney acting as advisor to the Meteorological Council during these experiments. Each camera was supported on a theodolite base fitted with altitude and azimuth circles. One of the cameras was mounted on the roof of the Observatory, the second was positioned in the Old Deer Park. The chief observer, stationed at the Observatory camera, decided which cloud should be photographed and telephoned the altitude and azimuth bearings to the observer by the second camera. When the latter reported that his camera was adjusted and the shutter set the chief observer triggered both cameras simultaneously. The procedure was repeated one minute later and from the four photographs the height and velocity of the clouds could be obtained, although the interpretation of the photographs was a complicated process.[15]

Some time later the procedure was simplified. Both cameras were set to point vertically upwards and a plotting table and strings were used to analyse the observations. This simplified technique was devised by the then Superintendent of the Observatory, George Whipple. Many years later his son, Robert Whipple, who joined the Company in 1898, noted that Darwin had admitted having considerable difficulty in design-ing a satisfactory synchronised electrical exposing system for the two shutters and in 1884 the Kew Committee, in its annual report com-mented: 'Some difficulties having been met with in working the electrical instantaneous shutters, part of the apparatus was returned to the makers, the Philosophical Instrument Construction Society, Cambridge, and rectified.'[16] Rarely can the name of the firm have been more tastefully distorted!

The cathetometer, which Darwin had begun to design for Professor Poynting in the autumn of 1880, was one of his first major essays at kinematic (geometric) design. Throughout his working life Darwin was a vigorous exponent of Clerk Maxwell's theories on good design and wherever possible he attempted to apply them in his own work. (Even the

supports for the micrometer for the worm stone at Down House—one of
the first instruments designed by Darwin in 1877—were designed on these
principles, with cylindrical trunnions resting in V-blocks.) As a result
Darwin was able to produce relatively simple instruments but with
significant improvements over the earlier designs of others. When assessing the design of an instrument Darwin advocated that one should
consider separately the effects of bad workmanship, the bending of
component parts, and wear. Ideally the functioning of the instrument
should not be affected by these defects and the application of geometric
design principles would often assist greatly in achieving this target. To
illustrate the principle of geometric design Darwin once cited the very
simple example of a wheelbarrow with a metal axle and wooden wheel
(*Fig.* 2.2): 'The axle of the wheel usually consists of two round iron pins
running in holes in wooden rails forming the frame of the wheelbarrow.
Both the wood and the pins wear; the pin gets smaller but keeps circular,
and wears its way into the wood and always fits it properly on the side
where pressure is taken. The wheel will work perfectly till either the holes
break out of the wood or the pin wears down very small and itself gives
way. But sometimes the axle is made differently, an iron rod is fixed to the
two wooden rails and passes through a hole bored along the centre of the
wheel. With use the iron rod wears on the underside and does not remain
circular and the hole in the wheel gets larger; the result is increased
friction and a loose and shaky bearing.'[17]

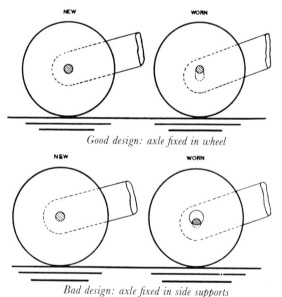

NEW   WORN

Good design: axle fixed in wheel

NEW   WORN

Bad design: axle fixed in side supports

*Figure 2.2 Geometric design applied to axle for wheelbarrow wheel.
(Diagrams: Aeronautical Journal, 1913, Vol. XVII, pp. 181–2.)*

The correspondence with Poynting shows that Darwin gave a great deal of thought to the design of the cathetometer and that he also sought the advice of R. T. Glazebrook, who was at that time a Demonstrator at the Cavendish Laboratory. As with many of Darwin's early designs the work took a considerable time to complete to his satisfaction and the instrument was not sent to Professor Poynting until September 1882. Despite the amount of work it had entailed the invoice was made out for the sum of £37.10s.0d. Darwin obtained a patent for the essential (geometric) features of the design in 1883 and used them again two years later in his surveyor's level (*Fig. 2.3*).

Figure 2.3 Surveyor's level c. 1885. (Photo: Zeitschrift fur Instrumentenkunde, 1886, pp. 55–8.)

In 1884 Darwin designed a reading microscope for Lord Rayleigh, for use in the Physical Laboratory at Cambridge. Used to measure small differences in length, this instrument comprised a pair of microscopes fixed in a vertical position to a pair of frames which could be slid along a gun-metal bed. Each microscope was fitted with a cross-wire eyepiece and each frame was provided with a micrometer screw, which could be read to 0·0001 of an inch, to give it a slow horizontal motion of one inch. As with the cathetometer the moving parts were designed on kinematic principles.

During 1882–3 Caldwell and Threlfall, working in the Department of Comparative Anatomy at Cambridge, invented the automatic microtome and during the following eighteen months or so the Company made a few microtomes based on Caldwell and Threlfall's design. The instrument was, however, expensive to make and this led Darwin to produce a much simpler design, again based almost entirely on kinematic design principles. It was so much simpler to make that, in 1885, the Company were able to price 'Darwin Rockers', as they became known, at £5.5s.0d. each, compared to £31.10s.0d. for the Caldwell and Threlfall instrument. Seventy years later the 'Cambridge Rocker' was still being made by the Company, in fundamentally the same form as the original Darwin design. In the intervening years it sold in great numbers all over the world, many of the early instruments manufactured by Darwin still being in constant use after fifty or sixty years of service. The history of the invention of the automatic microtome forms the content of Chapter 8.

With the many varieties of small electric motors which are now available it is difficult to appreciate just how handicapped the experimental scientists of the latter part of the nineteenth century were. Instruments had to be operated by hand or powered by clockwork motors or water pumps, which could only supply limited amounts of power. Gas engines and shafting were coming into use, to drive machinery, but this source of power was awkward and unwieldy when applied to instruments. As one solution to these problems Darwin devised a novel system of endless running cords and pulleys, which was more versatile and less cumbersome than shafting. By this means power could be transmitted from a central motor, usually an Otto gas engine in the basement, to various rooms throughout a building, the running cords being taken along the sides of the tables on which the instruments were placed. The system was marketed in 1883 and was first supplied to the Physiological Laboratory at Owens College in Manchester, and later to the Physiological Laboratory at Cambridge. Despite its astonishing complexities the system obviously helped to satisfy a pressing need at the time.[18]

Charles Vernon Boys was an experimental physicist with a talent for using unconventional methods. The son of a rector he studied mining and metallurgy at the Royal School of Mines in South Kensington and, after graduating in 1876, he taught physics there. He is mainly remembered for his method of making extremely fine glass and quartz fibres by shooting a filament of hot material from a specially constructed bow and arrow. Using this technique glass fibres 0·0001 mm in diameter and ninety feet in length could be obtained.[19] Such fibres were ideal for suspensions and about 1886–7 Boys used a quartz fibre to suspend the coil in the radiomicrometer which he designed at that time.

In this instrument heat radiation was received on a small rectangular piece of blackened copper foil. Two very small strips of bismuth and antimony were soldered to the upper edge of the foil, thus forming a thermojunction, the free ends of these strips being linked by a single loop of fine copper wire. The whole system was suspended between the poles of a permanent magnet by the fine quartz fibre, to which was attached a small mirror. This instrument was so sensitive that it would detect the heat radiation falling on a blackened copper foil from a candle nearly two miles away, and between 1888 and 1890 Boys made several attempts to measure the heat radiation from stars with the instrument, working in the garden of his father's rectory at Wing. He was unable to detect any radiation and, confident of the sensitivity of his instrument, he correctly concluded that the results of earlier workers were spurious.[20]

In 1890 The Cambridge Scientific Instrument Company published a preliminary leaflet announcing that it was making the radio-micrometer to Boys' design. A note at the end of the leaflet advised potential purchasers that 'All circuits are made and examined under the direction of Mr C. V. Boys and a certificate is given with each.'[21] For spectroscopic observations a special version of the instrument was made in which the 4 mm long piece of blackened copper foil was only 0·5 mm wide instead of the standard width of 2 mm.

Boys is also remembered for his experiments, during the early 1890s, to determine 'G', the Gravitational Constant, and hence the density of the earth. He used Cavendish's torsion balance technique of 1798 but was able to reduce the length of the beam from 6 feet to 0·9 inches by making use of a quartz fibre as the suspension. The Company made this apparatus for Boys in 1890, for £61.0s.5½d.

The Company continued to work closely with Boys for a number of years and marketed his apparatus for determining the Mechanical Equivalent of Heat, 'J' (in 1884) and his wheel of lenses (1891) the latter being used to study the oscillations of electric sparks.

About 1884 the Board of Trade asked Darwin to investigate the automatic temperature regulation of a standards bath with a view to improving the comparison of standards of length at the Standards Office. Darwin visited the Bureau International des Poids et Mesures at Sèvres to study the equipment in use there and after some preliminary trials constructed a regulator similar to that in use at Sèvres, but with a compensating barometer to eliminate the effects of atmospheric pressure variation. Although the apparatus was only experimental the results were highly satisfactory. During a test period of fourteen days, during which it was not adjusted, the temperature of the standards bath did not vary by more than 0·04 °C. A detailed description of this equipment is given in Chapter 11.

The first mention of the Anthropometric Apparatus occurs in the February 1885 List. These sets of instruments were used to measure and test the chief physical characteristics of the human body. The instruments were based on those used by Francis Galton which had been exhibited at the Health Exhibition in London in 1884. A twelve-page catalogue of the apparatus and tests was published in 1889. A set of instruments then comprised apparatus to measure over twenty different parameters including colour of eyes, hair and skin; head length, breadth and height; height standing and sitting; arm span; strength of grip and strength of arm when drawing a bow; eyesight keenness and judgement; hearing keenness and pitch appreciation; and reaction times to sound and sight.

In the Foreword to the List, the use of the apparatus was advocated, to 'draw attention to faults in rearing, to be diligently sought for and remedied lest the future efficiency of the child when it grows to manhood or womanhood be compromised.' Striking a slightly regretful note the Foreword continued: 'The necessity of periodical measurements is thoroughly recognised by those who have studied the subject of health, but it has not yet obtained that hold in England on popular opinion which it deserves, and which it will hereafter undoubtedly exercise.'[22]

Professor James A. Ewing (later Sir Alfred Ewing) is as famous for the seismographs which he designed whilst at the University of Tokio as for his later work on magnetism. Ewing was awarded a gold medal at the Edinburgh International Exhibition of 1886 for his work on seismographs and an account of this work is given in Chapter 9. The Cambridge Scientific Instrument Company began manufacturing these instruments in the mid-1880s and by 1889 they were in use in seismic observatories in several countries, including Manila, Sydney (New South Wales), San José in Costa Rica and the Lick Observatory and University of California in the United States of America. Four sets were also installed at various locations in Great Britain. Ewing later became Professor of Mechanism and Applied Mechanics at Cambridge after James Stuart resigned his post in 1889. He designed a number of other instruments which the Company manufactured, perhaps the most significant being the Ewing Extensometer for tensile testing.

Right from its inception the work undertaken by the Company was thus of a very varied kind—and occasionally not always of a strictly scientific nature. There was, for example, the order placed by Dr Sheridan Lea on 11 July, 1887, entered in the Order Book simply as 'To make sundry pieces of Fishing Tackle to instructions.'[23] Perhaps Dr Lea required this apparatus in connection with his duties as University Lecturer in Physiology at Cambridge at that time, but, then again, perhaps Dr Lea simply enjoyed fishing as a hobby. Whichever was the case, the Cash Book shows that he was subsequently charged five shillings.

Just over a year after The Cambridge Scientific Instrument Company was formed in January 1881 the Company moved to new premises in St Tibb's Row, Cambridge, quite close to Michael Foster's Department of Physiology. The two-storey building was rented from Robert Sayle from 25 March, 1882, at a rental of £115 per annum. The house at 2 Belvidere Terrace was given up from 24 June, 1882, a cheque for the rent for the last quarter (£7.10s.0d.) and the key of the house being sent on that day. At the same time, since William Pye was no longer

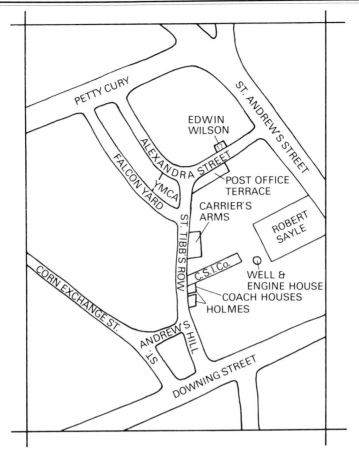

Figure 2.4 Map showing the location of The Cambridge Scientific Instrument Company's premises in St Tibb's Row (1882–95) and Edwin Wilson's business in Alexandra Street (1895–1900).

provided with a house, his salary was increased to £180 per annum: 'This sum being one hundred and fifty pounds per year as salary and thirty pounds per year in lieu of house rent, rates and taxes.[24] Pye was also given five pounds towards the expenses of moving house. The letter setting out the change was signed by both Darwin and Dew-Smith, as had been the earlier letters offering him the position of foreman.

Soon after the move to St Tibb's Row Darwin and Dew-Smith wrote to the Inspector of Factories in Norwich to verify that their workshop complied with the conditions of the Factory Act. The Inspector required answers to various questions, one of which evoked the reply in a letter from Dew-Smith: 'At present we use neither steam, water or other mechanical power. We do not employ women; we employ, however, two boys aged 15 and 15 respectively next birthday.'[25]

Although the premises in St Tibb's Row were small for a factory they were a great improvement on those in Panton Street. Initially all the machines were driven by foot power, but after some time a gas engine with shafting under the floor was installed. According to George Meaden, for many years the oldest mechanic in the firm, the basement in which the shafting ran was a 'dirty glory-hole.' A saw-bench installed at this time remained in use for over fifty years. Darwin occupied a corner of the workshop where he could keep in close touch with the jobs in progress and Michael Foster was a frequent visitor. In fact it became quite an institution for Michael Foster, Dew-Smith and Horace Darwin to meet in the small office in the works in St Tibb's Row to discuss instrument designs over a cup of tea.

Price List No. 2 was published a few months after the move to St Tibb's Row, in September 1882. The reasons for the move were set out in a Foreword to the List:[26]

> *THE CAMBRIDGE SCIENTIFIC INSTRUMENT*
> *COMPANY has moved from Panton Street to St Tibb's Row.*
> *The reason for this change is that the place formerly occupied*
> *was found to be too small for the work that has lately had to be*
> *done. Increased space will do more than make it possible merely*
> *to increase the amount of work done; it will make it possible for*
> *the Company to do that work more completely in accordance with*
> *their desire to make it as practical and accurate as possible. The*
> *Company is, as it always has been, anxious rather to strike out*
> *or adopt and improve new forms of instruments than to direct its*
> *energies to the reproduction in a dealer's spirit of familiar and*
> *more or less stereotyped models. The nature of the machines*
> *which the Company is now prepared, and hopes in future, to*
> *supply is indicated by the catalogue appended. This catalogue,*
> *however, is necessarily not altogether complete as regards the*
> *present, and is of course still less complete as regards the future.*
> *Fuller information may be given in answer to special requests,*
> *and in the case of less known and more complete machines, it*
> *will be possible to convey a better notion of them by means of*
> *photographs to those who have a special interest in obtaining*
> *them.*

R. D. Archer-Hind, at Cambridge, subsequently translated the Foreword into Greek and included it in a collection of translations which he published in 1905.[27] In addition, a letter sent in 1933 to Sir Charles G. Darwin by T. L. Heath—an eminent scholar in Greek Mathematics—implies that the Foreword may also have been used as a translation exercise for the undergraduates at Trinity College in 1882/3:[28]

> *Dear Darwin,*
> *It is a great pleasure to me to be able to send you this*
> *glorious piece of Greek Prose done by Archer-Hind. It seems it is*
> *almost exactly 50 years ago since he set it as an* alternative,
> *you will observe (the other passage was something of Emer-*

. son's). It is a thing to linger over—the perfect Greek idioms and the resounding long words! I think it is probably included in Archer-Hind's translations into Greek Verse and Prose published by the Cambridge Press (2/6) but I do not happen to possess that volume. I have it among the copies which I collected at Trinity from 1879 to 1883 and bound up in a volume to keep.

Yours sincerely,
T. L. Heath

It was customary for such passages to be given out as printed sheets (headed 'Trinity College Lecture-Room'), fair copy translations being distributed the following week. There is a collection of these exercises from the 1880s in Trinity College archives, although, unfortunately, the Foreword to the Price List is not amongst them. The Emerson 'alternative', mentioned by Heath, would have been an easier alternative passage for translation.

As a result of their continuing involvement in the publication of the *Journal of Physiology*, a lithographic department was added to the activities of the firm in 1883, the aim being to provide good quality illustrations for scientific publications. Horace Darwin was not greatly interested in artistic matters and the lithographic department was left largely in the hands of Dew-Smith, who became an acknowledged expert. In 1883 he engaged an assistant, Edwin Wilson (father of J. Dover Wilson, the Shakespearian scholar) and in January 1884 he sent him to Jena to master the technique of lithography. When Wilson returned he brought back with him an experienced lithographic printer named Schneider. In List No. 6, dated August 1884, it was announced that: 'The whole of the processes are done on the premises of the Company, and only work of a high quality is turned out, competing with the best lithography in Frankfurt or Leipzig.' In the next List, February 1885, this was extended by: 'The Company also undertakes to make drawings of microscopic preparations, or other specimens.'[29] Many of the plates in the *Philosophical Transactions of the Royal Society* of that period are marked 'Cambridge Scientific Instrument Company'.

Although there is no doubt that the partnership between Darwin and Dew-Smith was initially a close one—a letter from Darwin to Dew-Smith dated 12 September, 1881, begins 'Dear Dew,' and is signed 'Yours Horace Partner'—as time progressed it is clear that Darwin emerged as the dominant force. Dew-Smith could not match his technical expertise in instrument design and, although Dew-Smith continued to derive considerable enjoyment from the part he played in the daily running of the business, in order to satisfy his need for creative work his interests turned progressively to the more artistic sciences of lithography and photography. Dew-Smith expanded the lithographic side of the business to include photolithography and the 1888 Price List included the note '... and also by means of photography to make reproductions in photogravure, type blocks, photolithography and various other processes.'[30]

In 1883 the island of Krakatoa had been the scene of a violent volcanic eruption. The island cracked at its base, allowing the sea water to mingle with the hot lava. The resulting pressure was such that it sent a fiery column of dust many miles into the air. The dust encircled the earth, turning sunsets so red that months later fire brigades were called out on the east coast of the USA. A report on the eruption, published by the Krakatoa Committee of the Royal Society in 1888, included six plates illustrating the colourings of the sky in England (at a point just west of London) in November 1883.[31] These plates, which were based on sketches made by W. Ascroft, are fine examples of the chromolithography produced by The Cambridge Scientific Instrument Company[†] and are reputed to be the work of Edwin Wilson who became an exceedingly good lithographic artist.

Dew-Smith, for his part, became one of the best photographers of his day and he produced a series of exceptional photographic portraits of contemporary men of eminence by the carbon process. Some of these are preserved in Trinity College Library, to which they were presented by Lady Maud Darwin in August 1940.[‡]

However, it must be emphasised that Dew-Smith took very seriously the responsibilities of his business partnership with Darwin. Darwin's health was generally poor throughout this period and he was working himself very hard, as his mother noted in a worried letter to his brother George on 2 April, 1884:[32]

> '... Horace and Ida set out tomorrow with their
> pleasant party of M. Foster, Mr Coutts and the body physician
> Dr Pye Smith. Horace looks very unwell and I don't know when
> he has had such a long bout—Ida is perfect in cheerfulness and
> tenderness and she thinks it is better for him to force himself to
> see people and exert himself a little, though attempting to go to
> the shop and coming back entirely done up was certainly bad for
> him. ...'

The workshop at St Tibb's Row, affectionately named 'Down Room' by Darwin, was visited by many eminent men of science, including some from overseas, but the visits on 23 November, 1887, which prompted

---

† An entry in the Company's Order Book, dated 9 July, 1887, records the order placed by H. Rix, on behalf of the Royal Society: '1000 copies in Chromolithography on two plates, all the colours being shewn, printing paper etc. being included £92.0s.0d.'[33]

‡ The collection (Classification No. 0.17.4.) includes portraits of Frank Balfour, Gerald Balfour, Revd Robert Burn, Arthur Cayley, Sir Julian Corbett, William Cunningham, A. G. Dew-Smith, Sir Michael Foster (see Fig. 1.4), Sir Francis Galton, Professor F. J. A. Hart, R. D. Hicks, Henry Jackson, Joseph Joachim, Sir W. D. Niven and Sedley Taylor.

the following, somewhat excited letter to Darwin from Dew-Smith at the works at St Tibb's Row were perhaps rather unusual:[34]

> *Dear Darwin,*
>
> *Please put in the enclosed envelope the place and hour of Mr Galton's lecture to Dr Lamborn. He is a customer and bought one thing today and will buy others. He is from New York.*
>
> *We had a real living Chinese Mandarin at the Shop today in a great purple fur cloak, shoes with wooden soles about 3 inches thick and a pig tail down to his heels.*
>
> *Yours*
> *A. G. Dew-Smith*

A visit to Cambridge by a Chinese official was a noteworthy event but it is, perhaps, significant that, in December 1887, Professor Michael Foster was one of the fifteen members of Council who reported favourably to the Senate of the University on the proposed institution of a Professorship of Chinese. Sir Thomas Francis Wade, who was elected to the professorship in April 1888, was already living in Cambridge in 1887 after travelling widely in the Far East for many years. Furthermore, Robert Sayle had a considerable volume of import/export business with the Far East.

Dew-Smith's letters to Darwin show his real concern that the business should continue to run smoothly during Darwin's absences. In 1888, during another bout of illness, Darwin told Dew-Smith that he was considering taking a chalet in Switzerland to aid his recovery. Dew-Smith wrote to him on 14 June from his rooms in Trinity College to bring him up to date with the news of the Town and 'Shop':[35]

> *Dear Darwin,*
>
> *. . . I am glad to hear that you are thinking of taking a chalet in Switzerland for the summer. I don't exactly envy you, for there is nothing I dislike so much as being in a Swiss chalet or indeed as being in Switzerland. It is fortunate however that everybody is not of my mind, else those poor Swiss would starve. . . . However I sincerely hope that the change may do you good and that you will enjoy it as much as I should hate it.*
>
> *Please don't hurry for one moment. I am very happy and don't a bit want to get away. We shall be at peace after tomorrow. Just now we have had the Prince of Wales and Lord Randolph Churchill and all sorts of vulgar people here receiving honorary degrees. (I wish I knew if you receive your Reporter regularly.) They are all clearing out now and we shall be able to retire into our shell again.*
>
> *The shop goes on fairly comfortably. B--- the Carpenter is a little profligate in his habits I find, but now that I have found him out I shall get him into trim. W--- the stone grinder pretends that he is laid up with rheumatism, meanwhile he attends Race Meetings at Newmarket. The next time he*

complains of Rheumatism I shall take him to the hospital. It will be fun for me, but perhaps not so much for him. Mr Smith has just limewashed the shop from top to bottom so that will pacify the Government Inspector. . . .

In contrast Dew-Smith's letter dated 16 May, 1889, on the Company's letter heading was business-like and to the point:[36]

> *Dear Darwin,*
> *Warner has been worrying me about his job and we think we have got it to act alright. On the drawing is marked 'Contact Clock here'. We don't know what this is, nor what function it is to perform. If you remember please send me a line and we will try to put it through. It will be a comfort to you to feel that this job is done. We hope to have the Radio Micrometers ready next week to send out, sensitive enough to satisfy Boys' ideas. I hope you are still improving.*
> *Yours very truly,*
> *A. G. Dew-Smith*

Four days later Dew-Smith was relieved to receive a note from Darwin:[37]

> *Dear Darwin,*
> *I was very glad indeed to see your own handwriting this morning for although I had enquired almost daily for your welfare I had got an idea that you were not quite strong enough to write. I am delighted to see you can write and to gather that you are pretty cheerful. . . .*

The partnership agreement in 1881 had stipulated a partnership period of ten years with power to dissolve at the end of five. By the autumn of 1889, despite his persistent bouts of ill health in 1888 and 1889, Darwin had begun to plan changes to the firm. Dew-Smith returned from a holiday in the Isle of Wight to find that Darwin had prepared notes of his proposals for him to consider whilst Darwin took a short holiday before the winter. On 6 October, 1889, Dew-Smith wrote to Darwin from Trinity College.[38]

> *Dear Darwin,*
> *Please do just as you feel inclined as to coming to the Shop on your return. It is doing unusually well I think in every Department, and this Sunday morning I found more than a hundred pounds in the letter box. Several orders for physiology traps have come to hand. . . .*
> *As to our proposed rearrangement of the Partnership, I have read and thought over your notes many times, one question however always occurs to me which I had hitherto lost sight of.*
> *In what way would it be advantageous either to you or to me to alter the present arrangement. It would give you a good deal of responsibility, and necessary attention to detail which you have never had before. It would deprive me of a great deal of very pleasurable amusement.*

I do not suggest these things as arguments for not altering the present position of affairs, but it has occurred to me that if we do alter we may both be very much the losers, you having too much of dreary detail, and I having a great part of one's amusements curtailed. Let us have a chat about this when you return.

Yours most truly,
A. G. Dew-Smith

Notwithstanding Dew-Smith's misgivings the partnership was dissolved on 1 January, 1891. Horace Darwin took over the instrument side and book debts of the firm, including those of the *Journal of Physiology*.

Figure 2.5 The Company's premises in St Tibb's Row, c. 1890, looking towards St Tibb's Row. The low buildings, with ridged roofs, in the centre left of the photograph, are coach houses used by Edward R. Holmes, a livery stable keeper. These fronted on to St Tibb's Row. An enlargement from the negative has revealed that the man at the top of the staircase is Dew-Smith. Although this part of Cambridge was largely re-developed in the 1970s the exact location of the Company's works has been determined from earlier aerial photographs, using the outbuildings and houses shown in this photograph. In particular, the Cambridgeshire Collection in the Lion Yard Central Library has a photograph believed to have been taken from a balloon about 1912 (Ref: A191 8839) which shows much detail of this area. (Photo: C.S.I.Co., Neg. SU 1944.)

Dew-Smith took over the business of lithographic printing and the publication of the *Journal*, trading as the Cambridge Engraving Company. At that time there were four men employed in the Lithographic Department: Wilson, Schneider, Bayley and Brand.

An agreement made between Dew-Smith and Darwin on 27 January, 1891, provided that Horace Darwin would occupy the ground floor at St Tibb's Row, consisting of a front office, or store room and the range of workshops extending from the front to the back with the show room and private office at the end. He would also have the use of the yard to the west side of the fence next to premises let to Holmes, together with right of entrance from the roadway leading from St Tibb's Row by the existing doors.

Dew-Smith, as the Cambridge Engraving Company, would occupy the upper floor, consisting of five rooms, and the portion of the yard and sheds attached on the east side of the fence and gateway which had recently been erected. He would also have the right of access from the roadway between six in the morning and six at night across the other part of the yard used by Horace Darwin, and the exclusive use of the staircase leading from the entrance lobby to the upper floor. Dew-Smith and Horace Darwin would jointly use and occupy the entrance from St Tibb's Row and the lobby at the foot of the staircase leading to the upper floor. The annual rent payable to Robert Sayle was apportioned as Horace Darwin £109 and Dew-Smith £92 per annum.

The partnership had started in 1881 with a capital of £2100, the partners having subscribed £1050 each. The accounts for the last year of the partnership recorded Sales for the year as £8621 and Salaries and Wages paid £3708. The year's trading had resulted in a loss of £772.1s.8d. which was shared equally between the partners, after which their Capital accounts showed balances in their favour as A. G. Dew-Smith £623.17s.4d. and H. Darwin £840.4s.2d. Darwin had also put money into the business by way of loan and his Loan Account showed a balance of £2417.6s.8d.

The Deed of Partnership in 1881 had given the object of the business as 'For the improvement of Scientific Instruments etc.' and this had certainly been achieved, although, perhaps because Darwin continued to be over-generous to his customers in his costing methods, it was not the financial success that had been hoped.

The value of the Lithographic stock taken over by Dew-Smith was £589.19s.5d. For some years he continued in business as the Cambridge Engraving Company, wrapt in the work which had brought together his love of apparatus and art. Apart from a brief holiday in the summer he was always to be found in the workshop on the top floor at St Tibb's Row, and those visitors who were allowed into his studio always found some new thing of beauty to admire. After a while, however, he

Figure 2.6 Albert George Dew-Smith. This photograph was given to Francis Jenkinson by Alice Dew-Smith in August 1903, after Dew-Smith's death. (Photo: Cambridge University Library Portraits Collection d.26)

tired of the business aspect of his work. In 1894 the Cambridge University Press, which had always printed the *Journal of Physiology*, also took over its publication, and, about a year later, when The Cambridge Scientific Instrument Company moved to Carlyle Road, Dew-Smith transferred the lithographic side of his business to Edwin Wilson, who had remained working with him as his assistant.

Dew-Smith kept his photographic equipment but from that time on used it only for his own pleasure or commissions for special friends. He had found a new interest in life, for in 1895 he married Miss Alice Lloyd. He gave up his rooms in Trinity and he and his wife lived happily in Chesterton Hall for five years until he was suddenly ill in 1900. He died in 1903.

In 1895 Edwin Wilson set up in business on his own as a natural history artist at 17 Alexandra Street (Post Office Terrace), Cambridge. About 1900 he moved to 16 Mill Lane and in 1913 he too disposed of his business, to the Cambridge University Press, although he continued to manage the business.

* * * * *

CHAPTER THREE

The Company under Darwin

ON 1 January, 1891, Horace Darwin assumed sole control of his 'Shop'. A circular had been printed in December 1890, informing customers that the business was to be split up and on 1 January Darwin sent out a further circular to his customers, ostensibly to tell them that he would shortly be publishing an illustrated catalogue, but in reality to maintain customer confidence in the business:[1]

> *Our staff of skilled instrument makers remains unchanged. The workshop is equipped with machine tools suitable for work requiring a high degree of accuracy; and great care is taken to ensure good workmanship.*
>
> *In the design of new instruments due attention has been given to accuracy of movement, convenience in use, and general simplicity.*
>
> *We hope that our past experience will enable us to carry out in a satisfactory manner any work which may be entrusted to us.*
>
> *Faithfully yours,*
> *Horace Darwin*

In March 1891 'List 12', the first illustrated catalogue of the Company's products, was issued. It had board covers, 122 pages, and was divided into twenty-eight sections. These included mechanics, the measurement of length, heat, recording apparatus, optics, sound and galvanometers plus comprehensive sections on physiological apparatus. Whilst this might appear to be a formidable range of instruments for a small company, with only a few workmen, the demand was small and the instruments were, in general, of a simple nature and sold for teaching and research purposes only.

Very few scientific instruments were in use in industry at that time. A few enlightened businessmen were beginning to see their advantages but any attempt to introduce improved methods of measurement usually met with strong opposition from the workforce who would not allow their acquired skill—which, it must be said, was often largely guess-work—to be taken over by a ' box of tricks', and sabotage was not uncommon. During the next twenty years a great revolution was brought about in this field and of all the instruments listed in the 1891 catalogue Callendar's platinum thermometer was, without doubt, the most significant in the influence it was to have on methods of industrial temperature measurement.

Hugh Longbourne Callendar was born in 1863 at Hatherop in Gloucestershire. A pupil at Marlborough School, he went up to Trinity in 1882 where he obtained first class honours degrees in classics in 1884 and in mathematics in 1885. It was while he was an Assistant Demonstrator in Experimental Physics from 1887–8 at the Cavendish Laboratory, working under Professor J. J. Thomson, that Callendar carried out his researches in platinum thermometry, largely at the instigation of Thomson, who had noticed that he was 'a beautiful manipulator.'[2]

Some fifteen years earlier Sir William Siemens had proposed that the change in resistance of platinum wire with temperature might be used as a means of measuring temperature. However, the thermometers which Siemens subsequently constructed proved unreliable in use and an adverse report by a Committee of the British Association for the Advancement of Science in 1874 had given the technique a bad name.[3] Thomson had been one of the members of this Committee although the tests had been carried out in Professor Carey Foster's laboratory. The Committee had included in its report various suggestions as to how the reliability of the thermometers might be improved, and Thomson had formed the opinion that with the proper precautions the method could be made to work. He encouraged Callendar to take on the project and, in 1887, after only eight months' work, Callendar showed that Thomson was right and that the resistance thermometer was indeed capable of highly accurate and repeatable results if proper precautions were taken during its manufacture and use.[4] In 1891 Horace Darwin obtained sole manufacturing rights from Callendar and began to make thermometers for industrial use.

In Callendar's original design the wire was wound on a hard glass tube. This construction was soon modified, the wire being wound on a cruciform mica frame. This cruciform arrangement is attributed to Ernest Howard Griffiths of Sidney Sussex College, Cambridge, a research associate of Callendar. Heycock and Neville were using resistance thermometers in their work on the determination of melting points of various metals and, apparently, were having persistent difficulties with shorted turns in the thermometers. It is said that Griffiths had been giving this problem a good deal of thought and the solution suddenly occurred to him one day while he was lecturing his class. He cut out a model from a postcard and sent it to Darwin, who worked out the constructional details and used the technique for many years afterwards.

Darwin's first thermometers were supplied with specially modified laboratory type Wheatstone bridges, which had temperature markings alongside the bridge wire, but the need for portable measuring equipment for use with the thermometer soon became obvious. In 1893 Darwin began manufacturing 'Callendar's Patent Electrical Pyrometer'. This was a self-contained unit with a battery and calibrated galvanometer, from which the thermometer temperature could be read directly. A large number of these pyrometers were made for the blast furnace and pottery industries. They were extremely sensitive, but quite robust and had a fast response time. At first Callendar, as the inventor and designer, checked and adjusted the production pyrometers, but when he accepted a post as Professor of Physics at McGill University in Montreal Griffiths took over the job of testing. A note in the 1893 catalogue reads:[5] 'In the absence of Mr Callendar as Professor of Physics in the McGill University, Montreal, Canada, each instrument will, before it is issued, be tested under Mr Griffiths' supervision in his laboratory at Cambridge and he will supply a form showing the corrections, if any, that have to be applied to each instrument.' A footnote added, 'Each instrument will be numbered and the correction form will be of a similar nature to that supplied by Kew with high class mercury thermometers.'

The practice of having his products checked by the designer was of considerable advantage to Darwin, and in many cases a necessity. The Company was at that time essentially a manufacturing workshop and whilst Darwin had test-room facilities he had no laboratory. However, scientists such as Callendar and Griffiths were able to make use of the equipment in their own laboratories to test his products and this situation, as well as having practical advantages, could also be used to help promote sales.

Because of the unsatisfactory performance of Siemens' thermometers and their subsequent condemnation by the British Association, there was, to begin with, considerable distrust in industry of the new thermometers being made to Callendar and Griffiths' designs. The British Association had somehow to be persuaded to give a lead in accepting their work. Griffiths raised the subject at the 1894 meeting. Not having tested Callendar and Griffiths' thermometers Carey Foster would not commit himself unequivocally but he did agree to make a statement in a letter to *Nature* which was published on 23 August, 1894:[6]

Platinum-resistance Thermometers

At the meeting of the British Association, just coming
to an end, it was pointed out to the Committee of Section A, by
Mr E. H. Griffiths, that the general adoption of the method of
thermometry, founded on the variation of the electric resistance of
platinum with temperature, that has been worked out by Professor Callendar and himself, is seriously hindered by the existence of a report presented to the Belfast Meeting of the Association in 1874 (British Association Report 1874, pp. 242–249) by
a Committee 'appointed for the purpose of testing the new pyrometer of Mr Siemens.' As I was secretary of this Committee and
drafted the report, and as all the experiments were made either
by myself or under my direction, I was desired by the Committee
of Section A to ask you to allow me to state in the columns of
Nature (what is indeed obvious to anyone who refers to the
1874 report) that the tests carried out by the Committee of 1874,
and the conclusions arrived at by them, had reference solely to the
pyrometers supplied to them for examination by Messrs Siemens
Brothers, and that they have consequently no bearing on the
question of the trustworthiness or accuracy of the platinum-
resistance thermometers of the kind devised by Messrs Griffiths
and Callendar.

G. Carey Foster

To reassure potential purchasers this letter was reproduced on
the back page of The Cambridge Scientific Instrument Company's
catalogue for Callendar's Pyrometers.

Lord Kelvin, at that time President of the Royal Society, had
already voiced his approbation of Callendar's Indicating Pyrometer in a
letter to Griffiths and Darwin the year before. Darwin, eager to obtain the
maximum advertising value from Lord Kelvin's letter, included an
extract in the pyrometer catalogue:

'It seemed to me most promising as an instrument for
practical use in the measurement of the temperature of furnaces. I
admired very much the arrangements by which the electric measurements which it involves are made practically convenient for
use in a factory, without losing the accuracy required to give
good results. I hope that it will prove a very valuable instrument
not only for factories but also in physical and chemical laboratories.'

It was while he was at McGill University that Callendar made
his next major contribution to industrial pyrometry with the invention of
the recorder associated with his name. Darwin quickly realised its
potential and by 1898 the recorder was in production and a comprehensive descriptive leaflet had been published by the Company. The recorder
was a self-balancing instrument, available either as a Wheatstone bridge
for use with resistance thermometers or as a potentiometer for use with

thermocouples and for potential measurements. It was the first of several generations of self-balancing potentiometric recorders and a detailed description of its operation is given in Chapter 12.

As the business expanded during the 1890s Darwin was faced with the need for larger premises and in 1895 he bought a piece of land, between Carlyle Road and Chesterton Road in Cambridge, for £301.2s.7d. A contract was placed with Rattee and Kett to build the first of the Company's workshops on the site. That same year the business was converted into a limited liability company with a capital of £10 000. It was registered on 11 May and the first Board meeting was held in the old premises at St Tibb's Row on 25 May, 1895. All four directors were present: Horace Darwin, Major Leonard Darwin, William Napier Shaw and Hugh F. Newall. William Pye was appointed Company Secretary, although the minutes were in fact written by Alfred Reed.

*Figure 3.1 Works outing on the river c. 1894. Present in the photo-
graph are:*   *Morgan, Meaden
Calcott, Horace Darwin, H. Pye, Jenkinson
C. Collins, Frost, Saunders, T. Pye, Murfitt.
(The harpist is not known.)   (Photo: C.S.I.Co.)*

At the next meeting of the Board, on 14 June, Darwin completed a conveyance of the land at Carlyle Road to the Company. The formal purchase of the business from Horace Darwin, as a going concern, was made at a value of £5200, Darwin receiving in return 1,040

fully paid up shares of £5 each in the Company. The first shareholders —Horace Darwin, Leonard Darwin, Francis Darwin, George Darwin, E. H. Griffiths, W. Napier Shaw and H. F. Newall—were then allotted one share each. To pay for the new building 4% debentures were issued: to Lord Farrer, £250; Lady Farrer, £250; George Darwin, £200; H. F. Newall, £200; William Darwin, £300; and Elizabeth Darwin, £200. The first instalment of £650 on the new building was then authorised to be paid to Rattee and Kett. Two months later debentures of £200 each were issued to J. Bonham Carter, The Honourable Mrs T. C. Farrer and William Pye.

Building work proceeded throughout 1895 and was sufficiently advanced for the directors to hold their first Board meeting at Carlyle Road on 4 September, 1895. The statutory General Meeting was held on the same day although only the minimum quorum of three persons was present. By the summer of 1896 the building was completed and in May Horace Darwin's mother visited the new factory. On 18 May she wrote in a letter:[7].

> '*I liked seeing the shop on Sunday. It is a perfect*
> *situation, surrounded with gardens and so quiet. I did not mount*
> *up to the show-room. Horace's room is so nice and airy and*
> *quiet. It made me think more of him to have such a shop.*'

The cost of the workshops had been £3208.1s.2d., but this price included a house at the entrance to the factory (later 22 Carlyle Road). This was known as the 'foreman's cottage' and it was let initially to Mr Pye at an annual rent of nineteen guineas.

Trading for the years 1895 and 1896 resulted in losses of £46 and £47 respectively but 1897 brought a profit of £333 and from this a bonus of $1\frac{1}{2}$% was paid to the workmen on their 1897 wages, 3% on Alfred Reed's salary and $4\frac{1}{2}$% on William Pye's salary as manager. A dividend of $1\frac{1}{2}$% was also paid to the ordinary shareholders and 6% to the holders of £300 preference shares. Up to this time the directors had not received any remuneration so at the meeting held on 26 March, 1898, the four directors, who were all present, voted themselves a share in this prosperity—£28; 3/8 of this was given to the chairman (Horace Darwin),

Figure 3.2 The first workshop in Carlyle Road c. 1900. The offices were in the left-hand building, with a show-room upstairs. The workshop took up the entire length of the right-hand building, as can be seen from the interior view.
A number of the personalities in the Company can be identified in the outdoors photograph. Alfred H. Reed is on the extreme left and George Meaden, bearded, is in the centre of the doorway. W. H. Apthorpe, wearing a cap, is immediately in front of Meaden, with William Collins, seated, in line with Apthorpe, fifth from the right in the foreground. (Photos: C.S.I.Co., Negs. 4463 and 8973.)

2/8 to each of the two directors resident in Cambridge (H. F. Newall and W. Napier Shaw) and 1/8 to the director not resident in Cambridge (Leonard Darwin). The shareholders had to wait a further seven years for the next dividend—and the directors for remuneration—although in 1902 the business did make a profit and as a consequence in 1903 the sum of £116 was divided amongst the employees as a bonus.

How Horace Darwin came to be introduced to William du Bois Duddell in 1897 is not recorded. It seems unlikely that Darwin would have attended the British Association Meeting that year for it was held in Toronto, but this was the meeting at which the twenty-seven year old Duddell first announced the details of his invention: an oscillograph galvanometer capable of accurately following the varying current and voltage characteristics of an electric arc. The instrument was exactly the type of research tool which would have excited Darwin's interest and he negotiated a royalty agreement with Duddell for the details of the design.

Duddell was an extremely gifted mechanical engineer although his ill-health as a youth had interrupted his education. He had refused to try for a place at Cambridge University but instead went to London University for a brief period before serving an apprenticeship with Messrs Davy Paxman of Colchester. When he was twenty-one he began attending the City and Guilds of London Institute in Finsbury. He studied at the College, working under Professor Ayrton, whilst at his home he fitted out the top floor of the house, which he shared with his mother, as a laboratory and a workshop with a number of precision machine tools.

His work on the oscillograph had stemmed from a study he was making at the College in 1896 of alternating current arcs, working with E. W. Marchant, a fellow student. Plotting the waveforms was laborious and time consuming and Duddell became interested in the possibility of designing an instrument which would enable these curves to be obtained more quickly. The technical details of the problems which he encountered whilst working on the design of his fast response galvanometer in his laboratory workshop are described in Chapter 14.

Darwin began the commercial manufacture of Duddell's oscillograph in 1898, working to Duddell's specifications and a set of working drawings prepared by him. The agreement document was a remarkable one in that, in addition to the usual commercial clauses, Duddell stipulated that the widths of the phosphor bronze conducting strips in the vibrator and the air gaps in the magnets should be accurate to 0;01 mm, the reason being that the efficiency of the damping depended on the extremely small clearances between the strips and the magnet as well as the viscosity of the oil.

For many years Duddell personally inspected every oscillograph before despatch and in the early years he also measured, with great care and exactness, the extremely fine tolerances. Subsequently, when modifications came to be made to the design, Duddell examined and criticised the modified drawings before they were released for manufacture.

The first oscillograph was completed by the Company in 1898 and when the invention became known, and its capability proved, it was received with enthusiasm by electrical institutions throughout the world. It was described in the Company's catalogue of 1899 as 'A powerful weapon of research for electrical engineers'.[8] The standard outfit consisted of a double element oscillograph, synchronous motor, arc lamp and tracing desk, all housed in a teak box, ready for use. The price was £59 and when, later, a rotating drum camera, with an automatic shutter mechanism, was added, the price was £79. The earliest outfits were the low voltage, high frequency pattern, the first high voltage outfit being supplied in 1910 for use at 15 000 volts. In 1911 a 50 000 volt outfit was made for Osaka University and, later, outfits for use at 250 000 volts were made.

In the years that followed Duddell developed a number of other electrical instruments, including his magnetic standard for the calibration of ballistic galvanometers, and the thermogalvanometer. This latter was an extremely sensitive instrument for measuring alternating currents, based on Boys' radiomicrometer, one of which was sent to Duddell by Darwin when he began work on the instrument in March 1900.

During 1898 there were two significant changes in the senior staff at the Company; in August Robert S. Whipple was taken on by Darwin as his personal assistant (at a salary of £180 per annum) and in October, William Pye gave notice of his intention to leave at the end of the year to join his son, W. G. Pye, who had started in business on his own account. Years later Robert Whipple could still vividly remember his first interview with Horace Darwin at 'The Shop'. It was high summer and the large wooden doors were wide open with the sun streaming in on the seventeen men at work at their machines. The interview included a talk with Mr Pye which was conducted whilst walking up and down in the yard to escape from the noise of the shafting driving the machines and to provide some degree of privacy. Further interviews followed with the two directors living in Cambridge; Napier Shaw at Emmanuel College and Professor Newall at his home at Madingley.

Robert Whipple was then twenty-seven years old. He came from a family of scientists, his father, George M. Whipple, being Superintendent at Kew Observatory. Robert had worked there himself, as an assistant, for eight years before leaving to become assistant manager to L. P. Casella for a short time. Whipple was to have an enormous influence on the growth and success of the Company. He was not only competent as a scientist but also as a businessman. At that time costing as a management tool was almost unknown but he immediately set about examining and analysing the Company accounts for the previous years, extracting manufacturing and administration figures, and set targets for profits. Notes still exist, in his handwriting, in preparation for discussions on how to make the Company 'a really going concern', supported by figures from the 1895–1897 accounts.[9] But, notwithstanding Whipple's desire to assist in making the business profitable, he soon discovered that Horace Darwin was first and foremost a scientist and engineer who involved himself in the problems of his fellow scientists.

Darwin had numerous personal contacts amongst the scientists of his day, particularly in Cambridge, and they had a high regard for his scientific knowledge. They frequently sought his advice on their problems, but the apparatus they wished him to make was usually of a special nature for some particular research problem and, all too often, the funds available for the project were not sufficient to meet the cost of making it. While the Company continued to manufacture a wide range of catalogued apparatus the profit from this side of the business was not always sufficient to make up for the losses on the specialist work, as was evident from the annual accounts for some years both before and after Whipple joined the Company. At the same time Darwin's enthusiasm and willingness to become involved in the design and construction of diverse and original instruments for his scientist colleagues, together with the skill of his workforce did much to build the high reputation the Company came to hold in the world of science.

William Pye's resignation in the autumn of 1898 marked the end of an era for the Pye family. At various times all three of his sons had also been employed by Darwin and there is a photograph, *Fig.* 3.1, taken at a Works Outing on the river Cam in 1894, in which both Mr T. Pye and Harry Pye are present. The third son, W. G. Pye had started with the Company as a boy when he was aged fourteen. After four years he left to gain further experience in London. In 1892 he returned to Cambridge to take charge of the workshop at the Cavendish Laboratory. He was an ambitious young man and whilst at the Cavendish he converted a wooden stable in his back garden in Humberstone Road into a small workshop. In 1896, with help from his father, he started up in business as W. G. Pye & Co. He specialised in producing well made and well designed apparatus at a moderate price, suitable for school laboratories or for elementary classes in universities—a product range uncomfortably close to Darwin's own. The business flourished to such an extent that William Pye was able to leave The Cambridge Scientific Instrument Company in 1898 and join his son full time.

Darwin was clearly not altogether happy with this train of events or the situation after William Pye's departure. On 2 February, 1899, the Company wrote to W. G. Pye & Co. asking for their price list and shortly afterwards Harry Pye was asked to leave the Company, although Darwin gave him a first class reference in his letter to Professor Barrett at the Royal College of Science in Dublin, on 21 February, 1899:[10]

'... He worked for us for about 8 years, beginning quite as a boy and learning his trade with us. Then after some experience in other shops he went to be Prof. Callendar's Mechanic in the McGill University, Montreal, where he was $2\frac{1}{2}$ years. On returning to England last year he again worked here. He is now leaving for no fault of his own. His father was Foreman and Manager to this Company for 18 years but left us a few months ago and is now in business as an Instrument Maker in this town. We had hoped that this would have made no difference with regard to keeping his son with us but after fuller consideration we came to the conclusion that it would be wiser for him to leave us although we had no fault to find with him.'

Harry Pye would seem to have been the victim of circumstances but a letter from Darwin dated 4 March, 1899, addressed 'Dear Harry' shows that he left on good terms with Darwin.[11]

Three years later, on 22 February, 1902, Horace Darwin reported to his fellow directors that W. G. Pye had approached him with a view to the Company purchasing the Pye business. It was agreed to communicate through solicitors for further information but at the Board meeting on 5 May, 1902, the directors were informed that negotiations had fallen through. A year later W. G. Pye moved his company to new premises in Mill Lane where it stayed until the move to the site in Newmarket Road in 1913. The partnership between W. G. Pye and his father lasted until 1908 when William Pye retired to live at Leigh-on-Sea. He died in June 1921 at the age of 74.

The years following the First World War were the threshold of a major recession which was to squeeze much of British manufacturing industry, but the creation of the British Broadcasting Corporation in 1922 did create a large domestic market for wireless sets. Whilst Darwin and his fellow directors decided that wireless was not in their line of business, W. G. Pye & Co., who were at that time short of work and looking for new products, began making the apparatus and, with a booming market, the wireless department rapidly outgrew the instrument side of the business. In 1928 Pye Radio was formed to take over the manufacture of wireless. During the height of the depression in 1931 a number of the Instrument Company's employees were 'loaned' to Pye, where more tool makers and skilled men were needed. Many of them became key men at the Pye Company and, with the roaring trade in wireless receivers and work just starting on television receivers, they never returned to the Instrument Company. Amicable relations were always maintained between the two companies and their employees frequently competed with each other in various sports and met at social events, but, with hindsight, it is interesting to speculate on the way The Cambridge Scientific Instrument Company might have developed had the proposed merger in 1902 taken place.

There is a further sequel to these links between 'Pyes' and the Instrument Company. In 1934 Sidney Stubbens, who was at that time employed as a foreman by the Instrument Company, had a disagreement with the management and subsequently left the Company, taking with him several of the men from his department. He started a small instrument-making business of his own in Arbury Road (about half a mile from the Instrument Company) which he named Unicam Instruments. This name resulted in some confusion and, to begin with, so much of the Instrument Company mail went astray that the Cambridge Board considered objecting to the registration of the name. No action was however taken and Stubbens' small company grew steadily. About 1947 the business was bought by Pye Radio and subsequently it became 'Pye Unicam', the instrument-manufacturing division of the Pye Group of companies.

When William Pye resigned his post at the Instrument Company in 1898 Robert Whipple succeeded him as Company Secretary (on 1 December) but a new foreman had to be found and W. Wayne was taken on in his place. Wayne had for some years previous been foreman at Elliott Brothers but he still had to serve an initial trial period. His letter of engagement dated 22 February, 1899, backdated his appointment as foreman at £3.10s.0d. per week to 2 December, 1898. Wayne took over the 'foreman's cottage' at the same annual rent of nineteen guineas and was allowed £5 removal expenses. Having had one foreman start up an instrument-making business in competition in Cambridge, Darwin did not intend to allow it to happen again and Wayne's letter of engagement included a clause noting that in the event of his leaving he agreed not to 'set up in business for the sale and manufacture of Scientific Instruments within 10 miles of Great St Mary's Church, Cambridge.'

Efforts to get the shareholders to attend the necessary Annual General Meeting in those early years were not always very successful. A meeting called for 1 April, 1899, had to be adjourned until the 8th because a quorum was not present. On 8 April there was again no quorum, and the meeting was reconvened for 25 April. Happily, on this occasion three shareholders appeared, which was sufficient to enable the business to proceed. Six years later, in 1905, the Annual General Meeting was held at Darwin's home, 'The Orchard', in Huntingdon Road, Cambridge, as there were two cases of scarlet fever amongst the employees in the works.

During 1899 a subsidiary company, the Sentinel Manufacturing Company, was set up to manufacture fire-alarms under patents held by Griffiths and Whetham.[12] The directors were Horace Darwin and W. C. D. Whetham, T. Whitely being Company Secretary, and the registered office was at Llandaff Chambers, 1 Regent Street, in Cambridge. The fire-alarm consisted of a steel tube attached to a thin-walled steel bulb with a wire passed down the tube but insulated from it. In the bulb a non-conducting material with a low melting point prevented a low-melting point alloy from completing the electrical connection between the wire and the bulb. Any rise in temperature sufficient to melt the alloy and non-conducting material caused the circuit to be completed and the fire-alarm bell to ring. As the top of the tube was hermetically sealed the alarm was resettable by warming the bulb and inverting it. The alarm appears not to have been a commercial success as there are no further records of the Company.

In 1900 William Napier Shaw was appointed Secretary to the Meteorological Council. Shaw was a fellow of Emmanuel College, Cambridge, where, as an undergraduate in 1876, he had been placed as sixteenth Wrangler and in the same year had obtained a First in the Natural Sciences Tripos. At the time of his appointment to the Meteorological Council he was Assistant Director of the Cavendish Laboratory but because of the work involved in his new post he gradually relinquished all his Cambridge posts over the following months, including that at the Cavendish and, in April 1901, his seat on the Board of The Cambridge Scientific Instrument Company.

Shaw's successor on the Board was Dr Frederick Frost Blackman, an eminent botanist. A former student at St John's College, Cambridge, Dr Blackman was appointed Demonstrator in Botany at Cambridge in 1891 and his association with the Department of Botany continued until his retirement in 1936. He had a very precise mind with the ability to indicate the best approach to any problem by marshalling and presenting all the facts in such a way that the path to follow became obvious. Blackman had a great love of the arts and one of his major interests was the preservation of the beauty of his college, particularly where extensions to the buildings were involved. He designed various instruments, most of which were used only in the Department of Botany in Cambridge, but one of the few instruments to attain worldwide use was his 'Air Current Commutator' (known to many as 'Clapham Junction') which was manufactured by The Cambridge Scientific Instrument Company in 1934. Using this instrument, analyses of a gas or liquid could be made at defined intervals. The instrument contained a rotating turret head with accurately spaced holes which could be brought adjacent to the entry and exit pipes in the main body of the instrument, thus allowing the flow of gas to be diverted or interrupted for specific periods of time.

As overseas sales of the Company's products steadily increased the first catalogues to be printed in French and German were published during 1901–2. By that time there were forty-four employees at the Company, and an extension to the workshop area was also built—Shop B—providing an additional 1600 square feet of floor area.

In those days the exposed metal surfaces of the Company's instruments were protected by a coating of lacquer. The trade secrets involved in producing the fine 'curly grain' finish were revealed some sixty years later by a retired employee writing anonymously in *Cambridge Comment*[†].[13]

> *We made our own lacquer from seed shellac which was dissolved slowly in a large jar of methylated spirits; after a month the liquid was strained five times and the right amounts of dragon's blood and gum arabic added to the brew. This produced the beautiful gold lacquer finish which is so very different from that given by the clear synthetic lacquers available today.*
>
> *The surfaces to be lacquered were carefully grained in the shops and we then gently warmed the work before applying the lacquer with a soft camel hair brush. If the surface to be covered was large we used a piece of best shirting on a stick, being sure to have singed off the hairs beforehand. It was a job that called for patience and a light touch and only needed someone to open the door at the wrong time for the job to be ruined.*

In September 1903 Major Leonard Darwin resigned from the Board. Horace Darwin's son, Erasmus, was then elected as a director. Erasmus had inherited his father's boundless enthusiasm and this appears in his letters to his father a few years later, when he was involved in the Company's negotiations with Taylor Brothers of the USA. 1903 was also the year that the premium bonus system of payment to the workforce was adopted and the year that the Company commissioned its first traveller to obtain orders.

Frank Doggett joined the Company in 1904. When he retired in 1957 he recalled his impressions of what it was like to be an apprentice in the early 1900s:[14]

> *It is interesting to recall the conditions at The Cambridge Scientific Instrument Company when I joined as a lad of 16. The hours were, in summer, 6.00 a.m. until 5.30 p.m., with a three quarters of an hour interval for breakfast and an hour for dinner. In winter the hours were from 7.45 a.m. until 6.30 p.m. with only the one interval of an hour for dinner. The works were closed on Saturday afternoons. The lads who lived any distance from the works found it strange to bring their meals to eat in the mess room, where a gas cooker was available for warming our food if we wished to do so. It was a small wooden building and quite comfortable as the gas stove was also used for heating during the winter.*
>
> *The lads who commenced at the works in those days were paid two shillings a week for a $53\frac{1}{2}$-hour week, from which one penny was deducted for the local hospital fund. Our work*

---

† 'Cambridge Comment': *The monthly Company newsletter published from December 1960 until about February 1969.*

*was interesting. Some of the other things we were expected to do
were not so interesting and took a lot of the time which we
would have liked to spend learning the trade. We swept out the
workshops and offices each morning and burned the rubbish on
the Alexandra Gardens, which were in those days a disused sand
pit. On Saturday mornings we swept up the yard, which we
quite enjoyed except in wet weather, destroying the rubbish in the
same way.*

*One of the jobs which we did not mind doing, or
rather, which I rather enjoyed, was going into the town with a
handcart, often to Addenbrooke's Hospital to replace batteries for
the X-ray machine, which were charged at the works. These
were heavy and it was some distance through the ward and we
took them to the machine to save the nurses having to carry them.
Other journeys into the town consisted of taking urgent packing
cases to the Railway Office on Market Hill and one wonders
how we should have liked this under present traffic conditions in
Cambridge. One can well imagine that lads at the present time
would not like very much having to do this kind of work. . . .*

*Visitors I can remember during my early days were
Sir Charles Darwin and Dr Gamgee. Also Dr Blackman,
Professor of Botany, and Professor Newall, Head of the Cambridge Observatory. Professor Newall was often driven by his
wife in a wagonette drawn by a pair of fine horses. Mrs Newall
was a former Mistress of Girton College. . . .*

*In 1904 the Test Room staff consisted of three persons
and the total number of employees was less than fifty. My first
job [in the Drawing Office] was to make a tracing of Mr
Foster's drawing of the Einthoven galvanometer. . . .*

Dr Arthur Gamgee was a physiologist. He had studied physics
and medicine at Edinburgh during the 1860s and for many years during
the latter part of his life he carried out research into the diurnal variation
of the temperature of the human body. When he published his results in
1908 he paid particular tribute to the assistance he had received from
Horace Darwin and Robert Whipple at The Cambridge Scientific
Instrument Company.[15] Gamgee experimented with various designs of
thermocouple thermometers. The experimental recording equipment was
designed and made for him by the Company and in the works he had a
corner under the stairs (near the old stores) with a bed for a 'patient',
where he refined and tested the apparatus before it was transferred to
Addenbrooke's Hospital.

In due course Frank Doggett became Head of the Drawing
Office and Chief Designer, a post he held for thirty years. He was also a
well known and respected citizen of Cambridge, serving on the City
Council for forty-one years. He and his wife, Marjorie, were Mayor and
Mayoress in 1946–7 and the following year Frank Doggett was elected as
Deputy Mayor and was also made an Alderman of the City until he

retired from the council in 1967. Then, in recognition of his long period of public service, he received the rare distinction of becoming an Honorary Alderman of the City.

In the early 1900s Charles Féry began to publish his work on a total radiation pyrometer.[16,17] Robert Whipple, who was fast becoming an authority on all forms of temperature measurement, was quick to realise the importance of Féry's instrument and obtained the manufacturing rights for the Company, which became sole agents for sales in the United Kingdom, British Colonies, United States, Norway, Sweden, Japan and China.

In Féry's first design in 1902 radiation from the hot body was focused by a lens on to a small blackened thermal junction, the output from which was measured using a d'Arsonval galvanometer, which could thus be calibrated to read the temperature of the hot body directly. Although the measurement was independent of the distance from the furnace or kiln a certain amount of the radiation was absorbed by the focusing lens, which led to some inaccuracies. In 1904 Féry eliminated these errors by using a mirror instead of a lens to focus the radiation.

The pyrometers had obvious merits. It was not necessary to insert a sensor to contact the hot body and the pyrometer was capable of measuring temperatures up to 2,000 °C, considerably higher than either thermocouples or resistance thermometers could be operated. Initially the Company manufactured both of Féry's designs but the early version was soon discarded in favour of the mirror type.

A very close and amicable working relationship was established with Féry who was a prolific designer. His absorption pyrometer was made by the Company and in 1909 a direct-reading version of the radiation pyrometer was added to the product list. In this instrument the radiation was focused on to a bimetallic coil. A pointer attached to the coil was thus deflected across a calibrated temperature scale as the coil partially unwound on heating. In 1912 the Company signed an agreement to manufacture the Féry Bomb Calorimeter (used for the determination of the calorific value of liquid and gaseous fuels) and this was put into production in 1913.

Callendar's recorder was considered by some industrial users to be too sophisticated for general temperature measurement work, and many wanted a more expanded scale than that on his electrical pyrometer. To satisfy this latter demand Whipple, in 1902, designed an indicator for use with resistance thermometers, which incorporated a manually balanced Wheatstone bridge circuit. The thermometer temperature was read directly from a calibrated drum, which thus provided a greatly expanded scale. Rapidly varying temperatures could be followed and the instrument was found to be especially useful for temperature measurements in boiler flues and annealing work. Over fifty years later

Whipple's indicator was still in production, its long equivalent scale length making it an ideal instrument for precision work.

It was, however, 1905 before the solution to the problem of how to design a cheap temperature recorder occurred to Darwin. Like all good inventions it was simple in essence, and, indirectly, it was Fred Culpan, the Company's pyrometry sales and installation engineer, who gave Darwin the idea. Having returned to the works one day, after a somewhat trying visit to a company in the north of England, Culpan stated firmly and emphatically to Darwin and Whipple that Callendar's recorder was not a suitable instrument for use with a thermocouple in that particular installation. In saying this Culpan was quite correct as the only thermocouple the Company had in use at the time was platinum against platinum/10% iridium alloy and the output was too low to give a satisfactory record on the Callendar recorder.

The following morning, when Darwin came into the works, he asked Whipple what he thought of the idea of pressing a galvanometer pointer on to an inked thread which in turn would be pressed on to a recording chart. He demonstrated the principle by means of an ivory rule pressed on to a pencil. Whipple was immediately taken with the idea and suggested that if two galvanometers were placed side by side the pointers might be depressed simultaneously, thus producing two records. In fact, four galvanometers were later put alongside each other, thus giving four records on the same chart.

Darwin worked on the design with Charles Foster, who was at that time Chief Draughtsman, and the first recorder was sold in 1906. The dotting thread recorder was so simple in principle and reliable in operation that it was manufactured for about seventy years before servo-operated recorders rendered it obsolete.

'Compensating Leads' for thermocouple systems were not introduced until about 1909. They were the invention of W. S. Peake, an employee of the Company. Instead of using thermocouple wire to join the thermocouple to the measuring instrument, 'compensating leads' were used, made from any suitable combination of cheap materials which had the same thermal e.m.f. characteristic as the thermocouple over the range of temperatures which the junctions with the compensating leads would experience. Typical materials were copper against a copper-nickel alloy. The technique considerably reduced the cost of thermocouple installations, which at that time always used platinum against either platinum-iridium or platinum-rhodium, and thus increased their use. Peake patented his invention and the Company paid Peake royalties on the sales of compensating lead.

Peake also patented his scale control board by means of which the zero could be suppressed and the range thus expanded in a thermocouple system. This, too, was marketed by the Company.

With only a small board of directors Darwin acted as both chairman and managing director and in November 1905 he informed his fellow directors that he wished to appoint Robert Whipple as managing director, as he was empowered to do under Article 24.2 of the Articles of Association of the Company. This was unanimously approved and Alfred Reed was appointed Company Secretary in his place. In June 1906 Keith Lucas also joined the Board.

Although only a young man Lucas was an accomplished experimenter in physiology. He had been made a Fellow of Trinity in 1904 and had a keenly analytical mind, particularly when working on mechanical designs. Like Darwin, he was a disciple of Clerk Maxwell, following the principle that the design itself should ensure the correct working of the instrument in spite of rough workmanship.

From the time he had been a pupil at Rugby he had had an interest in science. In his second term there he had arrived back from holiday with various pieces of electrical apparatus and an accumulator which he intended to charge from the newly-installed electric lighting system. Unfortunately the system was a.c. and not d.c. as he had expected. The headmaster, on hearing of his plans, promptly despatched the house butler to confiscate the apparatus, which the man did, although holding it at arm's length in some fear and trepidation of receiving an electric shock.

During that term Lucas developed an interest in boomerangs and this was followed by an analysis of the structural design of the bicycle when he made a model and carefully replaced each strut in turn with a string to determine which were in tension. Having completed his analysis he built a model to his design during the following holidays, which only failed when he tried to motorise it. However, his greatest interest during this period was photomicroscopy and this laid the foundation of his subsequent career in physiology. He began his experiments at Rugby with a cheap microscope and camera, but then he was given a Ross microscope with Zeiss lenses. The adjustment of this microscope so frustrated him, because of the delicacy required, that he designed his own instrument, making a set of working drawings from which he built a new microscope during the next vacation. Whilst the instrument worked, he was dissatisfied with its appearance, so he redesigned it and rebuilt it. This microscope is now in the Science Museum in South Kensington.

Having taken his degree in 1901, Lucas spent some months in New Zealand, on doctor's orders, after the death of a close friend. In 1903 he returned to Cambridge, and research in the Department of Physiology. In 1909 he married Alys Hubbard, but shortly before their marriage they were involved in a serious road accident in which his car was completely wrecked and his fiancée suffered concussion. Only the two-stroke engine could be salvaged from the car and this he subsequently installed in a motor launch. As the engine had no reverse gear, when he required to go backwards he excessively retarded the ignition so that the engine ran in reverse.

Lucas was very much a working director of The Cambridge Scientific Instrument Company, assisting personally with design work on new instruments, particularly mechanical apparatus and physiological instruments. His design for the slow-motion adjustment of a microscope (*Fig.* 3.3) is but one of the inventions by which he is remembered. It was patented in June 1908 and in November Lucas signed an agreement giving the Company sole manufacturing rights.[18] It was incorporated in most of the Cambridge instruments employing microscopes and was beautifully simple in action. The microscope tube rested in a double V-shaped cradle. On the same shaft as the focusing knob was a specially shaped friction drive wheel, bearing on a metal rod of semi-circular section fixed along the body of the microscope tube. One spring, bearing against the drive shaft, held the drive mechanism and microscope tube firmly in position, giving an adjustment both free from backlash and smooth in operation.

Figure 3.3 Lucas' slow-motion microscope focusing mechanism. (Photo: C.S.I.Co., Neg. SU 415.)

In List 124, the catalogue of physiological instruments published by the Company in 1913—the year that Lucas was elected a Fellow of the Royal Society—Lucas' name is associated with a number of instruments, including a pendulum and contact breaker (to switch electrical circuits at defined intervals during physiological experiments), an apparatus for drawing out glass capillary tubing, a muscle trough (to prevent tissues drying out during demonstration experiments) an electro-magnetic time signal generator (to provide a time base with photographic recording), a rectilinear myograph (apparatus used for recording the contraction of muscles) and an instrument for mechanically correcting the errors obtained when making photographic records of the moving meniscus of a capillary electrometer. His skill as a mechanical designer was backed up by his practical knowledge. In fact, Robert Whipple and Keith Lucas were quite able to cope with the running of the firm between them when Horace Darwin was away.

Figure 3.4 Settlement apparatus prior to installation in the Crypt of St Paul's Cathedral. c. 1903. (Photos: C.S.I.Co., Negs. 112 and 113.)

Darwin always took great delight in finding a novel solution to an unusual problem and the apparatus he placed in the crypt of St Paul's Cathedral in 1903 was no exception (*Fig.* 3.4). The public did not learn of its presence until three years later when a series of earthquakes throughout the world prompted Professor Belar, the seismological expert at Laibach, to suggest in the *Daily Mail* in December, 1906, that measurements should be made in St Paul's to test for any settlement as a result of the 'quakes.[19] Press reporters were surprised to find that equipment designed by Darwin to detect any movement of the building had in fact been installed in the cathedral for more than three years. Any permanent subsidence resulting from such tremors would be detected using this equipment.

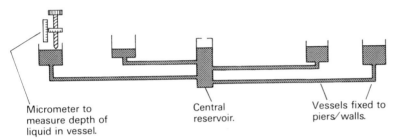

Micrometer to measure depth of liquid in vessel. Central reservoir. Vessels fixed to piers/walls.

Figure 3.5 Principle of operation of settlement apparatus.

In designing his apparatus (*Fig.* 3.5) Darwin may have been prompted by the method used by the Egyptians to establish a level at the time the pyramids were built. Under the floor of the crypt Darwin had fixed a system of four oil-filled tubes, radiating from a central reservoir in a similar manner to spokes from the hub of a wheel. Each tube terminated in an open vessel, two vessels being attached to points on the main piers supporting the dome and the two others to points on one of the walls of the South Transept. Metal flanges were grouted into the fabric of the building to support the vessels and to provide fixed reference points on which a micrometer could be placed. By adjusting the micrometer until the conical point just touched the surface of the oil (when the reflected image was immediately distorted) movement of the reference points relative to each other could be measured over a period of time. The micrometer used by Darwin could be read to about 1/400th part of a millimetre, but because of the effects of temperature the movement of the building could not be given to this accuracy. Micrometer readings of the four reference points had last been taken the previous July and as Darwin was not intending to take further readings until January 1907 he firmly refused to comment to the Press on the effects of the earthquake.[20]

As a result of experience gained with this equipment Darwin designed a set of three crack micrometers which were also tested in St

Paul's Cathedral before being marketed in 1914. When using the micro-meters, two cylindrical pins were first cemented into the wall on either side of the developing crack. Each micrometer had an inverted V notch frame to rest on one of these pins. With the first micrometer a conical point was advanced to just touch the second pin, thus checking the horizontal separation. The second unit incorporated a spirit level so that by adjusting a vertical micrometer until the level was horizontal, vertical movement of one pin with respect to the other might be measured (*Fig. 3.6*). In the third micrometer the point of the adjusting screw bore centrally on the end of the cylindrical pin and was adjusted until an arm on the frame just touched the end of the second pin, thus checking for relative movement of the faces on either side of the crack.

Figure 3.6 Level crack micrometer in position on supporting pins c. 1914. (Photo: C.S.I.Co., Neg. 1599.)

The micrometers were marketed in a case, complete with a gauge to set the separation of the pins in the fabric of the building. The resident engineer at St Paul's, Mr J. B. Thomas, still uses the set supplied to the Cathedral by the Company. Some fifty pairs of pins are fixed in various locations throughout the Cathedral and sixteen pairs are regu-larly monitored using the original micrometers from the set. The subsi-dence apparatus was, however, discarded many years ago and it has proved impossible to locate even the positions of the fixing plates.

Horace's son Erasmus may well have assisted his father to take his experimental measurements in St Paul's. Whilst a pupil at Marl-borough Erasmus had won an exhibition to Trinity and he went up in October 1901. In his second year he sat for the Mathematical Tripos, and was placed amongst the Senior Optimes. Two years later he obtained a second in the Mechanical Sciences Tripos.

No doubt, when Erasmus was made a director in 1903, his father hoped that he would eventually succeed him in controlling the Company. In 1905 Erasmus joined a Manchester company, Mather and Platt for about eighteen months, to gain practical engineering experience. Like his father he went 'through the shops', as well as having a spell in the design office and test room. Mather and Platt were designing machinery for the cotton industry and Erasmus frequently wrote to his father for advice on some tricky design problem he had encountered or idea he had had. At the same time he was always keen to have news of the Company's activities, taking his responsibilities as a director with the forthright earnestness of youth.

In May 1907 he returned to Cambridge to take an active part in the running of his father's Company. His father was away at the time and on 28 May Erasmus wrote to him:[21] '. . . Here I am sitting in your study, still feeling as if things were rather strange, but rapidly getting into harness. Everybody is very nice to me in the shop and I feel in rather a queer position. I know I shall enjoy the work very much—the first day I spent in breaking things but today I managed better. . . .' A week later, on 5 June, he wrote: '. . . I am at present working on a Thread Recorder—there are 28 on order besides 13 in the Test Room.'[22] And in another letter at about the same time:[23] 'I am enjoying my work very much; today I went through a repair recorder. I also had a good long and satisfactory talk with Whipple and Lucas about prices and microtomes and physiological instruments. I also had some talk with Foster about Gas Calorimeters. This evening I looked up the Fault Apparatus and I think we must have (or I at any rate) two days there before I go abroad. I thought of plotting the slip in a slightly different way which shows at a glance the degree of accuracy and the undoubted nature of the slipping movement. . .' This reference to the 'Fault Apparatus' almost certainly refers to the measurements Horace Darwin had been taking of the geological slip at Upwey in Dorset.

It was at this time that negotiations were begun with the large American instrument company, Taylor Brothers, for reciprocal manufacturing and marketing arrangements. Because Horace Darwin was away Robert Whipple and Erasmus Darwin carried out the initial negotiations when one of the Taylor brothers visited England on a three-week business tour in June, 1907. In a letter to his father, dated 11 June, Erasmus wrote:[24] '. . . Whipple has seen Taylor and Taylor said to him I think your demands are somewhat exorbitant and I think you will admit it yourself! They then had a lot of talk. He seems willing to come a good way to give us the Hohman-Maurer thing and to pay royalties, but he is now drafting out some sort of sketch agreement. He will not touch the thing unless he has a good man out there; he wants Whipple to go or Foster, you see as it is we have no-one who is any good to send except Harper and we should be in a hash if he went. He will promise not to touch English pyrometric work and will buy parts from us. I am going through the papers tonight and then have another talk with Whipple. Then there is really not much more to do until his rough draft comes, then it shall be sent out to you. ....'

The agreement was finalised and signed in November 1907, Horace Darwin and Erasmus Darwin signing on behalf of The Cambridge Scientific Instrument Company, the two Taylor brothers, President and Vice-President, signing on their part. Foster, the Chief Draughtsman at the Cambridge company, evidently agreed to go to the USA to satisfy Taylor's insistence for a good technical man.

Charles Foster had joined the Instrument Company about 1903 or 1904. He was an able engineer and was at one time in charge of the Test Room. In 1905 he assisted Darwin with the design of the thread recorder and two years later he obtained a patent for an improved relay mechanism which could be used to actuate the movement of the pen/pointer system in recording and indicating instruments.[25] Such a mechanism was, naturally, of considerable interest to The Cambridge Scientific Instrument Company. Before Foster sailed for the USA in the winter of 1907–8 he agreed to construct a prototype recorder in America and to send it over to England for the Instrument Company to evaluate. The Cambridge Company would then have four months in which to decide whether to exercise an option to sole manufacturing rights.

The agreement between the Cambridge Scientific Instrument Company and Taylor Brothers was a broad one. Taylor Brothers were to receive manufacturing information on the full Cambridge product range, paying a royalty on sales, and with preferential terms for the purchase of parts or finished instruments for those items which they did not wish to manufacture. All sales of the Cambridge products throughout North and South America were to be through Taylor Brothers. In return the Cambridge Company was to receive manufacturing information on the Hohman-Maurer range of thermometers and regulators, and various Short and Mason products, with sole marketing rights throughout the world, except for the Americas and Germany.

The Hohman-Maurer mercury-in-steel thermometers could be made either as dial thermometers or 'thermograph' recorders. The temperature sensor was a steel bulb filled with mercury and connected to a bourdon tube in the indicator or recorder by a metal capillary. A rise in temperature caused the mercury to expand and the bourdon tube to uncoil slightly. By means of a simple linkage this movement of the bourdon tube was converted to a pointer movement on a circular scale in a dial thermometer or a pen movement across a disc chart in the thermograph. In later variations of these instruments additional systems were built into the recorder case so that temperature and pressure, or temperature and humidity could be recorded on the same chart. The instruments were rugged, and admirably suited to industrial use.[†]

In March 1908 Erasmus journeyed to the USA to take over and sort through the manufacturing information on Hohman-Maurer thermometers and regulators. He arrived in America during the first weekend in March and after a few days spent sight-seeing in New York he travelled up to Rochester to the Taylor Brothers' factory. The following Sunday he had lunch with the Du Puys (his uncle George's wife's family) and then went to call on the Fosters. '. . . They have at present a very nice furnished house but they are going to leave it as soon as they can find a house to move into of their own. . .', he wrote to his father later that evening.[26] Erasmus had by then decided that he did not wish to confine his career to his father's company and, whilst he would remain a director, he was preparing to join Bolckow, Vaughan and Company, Ltd, in Middlesborough, as Assistant Company Secretary, on his return to England. The news did not please Taylor as Erasmus reported in his letter: '. . . Taylor was very polite in his regrets when he heard of my decision to leave; he talks of demanding an indemnity. He was relying on myself for the business and W [Whipple] for the scientific end so he says . . .'

Erasmus stayed in the USA until mid-April. It became apparent quite early on in his visit that Taylor Brothers were at that time much more accustomed to thermometric than to scientific instruments. On 10 March he wrote home: '. . . I wish that we had originally only handed over to Taylor Brothers the thermometric end of our stuff—as the purely scientific end hardly really suits them. . . .'[27] Three weeks later, in his letter dated 30 March, he mentioned Foster again:[28] '. . . I have seen a good deal of Foster and we have been very friendly. He is not well, suffering much from headaches, the results of nervous strain and I hope he won't break down—he is depressed with the way things are going out here, but he should really wait until the next three months show to us how the land really lies. . .'

In April 1909 Foster sent Horace Darwin the promised prototype of his new recorder. In manufacturing cost there was little to choose between Foster's design and Callendar's instrument and, when the instrument had been tested, it was found that the same was true of performance. Despite the disadvantage that Callendar's recorder was becoming dated—his patent and his agreement with the Company would both expire in July 1911—there was the significant point in its favour that the instrument was reliable and produced no customer complaints. The Company's royalty agreement with Callendar was, in point of fact, a complex one for in 1902 Darwin and Moses Wayne had produced a very

---

[†] *Instruments working on this same principle are still manufactured as part of the Kent Industrial Measurements 'Foster-Cambridge' product range.*

similar design to Foster's instrument. A patent had been filed but never completed, but a supplementary agreement had been made with Callendar that if ever recorders were produced to the Darwin/Wayne design Callendar would receive royalties, albeit 10% instead of his usual 20%. There was thus the further point to be considered: if the Cambridge Company took up Foster's design would they be morally obliged to pay Callendar a royalty of 10%?

Despite the failure of his American patent application Foster had intimated his determination to market his own design in the USA in place of the Callendar instrument. But Foster was not happy in the USA and it was probably during the autumn of 1909 that he made up his mind to return to England. Rather surprisingly, in October 1909, he agreed to assign his rights in the British patent to the Cambridge Company for £120, thus solving a difficult problem for Darwin who was not yet ready to commit himself definitely to a design change.

Foster had plans to start his own company and in April 1910 he proposed to the directors of The Cambridge Scientific Instrument Company that they co-operate with him in the manufacture and sale of pyrometric apparatus. The Board declined and Foster went ahead independently, founding his own company—the Foster Instrument Company—later that year, at premises in Works Road, Letchworth. In many ways the product range was similar to that of The Cambridge Scientific Instrument Company. Over the years Foster's instruments (including his recorders) gained a good reputation and competed with the products of the Cambridge Company, which must have been a source of continuing concern to Darwin.

By 1913 Darwin really needed a replacement for the Callendar instrument and an agreement to manufacture the American Leeds and Northrup recorder was signed with Elliott Brothers, the British licensees. However, this agreement does not seem to have been acted upon, possibly because of the intervention of the 1914–18 War.

On 17 February, 1925, fifteen years after the Foster Instrument Company was founded, Horace Darwin wrote the following note to Robert Whipple, really with the aim of clarifying his own thoughts:[29]

> *Dear Whipple,*
> *I have been thinking about the instrument maker who I will call F. I assume that the firm is a Company Ltd.*
> *If we took shares or debentures to a comparatively small amount it would not give us absolute control but would lead to a certain amount of friendly relationship between the two firms and might do real good to both. And the only thing to be said against it is that it [would] perhaps be better to invest our reserve fund in something which can be easily realised and something perfectly safe. If we took more than half the shares we should have absolute control. This would be bad and might lead*

> *to most unfriendly relations between F. and us. First because we*
> *are suggesting something he ought not to do. Secondly, it is not*
> *such a good form of control as amalgamation. Then, circum-*
> *stances might arise when it would pay us to make F. do*
> *something which would be very harmful to him. We as Instru-*
> *ment Company directors are bound to do the best for our share-*
> *holders, and this something might reduce F.'s dividend by a great*
> *amount and increase our dividend by a small amount. As share-*
> *holders in F. & Co. we should lose but we might gain on the*
> *whole. It would be a bad position to put the Instrument Com-*
> *pany in. This is as far as I have got.*
>
> > *Yours,*
> > *Horace Darwin*

Almost certainly 'F' refers to the Foster Instrument Company. Although nothing further seems to have come of his deliberations this letter does serve to illustrate Darwin's highly moral attitude to business deals. Thirty years later, in 1956, talks began with Philip Foster, Charles Foster's son. The directors of the Foster Instrument Company were then quite keen to establish some form of friendly association between the two companies, but the Cambridge Board could see little point in this and proposed a financial link. The talks lapsed but were re-opened in 1959, only to be abandoned after a few months when the Foster directors absolutely refused to consider any form of financial merger, regarding it as a takeover.

Fate was, however, determined to have her way, and in 1968 the Foster Instrument Company was taken over by George Kent. Within a few weeks The Cambridge Instrument Company had also become part of the George Kent Group. In 1971 the Cambridge Industrial Instruments division of the Company, in Muswell Hill and Finchley in London, which manufactured a range of instruments for industrial use, was merged with the Foster Instrument Company to form Foster-Cambridge Ltd. This company later formed the nucleus for the Kent Industrial Measurements division of Brown Boveri Kent, plc.

But to return to 1907. Amongst the special products made by The Cambridge Scientific Instrument Company at that time was a spectroheliograph for the Solar Physics observatory at Kodaikanal in South India, the equipment subsequently being used for a major study of sunspots. The instrument used the Janssen technique for monochromatic photography of the sun's disc and the dispersing prisms could be replaced by a diffraction grating for greater dispersion. A special feature was the mechanism used to drive the spectroscopic train. The whole unit was mounted on a rigid iron framework, which was supported by three steel balls on which it rolled. A cylinder of oil was used to control the rate at which the frame moved, the actuating force being provided by a suspended weight. The movement of the frame caused a plunger to force oil out of the cylinder through a valve. The orifice in the valve was provided with a micrometer adjusted so that photographic exposures up to an hour were possible, the motion being absolutely smooth. Similar traversing systems had previously been made for the Solar Physics Observatories at South Kensington and Mount Wilson in California.

In contrast to the spectroheliograph just described, there is a note further down the page in the same catalogue informing potential customers of a kite winding gear which the Company had manufactured for a Mr C. J. P. Cave of Petersfield in Hampshire. The equipment was driven by a 4 H.P. petrol engine and provision was made for paying out seven miles of steel wire from the winding drum. 'Under favourable circumstances a height of two miles has been obtained by the kite.' Still further down the page is a mention of a 50-metre Comparator for the National Physical Laboratory, for the standardisation of surveying tapes and bars. An elaborate series of microscopes and collimators was used to compare the tapes or bars against standard lengths.

The diversity of the Company's products indicates both the limited number of skilled engineering firms during this period and also the willingness of Darwin to tackle any engineering product which caught his imagination and would keep his workforce employed.

In 1908 the Company began to manufacture Méker burners and furnaces. The Méker burner, invented and patented by M. Méker of Paris in 1904, was essentially a highly specialised form of the Bunsen Burner and was designed to achieve very high temperatures by burning the maximum quantity of gas in the minimum size of flame. In an ordinary Bunsen burner the proportion of air to gas in the chimney is about two or three parts of air to one of gas. Complete combustion requires six parts of air to one of gas and in a Bunsen flame complete combustion only takes place on the outside of the flame, leaving a cone of unburnt gas in the centre. To correct this situation, in the Méker burner the size of the gas injector hole was precisely defined in relation to the size of the air inlet holes and the gas/air mixing chamber was specially shaped to ensure thorough mixing. A deep nickel grid at the top of the burner prevented flame flash-back, a common occurrence with the Bunsen burner.

From its very early days the Company had made apparatus for studying the action of the heart and physiologists continued to experiment with frogs' hearts for many years. In January 1899, when asked to supply frogs, the Company was happy to oblige, at 2*d.* each, although somewhat unsure of the husbandry of such animals:[30]

> Dear Sir,
>   Last year you were good enough to send for us some Frogs to Mr Chilton of Bristol. He now asks us to send him another 2 dozen and wants to know how you feed them, and whether you put earth and water or only one of them in their

*cage. Will you kindly send the Frogs on to him attaching the
enclosed label to the box and let us know what to reply in answer
to his query re feeding and oblige.*

Yours faithfully,
The Cambridge Scientific Instrument Company Ltd,
Robert S. Whipple

The Company's supplier, Mr Hall, at the Physiological Laboratory, replied very promptly and next day Robert Whipple was able to write to Mr Chilton:[31]

Dear Sir,
*We thank you for your letter and order of the 30th ult. We
have despatched the Frogs as desired. In reply to your query, in
winter time they should be kept in damp leaves and grass, but the
time is coming for them to be kept in running water with a few
worms given occasionally, but they don't feed well in captivity.*

Yours faithfully,
The Cambridge Scientific Instrument Company Ltd,
Robert S. Whipple

At that time the arterial or venous pulse and respiration movements were recorded using a Franck capsule or Marey tambour and the 1891 catalogue lists such a recording cardiograph, the design being 'Professor Burdon-Sanderson's pattern'. However, four years earlier, in 1887, Dr A. D. Waller, using a Lippman capillary electrometer, had demonstrated the feasibility of registering the electrical potentials associated with the action of the human heart beat.

The Lippman electrometer, although the best instrument available at that time, was not ideally suited to the work because of its inertia, and Professor Einthoven of Leiden University became interested in the problem of designing a galvanometer which would respond immediately to the minute heart currents so that accurate 'electrocardiograms' could be recorded.

As a student at Utrecht University Willem Einthoven had mainly studied optics—a subject for which the university was particularly renowned—and his first published papers were in this branch of science. He was a student of outstanding brilliance, so much so that when he was twenty-four, before he had fully completed his qualifications, he was appointed as a Professor at Leiden. The appointment was termed an 'appointment on credit' i.e. he was given credit for what he was expected to accomplish rather than for his past achievements. Already his interest had turned to electrophysiology and this became the subject in which he was to make his career and in which he was to become an acknowledged master.

Beyond his work and his family Einthoven had few interests. He did, however, enjoy music and at one time he played the violin. His main forms of recreation were walking and cycling and his bicycle remained his constant form of transport during most of his working life. In all weathers, night or day, he could be seen pedalling to and from his laboratory and in his early years even taking journeys to Amsterdam and back, some sixty miles in all, to attend the monthly meetings of the Royal Academy of Science.

Each morning Einthoven would arrive in his laboratory at about eleven o'clock, take off his shoes and put on slippers, and remove his collar and tie. He would then settle to uninterrupted work until the laboratory porter, on instructions from Mrs Einthoven, interrupted him at five o'clock to say 'Professor, it is five o'clock.' This message was repeated at half-hourly intervals, usually acknowledged by a nod and no cessation of work, until at some convenient point, often as late as eight o'clock, Einthoven would reclothe and cycle home.

After a considerable period of experimenting Einthoven perfected his string galvanometer in 1903 and, although the prototype equipment was large and cumbersome, the cardiograms which he obtained using the galvanometer were of outstanding quality. Detailed descriptions of the construction of the string galvanometer and of the electrocardiograph are given in Chapter 15.

Einthoven now wished to hand over further development and marketing of the equipment to a commercial concern on a royalty basis whilst he concentrated on its application. He therefore approached both Messrs Edelmann in Germany and The Cambridge Scientific Instrument Company. Darwin viewed the 'string and sealing wax' prototype with rather more caution than Edelmann. Whereas the German company went straight into production with a copy of Einthoven's design, the Cambridge company first put into production, in 1907–8, an improved version of the galvanometer, based on redesign work by William Duddell.

Complete electrocardiographs were not made in Cambridge until 1911, the first one being supplied 'on hire' with right to purchase to Dr Thomas Lewis. It was installed in a dark and unprepossessing basement in University College Hospital in London. Dr Lewis worked closely with the Company for many years and became perhaps the greatest authority in the UK on the interpretation of electrocardiographic records during that period.

The first Cardiographic Department to be set up is thought to have been that at The London Hospital where, in 1913, Dr John Parkinson had a clinic. Dr Parkinson published many papers on his work with the equipment. Further outfits were supplied to leading hospitals throughout the UK and during the four years to the end of 1915 the Company made eighty-four electrocardiographs. More than two-thirds of them were exported to hospitals abroad: twenty-two to the USA; eight to Canada; four to India, and others to most European countries. This was no mean achievement and amply justified the considerable amount of design effort needed to produce a commercial design from Einthoven's prototype.

In the meantime Professor H. B. Williams of the USA, following a visit to Einthoven, had built his own electrocardiograph with the aid of a mechanic named Charles Hindle. This was in 1910 and the demand for instruments was such that Hindle formed a private company, Professor Williams acting as adviser and consultant. Hindle was concerned only with cardiographs and the equipment which he designed was similar in many respects to the British instrument. Most of the early work of physicians and physiologists in America was carried out on Hindle instruments although, after 1913, the British instrument was sold in the USA through The Cambridge Scientific Instrument Company's marketing agreement with Taylor Brothers. The wording on the front of the Cardiograph catalogue distributed in the USA is interesting, and shows the closeness of the link between the companies at that time: 'Taylor-Cambridge division of the Taylor Instrument Companies. Another branch of The Cambridge Scientific Instrument Company.'[32]

The electrocardiograph proved to be a valuable diagnostic tool in advancing the study of the action of the heart. For many decades the Company maintained its position as a world leader in the quality and performance of the electrocardiographic equipment which it supplied, although its approach to the use of electronics in this field might be said to have been over conservative.

A further change in the Board of the Company was made in 1909 when Hugh Newall resigned his seat after being appointed to the new Chair of Astrophysics at Cambridge. Although initially a physicist at the Cavendish Laboratory, Newall had for many years been closely involved in the astronomical work of the University. The change in his early career had come about as a result of his father's amateur interest in astronomy. His father, Robert Stirling Newall, was, in fact, a scientist of some repute, being a Fellow of the Royal Society, but he was by profession a business man. At the Exhibition of 1862 it so happened that Mr Chance of Birmingham had on show two large discs of crown and flint glass. R. S. Newall bought them and had them polished to produce a 25-inch lens, with a focal length of 29 feet. This was used as the objective for a telescope which R. S. Newall then had erected at Ferndene, Gateshead (Hugh Newall's birthplace). At the time it was the largest diameter object glass in existence.

Hugh Newall went up to Trinity in 1876 and took both the Mathematics Tripos and the Natural Sciences Tripos examinations in 1880. He then began a career as a teacher but was dogged by ill-health and in 1885 he returned to Cambridge as J. J. Thomson's personal assistant at the Cavendish Laboratory. Two years later he became Senior Demonstrator at the Cavendish.

In February 1889 R. S. Newall offered his telescope, complete with its dome to the University, expressing the hope that it might be used in the development of stellar physics. The University authorities wished to accept the gift but could not afford the expenses of removing the telescope or of providing an observer. In April R. S. Newall died and his son, in order that his father's wishes should be carried out, offered £300 towards the cost of moving the instrument and sacrificed his prospects as a physicist by volunteering his own services as unpaid observer at the telescope for a period of five years. The gift of the telescope was then accepted, but with the proviso that Hugh Newall must live within 500 yards of the Observatory—which he had indeed already volunteered to do.

The telescope was erected at Madingley and Hugh Newall had a house built there—Madingley Rise—with a small farm attached, which produced mainly dairy produce for the family. His wife, Margaret, was an accomplished concert pianist and for many years Madingley Rise became a centre of hospitality both to visiting astronomers and music-loving people.

The vacancy on the Board created by Newall's resignation was filled by Cecil C. Mason in January 1910. In March 1911 Mason was appointed Joint Managing Director with Robert Whipple, a post he held until 1941, when he resigned through illness, although he continued on the Board until his sudden death in 1958. Mason was a Wrangler having obtained first class honours in the Mathematics Tripos at Cambridge in 1902 whilst at Trinity Hall. The following year he was also placed in Class 1 of Part 1 of the Mechanical Sciences Tripos. Early in his career he became a gunnery expert and during the 1914–18 war he was Technical Adviser to the Controller of Gun Ammunition at the Ministry of Munitions. In recognition of this work he was awarded the OBE in 1920. He was also a Freemason and in later life he became Grand Warden of Cambridgeshire and Grand Deacon of England.

Mason had an extraordinary flair for figures and was adept at unconventional mathematical 'short cuts'. (Typical of these was the perpetual calendar which he carried in his head. He always said that the key to this could be written on the back of a postage stamp.) This flair for figures stood him in good stead in his control of the Company's finances. On one occasion, before the introduction of machine accounting, when every account had to be listed and balanced by hand, the Accounts Department worked overtime to finish the annual accounts early. Alfred Reed, the Company Secretary went to Mason, with a certain amount of pride, to present the results of the year's trading. When he returned to the Accounts Office he blurted out 'What do you think? When I showed him the figures he opened a drawer, pulled out a piece of paper on which he had made some calculations and showed me a figure as near as dammit the same as ours!'

The Newall telescope was dismantled and removed to the Greek National Observatory in Athens in 1956. The fate of two self-recording electrometers which the Company loaned to Captain Scott's expedition to the South Pole is not so clear. The instruments, which were used to record atmospheric electricity, had been designed by the Company in collaboration with the Meteorological Bureau of Toronto. Each incorporated a quadrant electrometer and a thread recorder dotting mechanism (*Fig. 3.7*), but one had only 1/10 the sensitivity of the other (effected by shortening the quartz suspension fibre). This allowed the expedition to continue to record in snowstorms and other weather conditions when the potential difference between the air and the ground was very great.[33]

Figure 3.7 Self-recording electrometer (c. 1912) as used by the Scott Antarctic Expedition. To save weight the instruments taken by Scott were 'stripped down' models without cases. (Photo: C.S.I.Co., Neg. 1247B.)

Although, tragically, Scott and his companions perished, the return of the electrometers from Simpson's antarctic 'laboratory' was reported at the Board meeting on 29 August, 1913. A note was made in the minutes that in view of the historic interest attached to the instruments they should be presented to some institution. Tantalisingly, there is no record of which institution received the electrometers and efforts to find them have so far proved unsuccessful. However, the Royal Geographical Society does possess a photograph,[†] dated 31 March, 1911, which clearly shows the two electrometers in Simpson's laboratory.

C. T. R. Wilson's first photographs of the tracks of ionising particles in his cloud chamber were shown to the Royal Institution in May 1911.[34] They were the culmination of seventeen years' work; work which was to earn him the Nobel Prize for physics in 1927. The results of his experiments with his improved cloud chamber, detailed in his subsequent paper to the Royal Society in 1912,[35] caused great interest and excitement amongst physicists throughout the world and very soon The Cambridge Scientific Instrument Company was receiving enquiries asking whether they could supply cloud chambers as used by Wilson. With Wilson acting as adviser Darwin produced an instrument which was virtually a copy of Wilson's apparatus but with minor constructional improvements, and the first catalogue for 'Wilson's Expansion Apparatus' was published in 1913.

At the end of the 1914–18 war a young Japanese physicist, Takeo Shimizu, was studying the continuous emission of alpha and beta particles at the Cavendish Laboratory. To further his researches he designed a reciprocating system so that 50–200 expansions per minute could be obtained in a cloud chamber. The Company assisted Shimizu to patent this equipment and produced it under a royalty agreement with him, although it is doubtful whether Shimizu ever received the royalties due to him, as letters show that he returned to Japan and the Company was then unable to trace his address in order to pay him the monies due.

Special cloud chambers were made from time to time for various research workers. One was supplied to Dr Chadwick in 1927, who used it for his work on δ rays, and another to Dr Kapitza for his work on the effects of strong magnetic fields on particle trajectories. Dr Kapitza used a field of 40 000 gauss and obtained photographs showing the bending of the tracks of alpha particles in this field. In 1932 Dr Dee used a chamber made by the Company when he photographed the disintegration of lithium when bombarded by protons. His photograph showed a pair of oppositely recoiling helium atoms produced during the disintegration process.

In 1927 the Company brought out a simplified version of Shimizu's apparatus, for use in schools and colleges. To keep the instrument as simple as possible it was made with a fixed expansion ratio and was only suitable for showing the tracks of alpha particles. Large numbers of these demonstration models were sold. At the Festival of Britain, in 1951, two such instruments were put on display, for visitors to

---

† *Ref. No. 248; Negative No. 000978.*

operate. The Exhibition lasted for five months and it was estimated that some 3000 people per day operated the instruments. In addition, a motor-driven version of Shimizu's instrument, fitted with a mirror system, provided continuous displays of alpha particle tracks. It produced 50 expansions per minute for 12 hours a day, 7 days a week for 5 months—nearly six million distinct sets of tracks.

A brief account of Wilson's researches leading up to his development of the cloud chamber and descriptions of this instrument and Shimizu's equipment are given in Chapter 17.

In October 1913 the Board approved proposals to further extend the factory by building a new two-storey block and adding four new bays to the workshops. At that time the works consisted of the original Shop A, a newer Shop B (built in 1901), a two-storey building containing the offices over the stores and packing room (built 1906), and the most recent addition, Shop C (built in 1912), plus a test room and various smaller rooms. The older machine tools were in Shop A. Shop B housed the vertical and horizontal milling machines, various small lathes and a high-speed drilling machine of the Company's own make. In Shop C there were some seven or eight turret lathes of various makes and sizes. Part of this shop was also used as a grinding shop and the rest was partitioned off as the drawing office. Shop C was built with the latest design of saw-tooth roof with a large glass area and the east and south walls of the building were only semi-permanent to allow additional bays to be added as required. Inside the framework was covered with asbestos board.[36]

The ground floor of the proposed new two-storey building would extend the existing stores to feed new bays in Shop C and provide a larger despatch department. The upper floor was to be used for offices. To cover the cost the shareholders were offered one-eighth of their holding of ordinary shares at £6 each on condition that they also took up a number of £50, $4\frac{1}{2}\%$ debentures at par, the number being the nearest in face value below the one-eighth face value of their existing holding of ordinary shares. From the accounts for the following year it would appear that most of the shareholders took advantage of this offer.

The new extension covered 6740 square feet, bringing the total area of the works to 22 000 square feet. The number of employees at that time was about 180. To celebrate the completion of the extension about 650 visitors were invited to an open day on 22 May, 1914. They were shown round the works and were able to see the workshops and machinery as well as the various offices. There were many exhibits, both of instruments under construction and completed instruments waiting despatch, with some working demonstrations. The instruments under construction included chronographs for timing shell fuses, recording magnetographs for the Royal Observatory at Greenwich, high speed plate cameras, and torque and thrust dynamometers for testing aeroplane propellers. Amongst the static displays of completed instruments were various galvanometers and electroscopes, an aerodynamic balance for experimentally investigating the forces and couples on model aeroplanes in a wind channel [*sic*], a pyrheliometer for use in measuring solar radiation, crack micrometers, laboratory chronographs and a Rosenhain Coal Calorimeter for measuring the calorific value of coal. There were working demonstrations of a Duddell Oscillograph, a string galvanometer with a double vibrator for electrocardiograph work, a Callendar recording pyrheliometer, a Brearley curve tracer, Féry radiation pyrometers and absorption pyrometers, Boys' radiomicrometers and various automatic temperature regulators and other instruments for industrial use. The visitors included famous scientists and senior members of the University and many expressed surprise at the variety and accuracy of the instruments manufactured by the Company.

As a precaution against fire the Company had installed a Grinnell sprinkler fire-extinguishing system and to give the visitors a demonstration of its effectiveness a fire of wood, wool and shavings was lit in a temporary shed. Unfortuantely, the sensitivity of the system had not been tested beforehand and a cloud of dense, stifling smoke enveloped the onlookers before the fire bell rang and the sprinkler began to operate.

A month later on 20 June the Company's premises were the venue for a meeting of the members of the Physical Society, who were also entertained to luncheon in the Hall of St John's College at the invitation of the Company. A number of distinguished physicists were present and the meeting was presided over by the then President of the Physical Society, Sir J. J. Thomson. This time the directors decided not to demonstrate the Grinnell fire-extinguisher system.

* * * * *

CHAPTER FOUR

War work; 1914–18

THE outbreak of the First World War created an atmosphere of uncertainty in industry. The directors of the Company at first feared that there would be a drastic cut-back in orders and output. Accordingly, at a Board meeting held on the day war was declared (5 August, 1914) they passed a resolution 'that the wages of the whole of the staff be reduced by one-quarter starting from Saturday, August 8th, and that the staff be informed that, should the present situation continue, the wages will be further reduced to a half on August 22nd.' In the event the directors' fears proved groundless and on 9 September the directors were able to record a minute 'as the works are now fully employed, staff be paid full wages and any balance owing be at once paid.'[1]

Despite the doubts engendered by the war, the directors were still keen to grasp any opportunity to expand the business of the Company, particularly its export business. So, in May 1915, the Board considered opening a branch in Petrograd and noted in the minutes that one of the Company's agents, Mr Dannatt, was actively studying Russian. The Russian revolution in 1917 brought an abrupt end to these plans and in 1918 a realistic decision had to be taken to write off all amounts owing from Russia.

During the early months of the war the peaceful city of Cambridge seemed a long way from the battlefields of France. When, in April 1915, the first Zeppelin air raids began to take place over East Anglia, the Cambridge Board did not regard these raids with any great concern, so in June it was agreed that it was not necessary to insure the factory against air raids. However, by October Zeppelins had inflicted sporadic damage over a wide area of eastern England and the directors decided it would after all be prudent to take out insurance.

Because of the exigencies of the war effort the directors, at their Board meeting on 31 May, 1915, had fixed the maximum amount of summer holiday as one week. 'Wages in lieu of part foregone will be paid at the end of the year.' In July 1915 the Company was declared a 'Controlled Factory' by the Ministry of Munitions and from then on was only allowed to do work which the Ministry considered to be of national importance. The drafting of skilled personnel was halted and in November, with the ever increasing work load, proposals to create additional workshops, by extending Shop C, were accepted by the Board.

With a large part of the male population in the armed forces, of necessity women were employed for the first time in Britain in many fields traditionally regarded as male domains. The engineering industry was one of these. At the beginning of the war the Company had only five female employees—all of them shorthand typists. In 1916 the total number of employees was 227, an increase of 28% over 1914, 41 being women. By 1918 there were 488 employees, 200 being women. When women began to be employed in the factory in significant numbers a surgery was equipped and a qualified nurse engaged to attend to minor accidents and ailments, a practice which was continued after the war ended, when a doctor was also appointed to visit the surgery once a week for consultations. During the latter stages of the war, because it was impossible to find enough skilled workers, serving members of the Royal Engineers Regiment were drafted to the Company for special duties in connection with direct Ministry contracts.

In 1916 a full working week was $53\frac{1}{2}$ hours: 6 to 8 a.m.; 8.30 a.m. to 12.30 p.m.; and 1.30 to 5.30 p.m., Monday to Friday with a further $3\frac{1}{2}$ hours on Saturday. The minimum rate of pay for labourers in 1916 was $5\frac{1}{2}d$. per hour and the top rate for skilled instrument makers was $1s. 1\frac{1}{2}d$. per hour. Apprentices received $4s. 3d$. per week. In November 1917 the working hours were reduced to $49\frac{1}{2}$ hours per week but the weekly wage was maintained. With these long hours on highly skilled work, little overtime was worked as, to quote the annual report of 1917, experience showed that it was 'bad both for the workers and the work.'[2]

At that time wages were paid entirely in coins, which included gold sovereigns and half-sovereigns. Each employee's wage was put into a wooden cup bearing his or her clock number. The paying out clerk stood on a raised stand with the cups on a tray. As the employees filed past the clerk each called out his clock number and the contents of his cup were poured into his hand.

Since the Company was a controlled factory the salaries of its managers had to be approved by the Ministry of Munitions. In the summer of 1916 an application was submitted by the directors to make annual payments of £1000 to Horace Darwin, £1350 to Robert Whipple, £1050 to Cecil Mason and £750 to William Collins, until the end of the war. The Ministry replied that the 'question should be deferred until accounts for the Standard Period had been submitted for consideration,' and the management had to be content with temporary payments of 75% of the proposed figures in the interim period.[3]

Erasmus Darwin, Horace's son, was one of the early casualties of the war. When war was declared he joined the 4th Territorial Battalion of the Yorkshires. In April 1915 the battalion was put under orders for the front but just before he left England Erasmus was summoned to the War Office. There he was offered a staff appointment at home, connected with war munitions. Erasmus refused the post. As he explained afterwards in a letter: 'It would have been interesting and important work but of course there are plenty of older men who can do it just as well as I can.' A few days later the battalion crossed to France and on 24 April Erasmus was killed in the fighting at Ypres. His body was recovered by soldiers of the Royal Irish Fusiliers, who were fighting alongside, and he was buried, with his field captain, in a grave near a farmhouse outside Saint Julien.[4]

A year later Keith Lucas was also killed. He had resigned his seat on the Board in October 1914 and had applied to join the Honourable Artillery Company. He had already passed the medical examination when Darwin telephoned Lieut.-Colonel O'Gorman of the Royal Aircraft Factory. Darwin suggested that Lucas might be of more value to the nation at the Aircraft Factory than in the Artillery and O'Gorman promptly offered him work there. One of his first jobs was to design accurate, gyroscopically-controlled sights for bomb aiming. He then tackled the problem of designing an efficient aircraft compass and, with advice from Darwin, produced an instrument which was not affected by the banking of the aeroplane in flight nor by the vibration present during flight.

Because he was not a trained pilot Lucas had to fly as a passenger whilst testing his experimental designs. This irked him considerably and he submitted frequent requests to his superiors at the Royal Aircraft Factory for pilot training. In 1916 his request was at last agreed but, tragically, on his first solo flight in October 1916 his aircraft collided with another over Salisbury Plain and Lucas was killed.

In the early months of the war the military authorities did not appreciate the importance of utilising the inventiveness and talents of the many British scientists and engineers. (Surprisingly, a similar situation recurred during the first few months of the 1939–45 War.) So it required considerable pressure from respected men such as Thomson and Rutherford to persuade the Admiralty to set up the Advisory Board of Inventions and Research, which was constituted in July 1915 under the chairmanship of Lord Fisher. Sir J. J. Thomson, Sir Charles Parsons and Sir George Beilby formed the governing body with Lord Fisher, and the panel of scientific experts assisting them included Bragg, Crookes, Duddell,

Hopkinson, Lodge, Rutherford and (later) Threlfall.[5] The expertise of Darwin's skilled workforce was well known to many of these men and it is therefore hardly coincidental that by the end of the war the Company should have been involved in the manufacture of some of the secret devices designed as a result of the activities of this committee.

Even before the formation of the Advisory Board the Company was called upon to apply its skills in instrument design in support of the war effort. A number of the firms employed in making materials for munitions in this country were using a German optical pyrometer to monitor their manufacturing processes. The pyrometer, made by Wanner, had been distributed in England by a Company named 'Leskole' and in 1915 The Cambridge Scientific Instrument Company was asked to make a similar instrument and to take on the servicing of the German instruments already in use. Frank Wakeham, who had been a partner in Leskole, joined the Company when this work was taken on, becoming a director in 1919. Using the German instrument as a prototype the Company designed a new pyrometer and put it into production within two months.[6]

Figure 4.1 Wanner optical pyrometer in use in a foundry in 1923. (Photo: C.S.I.Co., Neg. 3069.)

The Wanner pyrometer (*Fig.* 4.1) was used extensively for high temperature work. Radiation from the furnace was compared visually with the light from a reference lamp and the light-polarising property of

Nicol prisms was used as a method of matching the intensities of the radiation from the two sources. The angle through which the prisms had to be rotated was then a measure of the temperature of the furnace.

Although, over a period, three hundred of these pyrometers were subsequently made for firms engaged in war work, there was a fundamental difficulty—the same difficulty which resulted in a chronic shortage in the British armed forces of other essential optical equipment such as field-glasses and rangefinders. Prior to 1914 Britain had imported the vast bulk of these products from the very country with whom we were now at war, and in Britain we had neither the materials nor the manufacturing expertise to make optical glass in any quantity. Consequently, in November 1915 Robert Whipple was sent by the Ministry of Munitions on a special mission to the USA to assess whether American resources might be used to boost the production of optical munitions in Britain.

But optical glass was not the only item for which British instrument makers had relied on German manufacturers. Porcelain sheaths for pyrometers, ebonite moulding material, magnets and clock escapements had all been largely imported. In 1916 the Board of Trade set up an Engineering Industries Committee to assess the performance of the engineering industry under wartime conditions. The minutes of the enquiry record that Robert Whipple was one of the two representatives of the British instrument industry to give evidence to the enquiry. Many of the initial problems had by then been overcome and Whipple reported that The Cambridge Scientific Instrument Company was obtaining pyrometer sheaths from the Royal Worcester potteries, optical glass from Chance Brothers, magnets from a Sheffield firm and clock escapements from a firm in Coventry, although this company was the only firm in Britain able to make them.[7]

On 22 April, 1915, at Ypres, the Germans used chlorine gas for the first time. It was a horrifying weapon, especially since even very small concentrations were dangerous. Some method of detection to provide an early warning of its presence, particularly at night, was urgently needed by the troops in the trenches. One such apparatus was devised by Dr G. A. Shakespear, Acting Professor of Physics at Birmingham University, where the Physics laboratories had been commandeered for experimental war work. It was a simple device that would detect a concentration of one part chlorine in 10 000 parts of air and within two seconds of exposure, ring an alarm bell or fire a Verey signal.[8] In the event detectors such as Shakespear's were not very satisfactory in the field. A booklet published by the Stationery Office in 1939 blamed their failure on the time lag of the detector systems[9] but in Shakespear's device the fragility of the wires in the sensor was a greater drawback. Nevertheless his work attracted the attention of the Advisory Board of Inventions and Research and in

September 1915 Shakespear was asked to design a hydrogen alarm system for use in airship sheds where explosive levels of as much as 4% of hydrogen had been reached.

Gilbert Arden Shakespear was an ingenious scientist whose special skill lay in adapting a simple technique into a method of precise measurement. Born on 19 August, 1873, he went up to Trinity at Cambridge in 1897 as one of J. J. Thomson's research students and obtained his BA in 1899. (This was under the 1895 University Ordinance whereby graduates from other universities might be admitted to Cambridge as research students and obtain their BA after two years of research by submission of a thesis. The first two such students in 1895 were Rutherford and Townsend.) In 1912 Birmingham University conferred their Doctorate in Science on Shakespear, who then lectured under Professor J. H. Poynting at Birmingham until Poynting's early death in 1914 when Shakespear became Acting Professor of Physics.

Shakespear's ability to design an instrument around a very unsophisticated process is nicely demonstrated in the following story from the 1930s, when he had a heated towel rail installed in his bathroom. He was at first disappointed to find that the wet towels which he hung over the rail fell to the floor when dry, but he soon discerned the cause. Whilst there was enough friction between a damp towel and the rail to support an uneven drape, as the towel dried the friction decreased and the towel slid off the rail. Shakespear realised that he could design a hygrometer using this principle: by draping a piece of fabric over a roller with a weight attached to one end and the other supported by a spring. If the roller was rotated at a constant angular velocity in the direction of the weight, the height of the weight from the floor would give an indication of the humidity. It is, of course, unlikely that Shakespear ever made such a hygrometer but its feasibility has been proved by the University of Birmingham Physics Department.[10]

In 1906 Shakespear had married a Newnham graduate, Ethel Mary Read Wood, who had received her doctorate the year before their marriage. Shakespear was perhaps overshadowed by his wife who was an eminent palaeontologist as well as being extremely active in social work during the 1914–18 War, assisting disabled servicemen and their dependants. For this latter work she received a DBE in 1920. Dame Ethel was also a masterly pianist. Indeed, before she settled on science as a career she had considered music as a profession. Whilst at Newnham she had starred in many college concerts, and on winter evenings when she practised on the only good piano the college possessed in the darkened college hall, the seats would silently fill with girls entranced by her playing.

The katharometer, the instrument Shakespear designed for the Advisory Board of Inventions and Research to measure hydrogen concentrations, was typical of his work. It utilised the variation in thermal conductivity amongst different gases as a means of gas analysis. The change in heat loss from a pair of electrically heated platinum spirals —one in a reference gas, the other open to the gas to be analysed—was monitored as a change in resistance of the open spiral by connecting the spirals in a Wheatstone bridge network.[†]

By 1916 Shakespear had designed not only a hydrogen level alarm system, but also a hydrogen purity meter which could be fitted to the delivery pipe of a gas generator, providing a continuous indication of the hydrogen concentration on a calibrated meter. Even an unskilled operator could see when the hydrogen concentration was sufficiently high for gas to be fed into the gas bag and the meter thus enabled savings to be made in the large quantities of gas which had previously been wasted.

Shakespear next turned his attention to measuring the gas permeability of the rubber-proofed fabrics used for the envelopes of balloons and airships. He found that in general more hydrogen was being lost through the seams of the material than through the fabric itself, although the fabric on the top of an airship envelope was more porous than that on the underside due both to the heating effect of sunlight and deterioration of the rubber by ultra-violet action. So that weak spots in the fabric could be found and repaired in the field he designed a portable gas permeability outfit. Shakespear was not allowed to make comparative measurements on the fabric from German airships, a fact indicative of the secrecy and importance attached to his work at that time.[11]

Strictly speaking, Shakespear was not the inventor of the thermal conductivity analyser. Prior to the war a German scientist, Koepsel, had experimented with an analyser using the principle and even earlier, about 1880, Leon Somzee, a Belgian, had suggested the principle as a method of analysis. However, Shakespear was apparently not aware of this earlier work and he was granted a British patent in 1919. A more detailed description of the work leading up to the invention and development of this method of gas analysis is given in Chapter 16.

The prototypes of Shakespear's instruments were made in his laboratory at Birmingham; Harold A. Daynes, one of Shakespear's research students, assisting him with the design work. There was soon a considerable demand for the analysers and The Cambridge Scientific Instrument Company manufactured the indicating and recording equipment. It was clear that the method of analysis had great industrial potential but little development work could be undertaken during the war. However, after the war Dr Daynes joined the Company and was

---

[†] *It has not been possible to establish the operating principle of Shakespear's earlier chlorine detector but it was not a thermal conductivity instrument. However, there seems a strong likelihood that it was based on a Wheatstone bridge network and it may have utilised the catalytic properties of platinum in the presence of hydrogen and chlorine.*

responsible for developing the technique into one of the most useful methods of continuous gas analysis available. This work was later continued by Dr Gilbert Jessop and the katharometer made a major contribution to the Company's profits for over half a century. These gas analysers are still manufactured by Kent Industrial Measurements, the design of the measuring unit being recognisably similar to Shakespear's original katharometer.

Darwin was one of the founder members of the Advisory Committee for Aeronautics, set up by the government in 1909 to further the development of aircraft. It is therefore not surprising that the Company should have become involved in the commercial manufacture of some of the few instruments used in aircraft at that time and also in equipment for use in wind tunnels, such as the aerodynamic balance. At the beginning of the war winged aviation was still in its infancy (the committee had been set up in the same year as Bleriot's historic flight across the English Channel) and the instruments were based on those in use at such institutions as the National Physical Laboratory, the Royal Aircraft Factory and the Army Flying School. During the war one workshop in the Company was given over entirely to the manufacture of engine cooling system thermometers. As the altitude at which 'planes flew increased these instruments became ever more important. At high altitudes it was essential for a pilot to keep a close watch on his temperature gauge so that should the temperature of the cooling water start to fall towards freezing point he could reduce the air flow through the radiator. More than 17 000 of these thermometers were made by the Company during the war and the milestone of 1 000 per week was celebrated with a social evening at the works.[12,13]

Cecil Mason's appointment as Technical Advisor to the Controller of Gun Ammunition led to the Company becoming involved in several items of gunnery work. A clinometer, used by anti-aircraft gunners for height finding, was designed and made in large numbers and the firm also took on the adjustment of the clockwork timers used in the fuse mechanisms of heavy calibre shells. These timers, which were made by various companies, had to be checked whilst spinning at a high rotational velocity on a test rig. Twenty-five years later, when the Second World War broke out, the Company was to resume this work.

During the early months of the 1914–18 War both the French and the German armies experimented with sound-ranging as a means of accurately locating the enemy's guns. The German system was never fully perfected. The system which the English artillery adopted was designed by M. Bull of the Institut Marey in Paris. In October 1914 he was recording heart sounds and using Einthoven's string galvanometer for electrocardiography, when he was approached by Charles Nordmann. Nordmann had been astronomer at the Paris Observatory before he was called up for service in the artillery. He had conceived the mathematical possibility of locating the position of the enemy's guns by measuring the time interval between the arrival of the sound of gunfire at different points on a measured base. At first he asked Bull for advice on the recording of faint low frequency sounds but then, having aroused Bull's interest, he went on to explain his whole idea. The two men set about constructing an experimental system using a string galvanometer recorder. Within a few weeks it was successfully demonstrated to some French generals and in February 1915 the first set was in use on the French front.

In October, Lieutenant William Lawrence Bragg (from a territorial horse artillery battery) was despatched to France to collect a sound-ranging outfit from Paris with instructions to experiment with it at the Front. In civilian life Bragg, like his father, Professor William Henry Bragg, had been an expert in X-ray crystallography and that same year, away from the battlefield, they were nominated joint winners of the Nobel Prize for Physics.

This early sound-ranging equipment was not, in fact, a great deal of use. For a year Bragg and his assistants struggled to perfect it, hiding its ineffectiveness from superior officers who would have suspended further work had they known. The main problem was the microphones. The carbon granule instruments which they were using were fine for picking up high frequency sounds, such as rifle fire or people talking nearby, and in consequence the high frequency shell wave completely masked the low frequency gun report which they needed to detect. The solution was eventually suggested by Corporal Tucker from the Physics Department at Imperial College. Before the war he had been conducting experiments on the cooling effects of air currents on fine platinum wires. He noted the idea of using a heated platinum filament as a pressure wave microphone. The first crude hot wire microphone was constructed using an old ammunition box. It worked admirably. It was completely selective to low frequency sounds and from then on sound-ranging was a success. The only refinement to be added later was a small grid to keep out unwanted insects, attracted by the warmth of the hot wire. In due course these grids were added to the *Army List of Stores*—as 'Protectors, Earwig, Mark I'.

Each outfit consisted of six microphones spread out along a base line of some 9000 yards, about 4000 yards behind the Front, with an observer some way in front of this base line. Each microphone was connected to a string galvanometer, the six galvanometers being mounted in one photographic recording unit. On hearing the report from the gun the observer pressed a switch to start the recorder. This would be some two or three seconds before the report reached the microphones. As soon as the photographic record was complete it was cut off and quickly developed and fixed using strong solutions.

In addition to the six traces the photograph included timing marks generated in the recorder so that the time intervals as the pressure wave passed each microphone could be measured very accurately. A later refinement was to place the microphones at exactly equal distances in a straight line (*Fig.* 4.2). The regular pattern this produced on the record was a great help when picking out the report of one particular gun from a record confused by other gunfire.

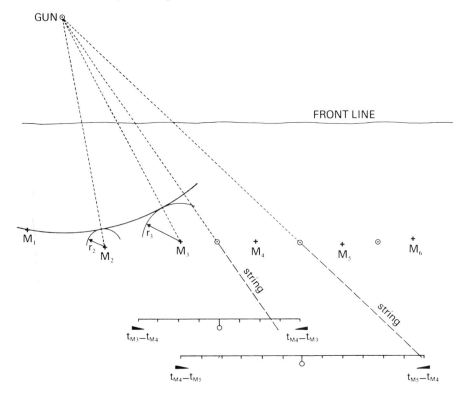

Figure 4.2 The principle of sound ranging. Since sound travels at 335 m/s, circles radii r_2 and r_3 can be drawn round microphones M_2 and M_3 to represent the delays in hearing the gun report at these microphones after it has been received at microphone M_1. An arc passing through M_1 and touching these circles would have the gun at its centre.

In practice a plotting board with a system of strings attached to the midpoints of M_1–M_2, M_2–M_3, etc. was used. The strings were laid across scales drawn on the plotting board, the time calibration of each scale corresponding to intervals between the receipt of the gun report by each microphone. This method of obtaining bearings of the gun's position is shown in the diagram, for microphones M_3, M_4 and M_5.

A considerable number of the sound-ranging outfits were made by The Cambridge Scientific Instrument Company, detailed manufacturing drawings being prepared in the Company's drawing office under the supervision of Frank Doggett. Both Lawrence Bragg and his father (who was at that time Director of Research at the Naval Laboratory at Parkeston Quay and working on hydrophones for submarine detection) are reputed to have kept an eye on the manufacture of the equipment but it is unlikely that either would have been able to spare much time. Indeed, Lawrence Bragg, in an account some fifty years later, criticised the 'tidy-minded instrument designer' who changed the microphone container from a discarded ammunition box, which was heavily damped, to a smart metal container which resonated.[14] Towards the end of the war a fully automatic developing recorder was produced—the first instrument of its type to be manufactured—in which the photographic processing took less than a minute, although it was regarded by Lawrence Bragg as 'horribly messy'.

Sound-ranging also claimed the attentions of another member of the Darwin family—Charles Galton Darwin, Horace Darwin's nephew. He was a mathematical physicist and during the war he commanded a sound-ranging section in one of the Royal Engineers units. Later, in 1917, he was attached to the Royal Flying Corps to work on aircraft noise. After the war, in 1919, he became a director of the Company.

There were eventually about forty sets of sound-ranging equipment in use at the Front. Tradition also has it that General Allenby used sound-ranging to locate the Turkish guns before his advance on Jerusalem. During the Second World War the technique was again used by the artillery and later in the war an experimental system of 36 microphones was set up across south-east England, linked to six synchronised recorders at Canterbury, in an attempt to determine the launch sites of the first V2 rockets aimed at London. The military authorities, aware of the imminent use of these 'secret' weapons gave the Cambridge Company just six weeks in which to construct a plotting table. The table was finished before the first rocket arrived but in this instance the technique proved too cumbersome and the chain of listening posts was soon abandoned. However, a few months later sound-ranging was used to locate the launching sites of the V2 rockets fired at Antwerp by the retreating Nazis, as the spread of possible launch sites was too wide for adequate coverage by the radar systems then available.

During the period of peace following the 1914–18 War ex-army sound-ranging equipment was used for upper atmosphere research at the University of Birmingham. Professor P. B. Moon has recorded Sir Arthur Vick's description of this work.[15] Several hot-wire microphones were set up in the grounds of the University, the microphones being mounted in the necks of dustbin-sized resonators. The string galvanometer recorder (one of the fully automatic developing units) was located in the basement of the Poynting Building. An arrangement was made that when the heavy guns at Shoeburyness were to be tested, or guns fired during a Royal review of the fleet in the Solent, the Department of Physics at Birmingham would be warned. The instant of firing of the guns would be given by the superimposition of four 'pips' on a radio programme. Eleven minutes later the recorder was switched on at Birmingham and the time of arrival of the sound wavefront at each microphone recorded using time signals from the Department's master clock. Analysis of the results enabled the angle of descent of the wavefront and also the temperature gradients in the upper atmosphere to be calculated.

Historians have pointed out that the British Navy had no real answer to the German submarine menace during the early years of the 1914–18 War and Lord Fisher's board was told that work on anti-submarine warfare was its highest priority. The answers were not easy to find and it was not until 1917 that effective means of detection and weaponry began to be produced. The Company manufactured some of these weapons at a secret factory—a roller-skating rink in Magrath Avenue, not far from their premises in Chesterton Road. The adjoining house, 24 Gloucester Street, with its garden and paddock, was rented by the Company in 1917 'for a period not exceeding one year after the duration of the war', according to the terms of the lease,[16] and the Admiralty erected a temporary 'Test House' in the paddock.

There are no public records detailing the devices which were made at the Skating Rink (and very few ex-employees of the Company alive now have personal knowledge of the factory) but from the clues available it is possible to draw some fairly definite conclusions. In the article published by *Engineering* to celebrate the 50th anniversary of the Company (subsequently reprinted as a Company monograph) a brief reference is made to the secret workshop '. . . where, under the guidance of the late Sir J. C. McLennan, anti-submarine devices were made from the designs of Mr F. E. Smith, . . .'[17] The later monograph, which was published to celebrate the 75th anniversary of the Company, expands on this '. . . a special secret factory was equipped for the study and development of anti-submarine devices and for mine detectors. At the close of the war, active work was in hand in relation to the possible menace of magnetic mines; this development work bore valuable fruit in later years when magnetic mines were widely used in the second world war.'[18]

Frank Edward Smith was an expert on electrical units and standards at the National Physical Laboratory. In 1914 the NPL turned to war work and when Lord Fisher's Advisory Board was set up Smith was drawn into its activities, and began working on mines. As Admiral of the Fleet, Earl Jellicoe, commented after the war in his book, *The Submarine Peril*, the mines which the Navy had for use during the early part of the war, prior to 1917, proved ineffective against both surface vessels and submarines, not being sufficiently sensitive.[19]. Smith invented the first magnetic mine, and these mines were responsible for the sinking of several enemy submarines. At the end of the war Smith received the OBE for his war work, one of a number of honours to be awarded to him during his lifetime.

The trigger mechanism for Smith's magnetic mine has been described by Dr A. B. Wood in an article published in the *Journal of the Royal Naval Scientific Service* in 1965.[20] It consisted of two bar magnets, one with a large moment of inertia and the other having a small moment of inertia. The magnets were pivoted vertically above each other and, at rest, pointed N–S. Each magnet carried a contact wire so that a small deflection either way of one relative to the other (such as would be produced by the passage of a steel ship nearby) would make a contact and fire the mine. A delay mechanism prevented accidental firing during laying and an anti-shock device was also fitted to prevent series triggering from adjacent explosions. A fair description of such a device would be a 'mining compass', and in the minutes of The Cambridge Scientific Instrument Company Board meeting held on 10 June, 1918, reference was made to a letter from the Director of Navy Contracts regarding the proposed charge for making 'mining compasses' at the Skating Rink. Further support for this theory that the anti-submarine devices referred to earlier were the trigger mechanisms for F. E. Smith's magnetic mine is provided by the recollections of a Cambridge octogenarian, Mrs Violet Tolliday, whose aunt was a munitions worker at the Skating Rink. She recalls that the women munitions workers were under strict instructions not to wear any steel objects such as combs. Corsets were much in fashion at the time and particular instructions were given that all steel inserts had to be replaced by whalebone.

Although John Cunningham McLennan was mentioned in the 50th Anniversary Monograph as advising the Company on the manufacture of Smith's 'anti-submarine devices' he was himself involved in the design of other such devices. A Canadian physicist with a dynamic, thrusting personality, he had first come to England in 1898. Then in his early thirties, he had worked for a year at the Cavendish under J. J. Thomson, and for years afterwards he was in the habit of visiting Thomson whenever he felt in need of intellectual refreshment. As an associate of Thomson, McLennan must have known Horace Darwin and may well have visited the Company's works during one of his visits to Cambridge. Early in 1915, before the formation of the Advisory Board of Inventions and Research, McLennan wrote to the Admiralty, suggesting the need to make more use of science in naval defence measures. His plea fell on deaf ears, but in 1916 he was invited to the British Admiralty for three weeks, to have discussions with Thomson and Fisher, and to assist with 'special work'. In April 1917 McLennan was again invited to join the staff of the Advisory Board for the summer, to assist in anti-submarine work. He actually stayed for the rest of the war and during the winter of 1917–18 he also brought over a team of his assistants from Toronto University, where he was Professor of Physics.

Lord Fisher has written that his committee suffered badly from obstructionism within the Admiralty from 'permanent-Expert Limpets', who could not see its merits.[21] McLennan, however, was one member who would not allow 'red tape' to stand in the way of getting things done quickly. He operated on the assumption that a professor was equal in rank with an admiral and that he thus reported directly to the First Sea Lord. On one occasion he used this principle to over-ride the objections of senior Navy personnel when he wanted the speedy isolation of a submarine in a dock at Portsmouth so that a magnetic survey of its magnetic moment —up till that time an unheard of quantity—could be obtained.

One of the anti-submarine measures for which McLennan was responsible was the electromagnetic detection of the passage of a submarine along a channel by laying a loop of wire on the sea bed. These loops were laid in the channels through mine fields at harbour entrances. The enemy submarine, once detected, would then be blown up by detonating a mine remotely, using an electrical signal—another of McLennan's ideas.

Whether experimental work on any of McLennan's anti-submarine ideas was carried out at the Skating Rink cannot be definitely established but his measurement of the magnetic moment of a submarine was certainly relevant and so is the hint in the *75 Years* monograph that early work on the Second World War concept of degaussing a ship was under way at the Skating Rink in 1918.[22]

Similarly, the meaning of the reference to 'mine detectors' in the *75 years* monograph remains a topic for conjecture, although here Dr A. B. Wood's memoirs are again of value. Dr Wood recalls that early in 1917 Professor W. H. Bragg suggested that sound ranging might be used under water.[23] The first experiments were carried out at Parkeston Quay by R. S. H. Boulding. Boulding was William du Bois Duddell's assistant. Prior to his early death in 1917 Duddell was also involved in anti-submarine work and in 1915 he wrote a report for the Advisory Board of Inventions and Research on 'The general question of detecting submarines by electrical and electromagnetic means.'[24]

Boulding's tests proved very successful and an undersea sound-ranging system later installed at Easton Broad near Southwold was used to fix the positions of minefields laid off the Belgian coast to an accuracy of 100 yards. Undersea sound ranging was further developed by Dr Wood in the years immediately following the war, the Einthoven galvanometer-recorder being replaced by a phonic chronometer—a stop clock operated electromagnetically and fitted with three sets of dials for measuring three independent time intervals. Dr Wood noted that in February 1921 he made an official visit to The Cambridge Scientific Instrument Company where he met Horace Darwin and discussed with Whipple and Collins arrangements for the construction of triple-dial phonic chronometers, tuning forks, etc.[25]

Both Robert Whipple and works manager William George Collins (who became a director in 1918) were considerably involved in the work at the Skating Rink and the directors' minutes dated 18 March, 1918, noted that two-thirds of their salaries were to be charged against this work. After the war the rink returned to its former function of providing entertainment for the citizens of Cambridge. It was refurbished as a cinema and ballroom—the 'Rendezvous Cinema and Ballroom', the name later being changed to the 'Rex Cinema and Ballroom'.[26]

As the war progressed the quantity of work undertaken by the Company continually increased. In 1917 the Company was working at the limits of its capacity and, largely to accommodate an order for 5000 transmitting thermometers, a new two-storey building was erected in Carlyle Road—Shop D. The Test Room was also extended in the grounds of 24 Carlyle Road. In July the trading agreement with the Taylor Instrument Company of America was terminated and in the autumn, when working hours were reduced at the time of the wage increase of $12\frac{1}{2}\%$ awarded to all skilled workers by the Ministry of Munitions, the directors took the opportunity to raise catalogue prices by between $33\frac{1}{3}\%$ and 60%.

Two important organisations for the employees of the Company were started in 1917. The first, in March, was a Works Committee of seven representatives of the employees, elected by proportional representation. Its function was to discuss with the management any matter which either side considered should be brought to the attention of the other. Just over a year later it was reported at a Board meeting that 'a letter of thanks had been received from the shops committee, on behalf of the workers, for the frequent meetings to settle various matters and expressing the opinion that the movement had been successful and of benefit to all concerned.'[27]

Also in 1917, a Trade School for the Company's apprentices, was started at 24 Carlyle Road, a three-storey house adjoining the factory. This was attended by the apprentices during working hours. Thomas Richard Byers BA was appointed schoolmaster and the subjects taught were mathematics, machine drawing, chemistry, physics and English. To begin with there were 39 boys in the school but by September 1919 this number had risen to 49, and the pupils included six boys from W. G. Pye and Co. To cope with the increased numbers Hugh Langdon-Davies, a graduate of Sidney Sussex College, was appointed as assistant master in May 1920, but during 1921, when the postwar depression began to take hold, the numbers fell sharply as the Company ceased to take on new apprentices. A small library, for the use of the boys, was started about 1918. A Cadet Corps was also founded, and for a number of years the apprentices ran their own football team.[28]

Spring 1918 brought a turning point in the war as American troops joined forces with the British and their allies in Europe and by midsummer the allied armies were beginning to advance on all fronts. On 3 June, 1918, Horace Darwin was awarded a knighthood for his work as a member of the Munitions Inventions Department Panel, an honour which also reflected to some extent the part played by the workers at The Cambridge Scientific Instrument Company in assuring the victory.

When the end of hostilities was announced on 11 November, 1918, Britain was in the grip of an altogether different adversary—an influenza epidemic. Four of the Company's employees died as a result of the epidemic and the first item minuted by Sir Horace and his fellow directors at their Board meeting on 15 November was the Board's sorrow at these deaths. The directors then turned their attention to planning the post-war future of the Company. During the war years the factory area had been significantly increased and industry in general was making use of many more instruments than ever before, particularly for temperature measurement, one of the Company's main fields. The Company had emerged from the war in a much stronger position than anyone could have foreseen. The outlook was bright.

*　　*　　*　　*　　*

CHAPTER FIVE

The Cambridge and Paul Instrument Company

THE year 1919 was an eventful one for the Company. With the war over the directors realised that the volume of government work would decline sharply. Immediate steps had therefore to be taken to strengthen the Company's sales force in order to compensate for this loss, and in January regional sales representatives were appointed in Newcastle and Manchester—the beginnings of what was to become a network of regional offices and service centres throughout the British Isles. In a move to expand the Company's overseas markets the Board joined with Ross & Company, Watts & Company, and Negretti and Zambra in a tentative agreement to form a company in Italy. This plan fell through within a few weeks but alternative proposals to set up a Belgian company were successful, and the consortium then began discussions with a view to forming a Canadian company.

Although it had been trading for nearly forty years The Cambridge Scientific Instrument Company had not so far made use of a trademark. Probably as part of the overall move to promote the Company's commercial image, on 7 February, 1919, Darwin put before the Board his idea for a mark to identify the Company's products.[1] It consisted of an electrical bridge with a cam inscribed in the centre (*Fig 5.1*) It was an inspired design. In a simple insignia Darwin succeeded in conveying the principle of precise electrical measurement combined with mechanical finesse, and yet the play on words linked the symbol unmistakably to the Company's name. The mark, which was to become indicative of the highest standards of technical excellence, was, of course, approved, and during the next few months the Company registered it worldwide.

The possibility of amalgamating Robert Paul's instrument-making business in New Southgate with the Cambridge Company was

Figure 5.1 Cam and Bridge trademark.

first discussed by the directors at a Board meeting in June. It seems highly likely that Paul may have made the original proposal to Robert Whipple for the two men were well acquainted. They were of similar ages and both were active members of the Physical Society. Moreover some of Paul's anti-submarine work during the war had closely paralleled that under-taken at the Skating Rink. Certainly, correspondence between the two men in later life shows that there existed between them for many years a deep and trusting friendship, Paul placing great reliance on Whipple's advice.

Robert William Paul (*Fig.* 5.2) was born in Highbury in 1869. His father, George Butler Paul, was a London shipowner and during school vacations Paul travelled the world in his father's ships, acquiring a taste for travel that stayed with him throughout his life. Paul's technical education was gained at the City and Guilds of London Institute, established in 1879, near Finsbury Square. It was here that Paul first began to show his talent for mechanical design. On leaving the College he went to Elliott Brothers for a while, in order to learn more of the practice of instrument-making and also to the Bell Telephone Company in Antwerp. In 1891 he started up in business on his own account, as an instrument designer and maker, in small premises in Hatton Garden.

At the City and Guilds Institute Professor Ayrton and his colleague Perry were busily engaged in designing electrical measuring instruments, work in which they were later assisted by Mather. Paul kept up his contact with the college and Professor Ayrton and his associates frequently helped Paul to find new products by putting forward their ideas for instruments. Although these instruments would then be sold bearing the inventor's name, their success owed much to Paul's own skills in mechanical design and the soundness of the craftsmanship in his workshop. Within three years his business in Hatton Garden had expanded to such an extent that it included a four-storey factory in Great Saffron Hill nearby.

Figure 5.2 Robert William Paul. (Photo: Institute of Physics.)

In the midst of this success Paul became interested in cinemato-graphy. In 1894 two Greeks, Georgiades and Trajedes, purchased some of Edison's kinetoscopes in America and brought them to London where they set them up in a shop near Liverpool Street station. The peepshows of 'living pictures' produced by forty-foot loops of film proved to be so popular that there were soon queues of would-be viewers outside the shop in Old Broad Street, all waiting to pay their twopences for a peep through the eyepieces. With business booming the Greek showmen asked Paul to make six more kinetoscopes. Paul at first declined, assuming the design to be patented in England, but when he discovered that this was not the case he readily accepted the commission. During the next year Paul made about sixty kinetoscopes, improving on the original design in the process. Naturally, the American inventors refused to supply film so Paul then joined forces with a photographer, Birt Acres, and together they designed a camera, based largely on Marey's design of 1890. But the partnership with Acres was shortlived and instead Paul began to make his own films, which, somewhat tongue in cheek, he offered to supply to Edison in America.

In making these peepshows Paul became interested in the possibility of projecting pictures on to a screen. The main difficulty lay in the design of a suitable mechanical arrangement which would advance the film a frame at a time (as opposed to continuous movement) as it was only by this means that a sufficiently high level of illumination could be obtained. Paul solved the problem by means of a Maltese cross ('Geneva escapement') mechanism. He called his projector the 'Theatrograph' and in *English Mechanics and World of Science* published on 21 February, 1896, it was described as 'a new mechanism for throwing on a screen, so as to be visible to an audience, theatrical scenes or events of interest, with their natural motions and in life-size. The apparatus is simple, and can be adapted to any lantern . . .'[2] Paul gave the first public demonstration of the theatrograph on 20 February, 1896, at the Annual Conversazione of the Finsbury Technical College, and a few days later he exhibited it at the Royal Institution. These were wise moves for by so doing the whole process of viewing films projected on a screen acquired a certain respectability and was no longer a showman's gimmick.

Paul became an acknowledged expert in cinematography. One of his most famous exploits was to photograph the Prince of Wales' horse, Persimmon, winning the Derby in 1896. Immediately the race was over he hurried back to Hatton Garden to develop the film, a process which was completed at one o'clock in the morning. When the negative was dry a print was made and that same evening Paul projected the film at the Alhambra in Leicester Square. The audience gave it a rapturous reception, standing on their seats and singing 'God Bless the Prince of Wales' whilst demanding two repeat showings of the $1\frac{3}{4}$-minute film.[3]

Figure 5.3 Robert Paul's factory at New Southgate c. 1905–12. The photograph cannot be precisely dated but was probably taken soon after the factory was completed about 1905. 'R. W. PAUL OFFICE' is set in the fanlight over the central door in the left-hand wing. (Photo: C.S.I.Co., Neg. 2533.)

Ever the entrepreneur, Paul began to make short 'playlet' films, staged in artificial sets erected on the flat roof of the Alhambra. 'The Soldier's Courtship' was the first, made in 1896. This had an appropriate if unexpected sequel a year later when Paul and his leading lady, Miss Ellen Dawn, were married. Paul's playlet films were so successful that in 1897 he bought a field in Muswell Hill and built a proper studio, which included a scene painting room where he used to work late at night 'after the day's work was over' as he said.[4]

In the early 1900s the cinema side of his business was extremely profitable but Paul began to resent the fact that it distracted him from instrument making, a part of his business which also continued to flourish. Indeed it grew at such a rate that in 1902 he commissioned a purpose-built factory on the Muswell Hill site (*Fig.* 5.3). There his standard product ranges were manufactured in a highly efficient manner in large batches. In an article in *The Electrical Review* in October 1914 the factory was described as '. . . not only his [Paul's] works but, also his own work, and it retains throughout the impress of his personality, which gives it the atmosphere of a living organism rather than of a complex machine.'[5]

At the heart of many of the instruments made at the new factory was Paul's own invention (in 1903) the 'Unipivot' galvanometer. This single pivot movement had a sensitivity comparable with the conventional suspended galvanometer but was even more robust than the double pivoted Weston meters.

Paul's instruments, like those of The Cambridge Scientific Instrument Company, won international approval. In 1904 he was awarded the gold medal at the St Louis Exposition and in 1910 the gold medal at the Brussels Exhibition. In the meantime he was becoming increasingly disillusioned with the show business side of cinematography. He foresaw the intervention of speculators pouring immense capital resources into lavish productions. Quite suddenly in 1910 he decided to discard popular film making and to concentrate on his instrument work. In a dramatic gesture he burned his large stocks of film and sold off the specialised film-making equipment. In reality he had always regarded this side of his business as a hobby, albeit a lucrative one, for even in its first year, from March 1896 to March 1897, it had yielded a profit of £12 838 on a capital of £1000!

His standard instruments sold well and profitably but, like Horace Darwin, Paul frequently preferred to devote time to the more interesting work of making specialised instruments for his friends as an aid to their researches. Fortunately he could afford to subsidise this work. In 1911 he opened a branch in New York where instruments shipped out from the Muswell Hill works could be tested and then calibrated to suit the specific requirements of his American customers.

When the war with Germany broke out in 1914 Paul addressed

his employees on the seriousness of the situation. His speech of 10 August, 1914, carries the echo of his dominant, at times intolerant, personality:[6]

We resume work under conditions so changed that it is scarcely possible to focus them. We, who have not lived the daily military life of our powerful continental enemies and allies, find it impossible to gain an idea of the forces now at work, which must, in any event rupture many of our commercial connections and for the remainder of our lives change our entire outlook. Practically all French and German trade is cut off, and all their able-bodied men are at the war.

We, as a nation, have awoke to the fact that security cannot be bought by the payment of professional soldiers, and that, if we are to hold our place in the world, all slackness, love of ease and selfishness must be thrown aside. The responsibility for the war is not upon our consciences, but we must reap its results from now onwards.

Let us consider our respective duties under these altered conditions, and how we can minimise the loss or suffering of those around us; we will confine our thoughts for the moment to our relations in the Works.

For my part, I conceive it my duty to carry on business as long as work, materials, and money for wages can be in any way procured. Already there is a shortage of certain materials, and it may be months, or even years, before regular importations can be counted on; therefore the greatest care must be exercised to prevent waste. A definite amount of stock should be now in each store, and I leave in a few moments to endeavour to secure more. A certain amount of work has been assured by Government contracts just placed, and more may follow from the same source if satisfaction is given. This work will be done under the Official Secrets Act, and to divulge information respecting it is treason. The payment of wages will be difficult on account of the nonpayment till September of due accounts, but I think I can surmount this difficulty. In order that workers shall not be subject to distressing anxiety, I will endeavour that two weeks' notice shall be given if it becomes necessary to largely reduce the number of employees. Any employee unpunctual, or negligent in his duties, or disobedient, will not be granted any notice. With regard to the duties of employees, those who are of suitable age for enlistment will find a job kept open for them on their return, if it lies in my power; others may serve by enrolment in the special constabulary, if unfit for military service. The rest of us have a duty to fulfil quite as important as that of a sentry guarding ammunition or provisions. As we have been entrusted with orders for signalling apparatus both for the Army and for the Navy, let each see that his share of the work is as thorough as the most strenuous effort can make it. Let us realise our responsibilities in this matter; war is not only a trial of moral character and of courage, but an engineering and scientific contest in which we can play our part. For example, aeroplanes are the eyes of our army, and their signalling apparatus as well as that of our battleships, is of vital importance. Imagine the feelings of a British workman responsible for a botched joint or a stripped screw and knowing that the faulty detail was liable to rob a British commander in action of his source of information, or, in other words, put out the eyes of our defenders. All of us must fight, not perhaps with rifles, but against our enemies of inefficiency, disorder and lack of hearty, cheerful co-operation; thus we shall learn the dearly-bought lesson of this great war.

We cannot predict the future; many great businesses may be crippled or wrecked in the scarcity following on the war. One recalls that during the Franco-Prussian war the founder of the great optical firm of Carl Zeiss turned his hand to repairing rifles with one assistant, and that they lived on bread, flavoured with an onion or an occasional herring. Modern organisation, and the wise precautions of our leaders and financiers, may, we hope, keep most of our factories at work, but an extended war will entail much personal strain and sacrifice both on employers and employed, and it is only by working cordially together that continuous employment will be rendered possible. The workers must assist each other, so as to reduce supervision, in order that the office staff may be free to tackle their work of providing material and money.

 I wish to take the opportunity of thanking, on your behalf and my own, those who have cheerfully given up part of their holidays in order to overhaul the premises and prepare for a fresh start. I would ask you to regard my remarks, not as those of an alarmist, but as an indication of my desire to respect our future welfare.

 Doubtless you will wish to think over these matters, and I will be at hand at this hour tomorrow to reply to any questions you may wish to put.

The contracts for signalling equipment referred to in this address probably included the early wireless equipment which Paul manufactured during the war for use in the trenches. Here, again, his continued association with the staff at the Finsbury Technical College can be seen; at that time the physical research laboratories at the college were working on short-wave equipment for trench use, under Dr W. H. Eccles and at the specific request of the Signals Experimental Establishment at the War Office.

Amongst other items of military equipment manufactured by Paul during the war was the Paterson-Walsh auto-aircraft height finder —once it had been officially adopted by the War Office. Dr Paterson has recorded his memories of that Saturday afternoon in 1915 when a demonstration of all the various height finders which were competitors for official adoption was given on a field at the National Physical Laboratory. The time appointed for the demonstration was 3 p.m.:[7]

> *All the height-finders, except Paul's, were erected on the field and got into working order by their sponsors in the morning; but Paul's failed to turn up, and when two o'clock came and the 'Brass Hats' began to assemble, it seemed clear that something must have gone wrong.*
> *At a quarter to three a cloud of dust appeared, and with it Paul's disreputable Gladiator car, driven by himself and with half-a-ton of height-finder on the back—depressing the back springs to the axle. The impact of the car on the boundary to the demonstration field caused it to bounce into the air and to continue to bounce and creak in a hair-raising way as it risked its heavy load to the erection site. Here, with no particular care, the height-finder was dragged down and by three o'clock it was set up and ready for trial.*
> *There was more than a suggestion of remonstrance at taking such risks on a critical occasion, but Paul's only response was that if the thing had to be handled in practice by Army personnel in the field it was just as well to test it for reliability as well as for accuracy. The gear was found to be in good adjustment, and this combined with Paul's demonstration and supreme confidence in his own design, resulted in the adoption of this height-finder for use at Field A.A. stations in the last war.*

Even in the midst of the gravity of war the showman in Paul could not be completely submerged!

Paul was also considerably interested in the problems of submarine warfare. Dr W. H. Eccles described Paul's personal contribution as 'suggestions and models for acoustic mines and magnetic mines, and the apparatus for the location of mines and submarines,'[8] whilst Dr A. B. Wood in his account of the war period (published posthumously) recalled one of the humorous episodes during Paul's visits to the testing laboratories at Parkeston Quay in the summer of 1917. Evidently Paul made frequent visits to Parkeston Quay, in order to test a magnetic system which he was developing for magnetic mines. On one occasion, when he wished to make an underwater test with a ship running past, he borrowed a slop-pail from the Alexandra Hotel at Dovercourt and carried it, without any wrappings, to the laboratory. Paul used the pail to house his pivoted magnet system but, unfortunately, the seal round the lid was faulty and when the bucket was submerged the system was flooded and put out of action.[9]

Early in 1918 his Muswell Hill factory was bought by the Signals Department of the War Office and Paul moved into temporary premises in Fortis Green where he continued his experimental work, assisted by thirty of his best workmen from the factory. When the war was over he bought back the factory in March 1919, and almost immediately began negotiations to sell the Company to The Cambridge Scientific Instrument Company. As the negotiations progressed William Herbert Apthorpe, head of the Test Room at Cambridge, moved to New Southgate. On 3 November the agreement to purchase Paul's business was sealed, and Apthorpe was appointed Works Manager of the Muswell Hill works. Two weeks later a new name for the combined companies was approved at a meeting of the shareholders: 'The Cambridge and Paul Instrument Company'.

From February 1920 Robert Paul had a seat on the Board of the new Company but he gradually withdrew from instrument design, concentrating instead on financial matters. However, in his workshop at home he would still work on particular projects that attracted his interest. One such was a request for help from his friend, Sir William Bragg, in September 1933. Bragg had a friend who was suffering from progressive muscular atrophy and who needed constant artificial respiration to assist his breathing. At first this had been carried out by teams of relatives and nurses. Bragg had then made a simple bellows device to inflate a football bladder bandaged to the man's chest. This was less exhausting for the operator but the device still required continuous manual operation. Paul designed and constructed a small hydraulic machine, worked by the mains water supply, which alternately compressed and relaxed a thick rubber bellows. The apparatus worked successfully for many months, only failing once when the water froze in the pipes. It soon attracted the approbation of the medical profession and 'Bragg-Paul Pulsators'—

forerunners of the 'Iron Lung'—were used by a number of hospitals.[10]

In December 1919 two members of the Darwin family were elected to the Board. One was Dr Charles Galton Darwin, Horace Darwin's nephew, the son of George Darwin and Maud du Puy. The other was James Alan Noel Barlow, who had married Horace Darwin's daughter, Nora, in 1911. It is through the Barlow side of the family that the family links with the Company continue to the present day.

Alan Barlow was the eldest of the three sons and two daughters of Sir Thomas Barlow. Sir Thomas, who was physician to Queen Victoria, Edward VII and George V, and President of the Royal College of Physicians, had been created a baronet in 1901. The family forebears were Manchester cotton spinners who had made a fortune during the Industrial Revolution. They had then set up as landed gentry in Buckinghamshire. Educated at Marlborough and Oxford, Alan Barlow followed a career as a civil servant and in 1916 he was appointed Private Secretary to the Minister of Munitions. After the war in addition to becoming a director of The Cambridge and Paul Instrument Company there followed one of the most successful periods of his career, when he served as Principal Assistant Secretary in charge of the Training Department in the Ministry of Labour. This period culminated in his appointment in 1933 as Principal Private Secretary to the then Prime Minister, Ramsay Macdonald. At the time of this appointment he felt it appropriate to resign his directorship of the Company but he was re-elected to the Board when he retired from public service in 1948.

Dr Charles Darwin was a Trinity man. He was a Wrangler in 1909 and obtained first class honours in part 2 of his degree in 1910. On leaving Cambridge in 1910 he took up a career as a mathematical physicist, working for a while with Rutherford on atomic physics in Manchester, at about the time when the atomic nucleus was discovered. During the war Darwin served in the Royal Engineers and his connection with sound-ranging has already been noted. In 1922 he was elected a Fellow of the Royal Society and in 1924 he became Tait Professor of Natural Philosophy at Edinburgh University. At this time he resigned from the Board but later rejoined as chairman when Horace Darwin died in 1928.

At the time of the expansion of the Company's sales force during 1919 the directors had seen the need for an office and show room in London. Kingsway or Lincoln's Inn Fields were originally suggested as appropriate locations but in the spring of 1920 a twenty-year lease was obtained on 45 Grosvenor Place in SW1, at an annual rent of £600. The house had previously been the Spanish Embassy and the Spanish Ambassador's brother, evidently himself a good salesman, persuaded the Company to buy the furnishings as well—carpets, furniture, even the pictures on the walls. After eighteen years, when the expiry date of the lease approached, the Company moved its office a few hundred yards down the road to number 13. The site of the first office is now occupied by the National Coal Board's Hobart House.

In the early 1920s William Collins devised a method of recording mechanical vibrations by means of a lightly loaded stylus moving over a strip of celluloid.[11] By examining the record under a microscope it was observed that if the stylus was given a rounded point approximately 0·02 mm in radius it would produce a moulded groove in the plastic instead of scratching the surface. This moulded trace had the advantage that when optically magnified it gave a much sharper picture than did a scratched record.

One of the first uses of this method of recording was as a means of measuring the torsion in a ship's propellor shaft. For this, two tuning forks vibrating at exactly the same frequency were used. Each carried a stylus on one prong and the records were produced on strips of celluloid wrapped around the shaft a known distance apart. The twist in the shaft could be determined by measuring the lag of one record with respect to the other.

Over a period of time a series of vibrograph instruments working on the seismograph principle were designed. They could be used to record vertical and horizontal vibrations, acceleration and stress.[12,13] Some of the early vibrographs were used experimentally by HM Office of Works during the re-leading of the roofs of the state apartments at Windsor Castle about 1925. It was feared that hammering or moving heavy loads on the roof might damage the paintings on the ceilings of the rooms beneath. However, tests on the ceiling joists, using a vertical vibrograph and an accelerometer showed that the effects were negligible. HM Office of Works subsequently bought several vibrographs which were kept in virtually constant use monitoring the historic buildings of London, including Westminster Abbey, St Paul's Cathedral and the Houses of Parliament.

Vibrographs were also frequently used during investigations into complaints of vibration from road traffic, pile driving etc. Often the sound of pile driving emanating from a building site would give an exaggerated impression of excessive vibration and there were instances where the evidence from vibrograph records prevented expensive litigation. Levels of vibration in aeroplanes and ships could also be checked in this way, not only to ensure the comfort of passengers, but also to avoid destructive resonances in the structure.

The first enquiry which the Company received for a pH meter came from the Professor of Pathology at Cambridge, German Sims Woodhead, who needed an instrument in order to standardise the media in which bacteriological cultures were being grown. This was about 1917, eight years after Professor Sorenson of Carlsberg Laboratorium in Copenhagen had published his paper on the importance of the hydrogen-ion concentration in enzyme reactions.[14] In it he had shown that the range of acidity is extremely wide and in order to define a standard of measurement he made use of a scale based on the negative logarithm of the concentration of the acid. Thus each step on the scale represented the hydrogen-ion concentration as a power of 10 and he therefore used the symbol pH to represent the major intervals of this scale, pH values from 0 to 7 measuring an acid condition, whilst the range 7 to 14 measured an alkaline state.

Although the use of pH revolutionised work in pathology, prior to 1918 the measurement technique was a relatively crude one using hydrogen and calomel electrodes with a simple straight wire potentiometer. With the increase in research work after the war there arose a demand for a more sensitive method of measurement, and about 1922 the Company began to manufacture a research instrument which made use of the Cambridge slidewire potentiometer (accurate to 0·1 mV). Not long afterwards a self-contained, but less accurate instrument—the H-ion potentiometer—with a built-in Unipivot galvanometer, was put into production.

In the late 1920s S. W. Cole of the Sir William Dunn Institute of Biochemistry in Cambridge suggested a modification to the potentiometer which enabled the Company to market the first direct-reading pH meter and in 1932 the electrometer thermionic valve pH meter was produced. Significant improvements in electrode design were made during the 1940s with the introduction of the sealed glass electrode and, a few years later, the Alki electrode, the latter considerably reducing measurement errors in the pH range from 10 to 14. pH measurement came to be not only a research technique but also a powerful tool in industry, pH meters being used in pharmaceuticals manufacture, brewing, sewage treatment, water purification, the textile and paper industries and the control of feed water purity in power stations.[15]

For many years the Cambridge Company remained a leader in pH measurement technology but in the 1950s it failed to keep pace with those companies who were making use of electronic methods. One company in particular, Electronic Instruments Ltd, founded by Paul Goudime, became highly proficient in a wide variety of liquid analysis techniques and it was largely a desire by the Cambridge Board to regain the leadership in this field which led to the takeover of EIL by The Cambridge Instrument Company in 1960.

During the 1920s several significant advances were also made in the constantly developing field of temperature measurement. Firstly, there was the demand for an instrument to measure the temperature of rapidly moving surfaces such as the hot rollers of calendering machines. Initially thermopiles placed near the rollers were used, but because of the difficulties of estimating heat losses the results produced were not very accurate. Then, in 1921, Cecil Mason suggested the use of an iron-constantan thermocouple with a rounded tip placed in contact with the roller, but it was difficult to obtain a correct temperature reading with this technique owing to the heat lost by conduction down the thermocouple. In 1926 John Liddon Orchard, at that time works manager at Cambridge, invented the strip contact thermocouple.[16] Two thermocouple metals were welded and rolled into a thin strip with the junction at the centre. The strip was mounted under slight tension so that when placed on the heated roller it took the shape of the roller. Thus a length of the strip on each side of the hot junction was in contact with the hot surface and errors due to conduction were minimised. The thermocouple was mounted in a frame with a handle and a built-in meter to make it portable. Various models of this instrument were manufactured for use with a variety of industrial processes such as textile and rubber calender rolls, drying cylinders, and the platens of moulding presses.

Temperature control of industrial processes had also become a practical proposition by the early 1920s. In 1923 W. H. Apthorpe patented his process controller system, described in Chapter 11. In 1926 an extension of the Hohman-Maurer mercury-in-steel filled system technique was introduced, providing process control by means of a hydrostatic system. Two Bourdon tubes were used, operated from one temperature sensing bulb. One Bourdon was used to indicate the actual temperature, whilst the desired control temperature could be set by means of a knob and pointer on another scale. Rotating the knob adjusted the mounting angle of the second Bourdon, the free end of which was connected via a simple linkage to a hydrostatic relay valve. When the temperature reached the desired value the Bourdon opened or closed the valve, thus controlling the pressure applied to the main control valve, and adjusting the flow of the heating medium—steam, gas, or oil.

Early in 1922 Frank Wakeham visited the USA. High duties were being levied on instruments imported into the United States and the Board was anxious to find a way to improve American sales. The obvious way was for the Cambridge company to join forces with an established American company, preferably one already selling into a similar market to that of the Cambridge company. Hindle's small business, making electrocardiographs in a disused church, seemed to fit the bill very well and as a result of Wakeham's visit Hindle was invited to England in March 1922 to negotiate terms for the sale of his company. The outcome of this visit was the creation of The Cambridge and Paul Instrument Company of America Inc., with a capital of $200 000, $70 000 from the English parent company and $66 000 from Hindle. It was arranged that this new company would purchase Hindle's business at Ossining on the

Hudson, and his offices in New York, on 1 July, 1922, for the sum of $92 000. Hindle was to be President of the new company for a term not less than five years at a salary of $10 000 p.a. plus bonus. The other directors of the American company were to be Professor H. B. Williams of Columbia University, Robert Whipple (Vice-President), Mason and Wakeham. C. W. Campbell of the London Office was appointed sales manager and Victor Digby from the Cambridge Test Room transferred to the Ossining Test Room (taking with him his new bride, Nancy McQuire, a typist from the Cambridge General Office). Within a relatively short time a number of new products were introduced, in line with those of the parent company, and the original staff of thirty was also increased.

Frank Wakeham's trip to the States in 1922 probably included a visit to the American company Cutler-Hammer since when he returned to England the Board meeting on 22 March discussed the negotiations with that company for the English manufacturing rights of the Thomas gas meter and calorimeter. (C. C. Thomas was a professor at the University of Wisconsin.) The gas meter was a simple method of measuring the total flow of large volumes of town gas, and utilised a small heater to raise the temperature of the gas by 2 °F. Resistance thermometers in a bridge network monitored the temperatures in the pipe before and after the heater and if the bridge became unbalanced as a result of a change in flow rate the current to the heater was automatically adjusted to restore the 2 °F differential. A measure of the electrical energy absorbed by the heater was thus a direct and accurate record of the gas consumed. The negotiations having been successfully concluded, production in England began in 1923/4.

The Company's interest in the Thomas gas calorimeter (*Fig.* 5.4) had arisen as a result of the British Gas Regulation Act of 1920, which required that gas distributed by the Gas Companies should not have a calorific value less than a certain prescribed figure. The market potential appeared considerable as a large number of companies were supplying gas in Britain. Unfortunately, they proved to be reluctant to buy the equipment until it had been approved by the Gas Referees, a process which turned out to be extremely lengthy. In July 1927 HM Fuel Research Station at Greenwich published a favourable preliminary report of their own tests on the calorimeter but there was still no word from the Gas Referees, and by that time relations with Cutler-Hammer had become decidedly strained. In fact Cutler-Hammer wanted to cancel their agreement with the Instrument Company, arguing that the Cambridge Company had not fulfilled its manufacturing and sales obligations. Somehow the agreement was kept alive and at long last in September 1928 the calorimeter was approved by the British Gas Referees—by which time 500 Thomas calorimeters were already in use in the USA.

The calorimeter worked on the principle that a stream of gas was burnt in the test chamber and the temperature rise of a heat-absorbing air-stream was measured by a differential bridge network of nickel resistance thermometers (*Fig.* 5.5). These formed the input circuit of a self-balancing chart recorder, which was calibrated directly in calorific value. Unfortunately, sales of the calorimeter in this country were never spectacular, although it remained in the catalogue for the next fifty years. There was a minor revival of interest when natural gas deposits began to be exploited in the 1960s and early 1970s, but manufacture (by Foster Cambridge Ltd) was finally discontinued in the late 1970s.

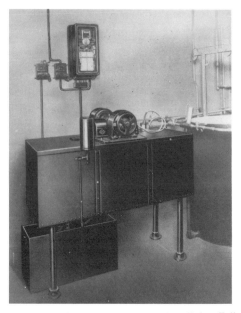

Figure 5.4 Thomas gas calorimeter installed at Fulham Gas Works c. 1929. (Photo: C.S.I.Co., Neg. 4584.)

In 1936 *Engineering* printed an article describing an interesting development of the Thomas equipment—a total-heat meter comprising a Thomas meter and calorimeter linked to an integrator.[17] The equipment, the only one of its kind in Europe, was installed at the Orgreave By-Product Plant of the Rothervale Collieries at Handsworth near Sheffield to measure the total heating value of coke-oven gas supplied through a three mile pipeline to the steel works of Steel, Peech and Tozer at Ickles. Both companies were branches of the United Steel Companies Ltd. Three more Thomas meters were installed by the Orgreave By-Product Plant, one with a capacity of 800 000 cubic feet per hour to measure the producer gas used for heating the coke-ovens, another, with a

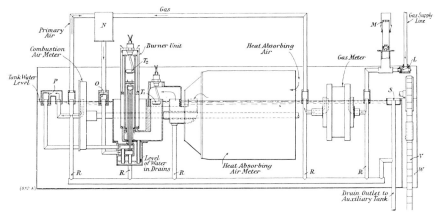

Figure 5.5 Principle of operation of Thomas gas calorimeter. L Pressure reducing orifice; M Bleeder burner; N Mixing chamber; O Mixture orifice; P Secondary air orifice; R Drain pipes; S Overflow weir; T_1 Inlet thermometer; T_2 Outlet thermometer; V Chain pump; W Chimney for chain pump. (Diagram: C.S.I.Co. Catalogues 1927–30, List No. 953.)

capacity of 500 000 cubic feet per hour, for measuring coke-oven gas delivered to a gas holder and a third with a capacity of 200 000 cubic feet per hour to measure the gas used for heating the gas ovens.

During his visit to the USA in the late summer of 1924 Robert Whipple met Ralph H. Kruse of Cutler-Hammer to discuss various matters relating to the manufacturing agreements for Professor Thomas' equipment. It was probably during this meeting that the proposal that Kruse and his colleague, H. N. Packard, also of Cutler-Hammer, might join the American Instrument Company was first tentatively discussed. Certainly, when he returned to England Whipple raised the matter in his report to the Cambridge Board. No immediate decision was taken at that meeting but over the next few months the proposal was approved and in July 1925 Charles Hindle transferred 1000 of his shares in the American Company to Kruse. In September 1926 the Cambridge Board formally approved an increase in the number of directors constituting the American Board from five to seven and noted that they would welcome the election of Kruse and Packard as directors of that company. So, at the annual meeting of the shareholders on 29 November, 1926, Kruse and Packard were elected to the board. The annual meeting of the directors followed but after the preliminary business had been transacted the meeting was adjourned until 1 December.

When the meeting re-convened the main business was first dealt with and then, in what was clearly an agreed and pre-arranged move, Charles Hindle resigned from his position as President of the Company and as a member of the board, claiming that he had 'several other interests occupying his time,' his resignation being on the understanding that he continued to receive his salary as a director until the end of June 1927, the termination date of his five-year contract.[18] Kruse was elected President in his place following which Whipple also stood down from his post as Vice-President to allow Packard to take that post.

Unfortunately the Board minutes convey only the stark outline of these intriguing changes in management with none of the background reasons for them but the subsequent correspondence between Kruse and Whipple confirms that Hindle's resignation was not voluntary. Perhaps the ensuing undignified shenanigans surrounding the delivery of the Company's mail are best forgotten.

Two further milestones in the history of the Cambridge Company occurred in 1924. The first was the conversion of the Company into a public company, the name being shortened to The Cambridge Instrument Company. The capital of the Company at that time consisted of 13 618 Ordinary Shares of £5 each and 5534 $7\frac{1}{2}\%$ Cumulative Preference Shares of £5 with a General Reserve Fund of £40 000. The trading profit for that year amounted to £42 406 and the total wages bill £93 024. A dividend of 12%, free of tax, was paid. The following year the Company made a bonus issue of one share for each two held and was able to maintain the same rate of dividend on the ordinary shares.

The second event of major importance in 1924 was the establishment of the Benefit Fund for Company employees. This had its origins in a fund set up at the Muswell Hill factory to assist the widow of an employee. The Company contributed £25 and the directors decided to set up a committee to consider the establishment of a Thrift and Superannuation Fund. As a result it was agreed to establish a non-contributory Benefit Trust, on similar lines to one in existence at Hall's Works at Dartford, with effect from 1 January, 1924. The Company started the fund with a donation of £1000 as capital and £200 as income. Income from investments was to be used to grant pensions, give assistance to widows of deceased employees, assist orphans of deceased employees or make grants in cases of prolonged and abnormal illness to either an employee or the near dependant relative of an employee. Initially three trustees were appointed: Alan Barlow and Robert Whipple as management representatives and George Meaden, representing the employees.

The scheme was welcomed by the Shops Committees of the factories, and they were asked to bring to the notice of the Trustees any cases that came to their knowledge where assistance was needed. Not all the employees were entirely happy with the scheme, some regarding it as a charity. To overcome this, at the suggestion of the Cambridge Shops Committee in March 1924, the Benefit Fund was modified to operate on a contributory basis, each employee paying in one penny per week and the

Company contributing a like amount. Thus the employees, as contributors, came to feel that they had a right to claim on the fund. Under the Trust Deed and By-Laws which were then drawn up a central committee of six members was made responsible for the expenditure of the income of the Trust and Benefit Funds. In addition, local committees were appointed by the Company's employees on the basis of one representative for every fifty employees. In general this resulted in each workshop or department having its own representative. The local committees were empowered to make minor grants but larger grants had first to be approved by the central committee. When the scheme started National Health Insurance benefits did not include an employee's wife and family, in consequence a fair proportion of the early grants were to help with doctors' bills.

As the Benefit Fund was a registered charity, dividends paid by, or accruing to, the Fund were exempt from tax. Generous gifts were made by the Darwin family and by 1970 the capital of the Fund provided an income of well over £3000, which enabled weekly grants to be made to widows as well as the standard grants to employees to help with expenses arising from births or deaths in the family of an employee. In a number of instances, when it was considered that an employee or dependant relative needed convalescence, arrangements were made, or a grant given to enable this to be done.

In 1926 a contributory staff pension scheme (with the London Life Association) was created to provide pensions at the age of 60. The premium was 5% of salary with the Company contributing a like amount. Those eligible to join were males, whose salaries were at least £200 p.a. at London Office, or £175 at the factories. A female employee over 25 years old, with a minimum of five years' service and whose salary was at least £120 p.a. at London Office, or £100 at the factories could also join. The scheme was optional for those in the Company's employ at the time, but from January 1927 membership of the scheme became a condition of service for new employees. It was anticipated that an employee with forty years in the scheme would be able to retire at age 60 with a pension equivalent to two-thirds salary.

In 1946, when it became known that a new National Insurance Act would come into operation in 1948, providing a pension for males at age 65, the age for retirement for new employees was raised to 65. At the same time contributions to the scheme were increased according to a scale from 5% for those up to age 35 to $8\frac{3}{4}$% at age 50 or over.

As in the present day, London in the 1920s was a particularly difficult area in which to find good rented accommodation at a reasonable price and many young couples could not raise sufficient capital to obtain a mortgage for house purchase through a building society. To help 'certain trusted employees' at the Muswell Hill factory the Company negotiated an arrangement with the Abbey Road Building Society, in March 1928, whereby the Society would lend 80% of the purchase price on houses valued up to £850 and the Company would make a temporary deposit with the Building Society (which paid 4% interest) of the remainder of the purchase price, so that the employee effectively obtained a 100% loan. The monthly repayment per £100 borrowed over 15 years in 1928 was £0. 17s. 9d.

A welfare problem of a different nature was noted in the Board minutes of March 1928. The Company had received a letter from the Russian scientist, Dr Kapitza, informing them of the poverty and illness of Princess Galitzin. Prince Boris Galitzin, who had died on 17 May, 1916, had designed an electromagnetic seismograph whilst a Director of the Meteorological Service of Russia, some of these instruments being installed in the Pulkovo Observatory, near Petrograd, in 1908.[19] In 1923 The Cambridge and Paul Instrument Company had begun manufacturing seismographs based on Galitzin's design. In view of this the Board felt it appropriate to take some account of Princess Galitzin's distressing circumstances and made her a small annual grant of £20, which the Princess later gratefully acknowledged. Galitzin's instrument was, in fact, extremely sensitive, so much so that on one occasion when one was being tested by G. S. Rayner at the Muswell Hill factory it recorded an earthquake in Japan.

With advancing years and deteriorating health Horace Darwin's visits to his 'Shop' became less and less frequent. As a consequence the reports of his managers became of ever increasing importance to him, both because of his interest in the welfare of his employees and also because of his instinct for good engineering. He never tired of reiterating the philosophy he had held to all his life: good design would go a long way to save bad workmanship but good workmanship could not save bad design.

*   *   *   *   *

CHAPTER SIX

Horace Darwin— engineer at large

D ARWIN'S life was marked by his concern for the well-being of his fellows—not only at his Shop and in the University of which he was a member, but also in the city where he lived for most of his life. His work for the city of Cambridge was shared by his wife Ida.

Emma Cecilia ('Ida') Farrer (*Fig.* 6.1) was the daughter of Thomas Farrer, later to become the first Lord Farrer of Abinger. Leonard was the first of the Darwin brothers to woo her, but it was Horace who stole her affections. All did not, however, go smoothly for the young couple. When, in 1879, the Farrers first became aware of their intention to marry, the family strongly opposed the betrothal on the grounds that Horace had 'very poor health, no proper profession, or likelihood of earning a decent living, and not much culture.'[1] Not until William Farrer, Emma's uncle and the family solicitor, had negotiated with Mr Hacon, the Darwin family solicitor for a suitable dowry, was the marriage allowed to proceed.[2] But on 3 January, 1880, Horace and Ida were wed at St Mary's Church, Bryanston Square in London.

Emma was known throughout her family as 'Ida' as a result of a childhood attraction to Hans Andersen's heroine 'Little Ida' in his story *Little Ida's Flowers*. She identified herself with the character to such an extent that the pet name stayed with her for the rest of her life. Gwen Raverat, Horace Darwin's niece, remembered her Aunt Ida as being a very kind but very correct person:[3]

> '. . . She never said anything critical, she was always kind, but we somehow felt that our hats or our legs or our manners were wrong (and so they were, particularly our manners). And what was worse, we never knew exactly how they were wrong, or what we could do about it. . . . her artist's nature was always driving

Figure 6.1 Ida Darwin. (Photo: Cambridge University Library.)

> *her on to aim at perfection in everything, and she could never*
> *herself attain satisfaction. In manners and in morals; in rising*
> *up and in lying down; in the roasting of the chicken, and in the*
> *trimming of Nora's garden hat; everything had to be perfectly*
> *done in the only right way.'*

Somewhat in contrast to Ida's clear-cut personality Gwen Raverat describes Horace Darwin as warm, tender-hearted and sympathetic. For his nephews and nieces he had a particular 'party piece' that clearly struck in their memories for years afterwards as Gwen Raverat describes:[4]

> *'However, his chief title to fame was that he used to amuse us by*
> *standing on a chair in the dining-room, holding a tin of treacle,*
> *and demonstrating that syrup always fell in a perfectly straight*
> *line from the spoon in his high-held hand, into a saucer on the*
> *floor. After a time, the exceptions that proved the truth of the*
> *laws of gravity became rather frequent, to the detriment of the*
> *carpet; and then Aunt Ida decided that he must conduct his*
> *operations in the veranda in future. After that, the experiments*
> *demonstrated the effect of the wind on treacle, more often than*
> *anything else.'*

As a young man Horace Darwin had also to overcome the prejudiced views of his family who were not at all convinced that he had the intellectual acumen to make a success of his business. However, his nephews and nieces, Gwen Raverat amongst them, did not always see Horace's failings in the same light:[5]

> '*A fact about Uncle Horace, which set him in a most amiable light, was that he had the greatest difficulty in learning to spell well enough to pass the Little Go. My grandfather did not spell very well either; all through the Beagle Journal he spelt broad BROARD, and yacht YATCH—a sympathetic weakness. It was understood by us children, that Uncle Horace and Mr Dew Smith had started a sort of concern called "The Shop", where they made clocks and machines and things; and where we hoped that poor spelling would not matter much. Nowadays it is called The Cambridge Scientific Instrument Company, and is not unknown; but then it was in a very small way, and was just The Shop, and was considered by my father as rather a doubtful commercial venture. Long afterwards Uncle Lenny said: "Of all my brothers, Horace was the one whom I should have thought the least likely to make a success in life." Yet he made a great success as a scientific engineer. But in those days they used to say: "Of course Horace is brilliant with machines, but will he really be able to make the business go? And his health is so bad, too . . ."*

Ida and Horace had three children: Erasmus, born in 1881, Ruth Frances in 1883 and Emma Nora in 1885. For the first few years of their marriage they lived at 66 Hills Road in Cambridge but on 16 August, 1882, Horace's brothers William and George jointly purchased 'The Grove', a large estate off Huntingdon Road and, at that time, on the city boundary of Cambridge. A year later Horace Darwin bought a piece of this land from them, at the city end of the plot, for £1200. During the winter and spring of 1884/5 he had a house built on this land which became his family home. Ida and Horace named this house 'The Orchard' since their land included the orchard which had originally belonged to 'The Grove' estate. It was a sizeable piece of land having a frontage of some 300 feet on to the Huntingdon Road, and extending back from the road about 380 feet. Even so, over the years Darwin bought other small adjoining pieces as the opportunity arose.

When Ida Darwin died in 1946 'The Orchard' was let, as a furnished property, to Byron House School, a small private school. Now, sadly, the house no longer exists as in 1954 the house and grounds were made over in a deed of gift to New Hall by Horace Darwin's daughters and today one of the University's newest colleges stands sturdily in its place. Horace's brother Francis built his house 'Wychfield' at the other end of 'The Grove' estate but this also has succumbed to modern development and Fitzwilliam College is now situated on that site.

Both Horace and Ida Darwin were deeply concerned about the low standard of public morality in Cambridge during the 1880s. When, in 1883 an Association for the Care of Girls was founded in the town, to assist girls who were 'in trouble', Ida Darwin became an active member. In May 1885 the Cambridge Association for the Protection of Public Morals was founded, largely at the instigation of various members of the University, as a further attempt to do something about some of the less attractive aspects of life in the university town. Horace Darwin was one of the founder members, the first president being the Master of Christ's College, and during its first year of operation the association succeeded in closing down eight brothels.

The Darwins had shown their concern over the social problem of the mentally handicapped a few years earlier, in 1880, when Horace had become a subscribing member of the Cambridge Committee of the Charity Organisation Society. After the report of the Royal Commission for the Care and Control of the Feeble-Minded in 1906 Ida Darwin and Mrs F. A. Keynes conducted an enquiry into the number of mentally retarded children living in Cambridge and in need of special training. As a result of this enquiry the Cambridge Association for the Care of the Feeble-Minded was formed, in 1908, as a sub-committee of the Cambridge Committee of the Charity Organisation Society. This sub-committee later became the Cambridgeshire Mental Welfare Association. In 1912, following a joint meeting with the Cambridge University Eugenics Society, the desirability of establishing a Home for mentally retarded boys, in Cambridge, began to be discussed and, as a result of continuing pressure by the Darwins and Mrs Keynes, Littleton House School was opened in Girton in 1914. The land for the school was provided by Darwin who became President of the governing body.

In 1924 Ida and Horace Darwin and Mrs Hume Pinsent gave £5000 to the University of Cambridge '. . . for the purpose of promoting research by studentship or otherwise into any problem which may have a bearing on mental defects, diseases or disorders.' In their letter to the Vice-Chancellor of the University they commented: 'We believe that the racial and social problems involved by the existence of such large numbers of mentally incapable persons in the community are of great national importance and that their solution may have far reaching effects.'[6]

Darwin's daughter, Ruth, assisted her mother with her work in this field and after the deaths of her parents she and her husband, Dr William Rees Thomas, kept up the family association with this work and provided generous financial support to the Cambridgeshire Mental Welfare Association. In May 1966 a tangible tribute was paid to Ida Darwin's own work when the new wing of Fulbourn Hospital, near Cambridge, was opened with places for 350 patients, and named the 'Ida Darwin Hospital' in her memory.

Figure 6.2 Horace Darwin as Mayor of Cambridge, 1896–7. (Photo: C.S.I.Co.)

As his business expanded so, too, did Darwin's involvement in the affairs of the town. By the mid 1890s he was a respected businessman and in 1895 he was elected to a seat on the Town Council. The following year he was elected Mayor of Cambridge (*Fig.* 6.2), a position of some importance during the Jubilee Year celebrations of 1896–7.

In those days the University and Town tended to eye each other from a distance, a fact of which Darwin was very conscious when he was elected to the Town Council. He set himself the task of bringing the two factions closer together whenever possible. In particular he wished to avoid his election to the Council being seen in any way as an infiltration by the University into the control of the Town's affairs. So when Alderman Spalding proposed Darwin for Mayor at the Council Meeting held at the beginning of November 1896 he was able to comment: 'Not very long ago Mr Horace Darwin described himself in the Council Chamber as a Cambridge tradesman.'[7]

Within a few months of becoming Mayor the 'Cambridge tradesman' was also appointed as a Justice of the Peace and a Director of the Cambridge University and Town Gas Company.

Darwin was always a keen cyclist so it must have given him particular pleasure to attend the Annual Dinner of the Cambridge Wanderers Cycling Club in December 1896 in his capacity as Mayor. He recalled in his speech that he had begun bicycling some thirty years earlier when few bicycles were made in England although he thought that the first he ever rode had been made in Cambridge. It was all of iron—long before the days of anything tubular—the spokes of the wheels being of crinoline steel. In 1877 he had bought a 'penny-farthing' bicycle ('I've got my new 56″ Bicycle and she goes very nicely,' he had written to his brother George from Down)[8] but about 1878 the discomfort of cycling in those early days had prompted him to write an article on 'Springs for Bicycle Wheels'.

Although spills were frequent with those early unstable machines they obviously left no lasting impression for, like his brother George, Darwin continued to be an enthusiastic, if rather unstable, cyclist all his life. Shortly before 'The Orchard' was built Ida Darwin wrote to George and his wife Maud:[9]

> '*Dear George and Maud,*
>   *This is meant to be a little joint letter from Horace and me and is only to say how glad we shall be to see you back again. Horace can't take his fair share in the writing because he has been tumbling off his bicycle and knocking about his arms and hands. Luckily his right arm has escaped most, but it will be some time before his left arm can again go about clothed like a Christian. . . .*'

A beautifully succinct description of Horace's injuries!

In later life Darwin exchanged his bicycle for a tricycle on which he would ride the half-mile or so from 'The Orchard' to the Chesterton Road works of his Company, his fine Alsatian dog accompanying him.

Above all else, however, Horace Darwin was an engineer. In 1880 a clergyman of his acquaintance had asked him what action he would recommend a young boy to take who wished to become a civil engineer. Darwin replied in a long letter, the nub of which would have provided good advice a century later.[10]

> '. . . *An Engineer will have something, and may have much, to do with governing men. I think a University education good for this, as it tends to give a man what is usually called the outside of a gentleman. Then an Engineer does not work with his hands but with his head, and a fair knowledge of mathematics and physics is of the utmost use. You must go through the shops, and you must work with your hands, and you do this to learn how things are done and not to learn to do them yourself in the same way as a workman, for it is impossible to become as good as a workman, but it is impossible to learn how things are done without working. . . .*'

By the time of his marriage and the beginning of the partnership with Dew-Smith the enthusiasm of youth had become tempered with practical experience, but many of Darwin's ideas were still too revolutionary for the era in which he lived. For example, on 18 February, 1881, he made notes of his idea for an automatic vote-counting system for the House of Commons. This was to be operated by compressed air. In front of each Member's seat there would be a voting box, the vote being registered by admitting compressed air to either the 'Yes' side or the 'No' side. An automatic counting device monitored the pressure in each Member's box in turn and totalled up the votes.

Later that year he had discussions with the Right Honourable Henry Fawcett (Postmaster-General under Gladstone) regarding the public display of the Greenwich Time Signal. It had been customary at the Cambridge Post Office for the duty telegraphist to monitor the 10.00 a.m. time signal from Greenwich and to call time to those members of the public who had come to set their watches. In 1881 the Cambridge Postmaster withdrew the facility because so many people were crowding into the post office that normal operation was impossible. Darwin therefore proposed a system whereby a galvanometer would be placed outside all post offices where the time signal was received and the time signal made to pass through the galvanometer.

His idea was turned down on the grounds of cost although he was prepared to carry out the installation in Cambridge at no expense to the Post Office. The Post Office authorities argued that anyone could have the time signal daily if they would rent a line and, in any case, The Cambridge Scientific Instrument Company was a trading concern which required the Greenwich Time Signal for trade purposes.[11]

In 1883 Darwin carried out a study of the water levels at Tillingbourne and the Abinger Mill Pond with a view to installing a water-driven dynamo to charge accumulators at the Farrer's country home, Abinger Hall. 'We can get 48 incandescent lights taking 10 lights to the horse power,' he wrote in a report. 'We have assumed that half the energy which leaves the dynamo is lost and that only the other half can be utilised at the house in the form of light. The 48 lights are supposed to burn for 4 hours a day.'[12]

As one might expect, when, in about 1885, a telephone exchange was installed in Cambridge, the list of the first twenty-five subscribers (published in August of that year) included all the members of the Darwin family living in Cambridge, i.e. Horace Darwin (No. 17), George Darwin (No. 10), and Francis Darwin (No. 18). All the other subscribers at that time were either tradesmen or businesses, the latter including The Cambridge Scientific Instrument Company (No. 6), Robert Sayle & Co. (No. 14), and W. Eaden Lilley & Co. (No. 13).

Horace Darwin was exceedingly proud of his profession as an

engineer and he held very positive views on the training of its members. Thus, when in 1889 James Stuart resigned from the Chair of Mechanism and Applied Mechanics at Cambridge, Darwin entered whole-heartedly into the ensuing fracas over the future of the Department of Mechanism.

During the latter part of his tenure at Cambridge, Stuart had become increasingly interested in the world of politics and business. In 1884 he was elected a Member of Parliament and in the autumn of 1889 he announced his engagement to Laura Elizabeth Colman, daughter of Jeremiah James Colman, the mustard manufacturer. His marriage was to lead, in due course, to a seat on the Board of that Company. However, the main reason for his resignation from the Chair of Mechanism undoubtedly lay in the increasing hostility to his actions—and particularly his insistence on workshop practice as a part of the course of study in the Mechanical Workshops—amongst many of the Members of the University Senate. In the spring of 1887 his proposal to establish a Mechanical Engineering Tripos at Cambridge was finally rejected after many months of argument in the Senate. When he tendered his resignation in December 1889 there were those amongst the Members of the University who saw it as the ideal opportunity to get rid of the embarrassment of the Department of Mechanism altogether, arguing that engineering training was better left to provincial universities in industrial conurbations. Fortunately, not all shared this view.

On 5 December, 1889, before Stuart had announced his resignation, a University Syndicate was set up to consider the way in which the Department of Mechanism was being run. But when, on 11 December, Stuart resigned his professorship, the Syndicate returned to the Senate asking for the scope of their enquiries to be broadened to cover the whole future of the teaching of Engineering at Cambridge. On one point they were unanimous: Engineering must continue to be taught at Cambridge.

The future of the Department of Mechanism aroused heated controversy within the University and several Members of the University published fly-sheets setting out their personal views, Horace Darwin amongst them.[13] He was by no means in agreement with the way James Stuart had been running his department and he was quite certain that the University ought to have an Engineering Laboratory. In the opening paragraph of his fly-sheet he stressed the necessity of a university education for the student who intended to become an engineer:

> '. . . *The scientific knowledge he will gain will be of constant use to him in his profession, and the other advantages of a university life are at least as great as to anyone entering another profession; advantages, I think, chiefly applicable to those professions which, like engineering, have constant dealings with men.*
>
> '*When he comes here he should devote most of his time to mathematics and physics; he will never again have such an opportunity. The value of this part of his training cannot now be*

*doubted; recently much work has been done to make mathematical
knowledge more applicable to engineering structures, and special
methods of calculation have been elaborated; far more is known
about the physical properties of the materials with which he has
to deal, and about the various forms of energy now in practical
use, than was formerly the case. The far greater use of iron and
steel in the place of masonry, in itself makes scientific knowledge
more necessary. It is true that the older engineers did good work
without such knowledge, but they would have done better still if
they had had it. George Stephenson is a case in point, as he knew
no mathematics beyond arithmetic. But he felt the want himself
and gave his son Robert the best available mathematical education.'*

On the subject of workshop training Darwin firmly opposed
Stuart, believing strongly that such training was best left until the student
had completed his university education:

*'If . . . the engineering pupil follows the course which I believe
Professor Stuart considers the best training, and spends a large
proportion of his time when at the University in the mechanical
workshops; and, on taking his degree goes through the shops in
the usual manner, he will lose far more than he gains; he will
lose wholly or in part the scientific training which should form
the basis of his profession, and he will have learnt what he could
have learnt more thoroughly in a commercial workshop
later. . . . An hour spent in the workshop here will save the pupil
less than an hour in the workshop afterwards; if we take into
account that the hour might have been spent in the Cavendish
Laboratory, we may say with more truth that the workshop
training here is a loss rather than a saving of time to the
student. . . .'*

The University Medical School was well respected and Darwin
emphasised the equivalent responsibilities of engineers and physicians in
the field of public safety:

*'. . . Both the medical and the engineering professions require a
scientific education, and in both, the safety of the public depends
on their work being well done. Certainly many deaths occur from
bad engineering. The engineering profession is not so large or
important as the medical profession; still it is very important,
and we must remember that engineers are in part responsible for
the welfare and safety of the very great number of people
working in connection with the machines and structures designed
by them; . . .'*

He concluded his argument by drawing attention to the opportunities for original experimental work in engineering:

*'. . . If an engineering laboratory were established, there is no
doubt it would produce valuable original work, resembling in
this respect the other laboratories here; . . .'*

He pressed his case,

> '... *there is a great field for such work,...*'

The arguments of Darwin and those who shared his views won the day. In 1890 James Alfred Ewing was appointed to the vacant Chair and the first steps were taken towards establishing an Engineering Laboratory at Cambridge.

Ewing was a Scot and the youngest of the three sons of a Free Church Minister. His childhood in the ministerial household had been a very happy one for, although his parents did not share his interest in science, his mother, in particular, encouraged him to develop his own talents. When the British Association met in Dundee in 1867 she took Ewing (aged twelve) to the meeting. Ewing later wrote of this period:[14] 'In a family whose chief interests were clerical and literary I was a "sport" who took his pleasure in machines and experiments. My scanty pocket money was spent on tools and chemicals. The domestic attic was put at my disposal. It became the scene of hair-raising and hair-singeing explosions. There, too, the domestic cat found herself an unwilling instrument of electrification and partner in various shocking experiences.' In 1871 Ewing became the first holder of an engineering scholarship from Dundee High School to Edinburgh University where he studied under Tait and Fleeming Jenkin. Thus began a life of varied scientific interests. Cable-laying expeditions in Brazil whilst still an undergraduate were followed by a period of research at Edinburgh and then five years as Professor of Engineering at the University of Tokio where Ewing laid the foundations for the design of effective seismographs. Returning to Dundee as Professor of Engineering in 1883 Ewing spent the next seven years on research in connection with magnetism before applying for the post in Cambridge in 1890.

When he arrived in Cambridge Ewing faced almost as difficult a task as James Stuart had on his own appointment. He had a workshop full of tools but no equipment for his laboratory—and, inevitably, the University was unable to provide the funds he needed. An appeal committee was formed with Horace Darwin as one of its most active members, for Ewing and Darwin were already well known to each other. The Cambridge Scientific Instrument Company had begun manufacturing Ewing's seismographs a few years earlier and, indeed, Darwin had personally supported Ewing's application for the post in Cambridge.[15] Darwin wrote letters to eminent scientists throughout the country to raise money for Ewing's equipment.

The response was considerable, much of it in the form of actual equipment for the laboratory. Some manufacturers offered oil and gas engines at reduced prices. Other donations were more conventional and quite substantial, as instanced by the following rather curious note from Darwin to Ewing:[16]

'I enclose Sir Richard's note but I am not sending you his £100
cheque now as this goes by one of the "Shop" boys and he might
drop it in the river or eat it or something as boys will be boys.
So I will send it on by post or by some other safer means . . . but
will you give me a receipt for the cheque although at present you
have not received it?

At a dinner held in Cambridge on 9 November, 1896, Ewing
made a public acknowledgement of his gratitude to Darwin. His speech
was reported in the *Cambridge Independent Press*.[17] He said that 'he had
profound reason to be grateful to Mr Darwin, that he was one of twelve
persons who had to divide among them the responsibility of bringing him
there. When an Engineering Laboratory was first talked of in Cambridge
it was Mr Darwin who put his shoulder to the wheel. With immense
enthusiasm he wrote letters all over the country, with the result that in a
very short time £5000 was raised for the formation of an engineering
laboratory.' Later, in a letter of condolence to Ida Darwin after Darwin's
death in 1928 Ewing wrote:[18] 'When I was appointed Professor in 1890 it
was largely (I believe) his doing, and it was to him more than to any other
that I turned for support and encouragement in the difficult early days of
the Engineering School. He gave help of many effective kinds—advice,
money, influence—and made his friends give theirs. The University
trusted his judgement; he was a veritable tower of strength.'

Over the years the University came to rely considerably on
Darwin's experience and opinions. Not only was he a Member of the
Board of Electors to the Professorship of Engineering, but he also served
on several University Syndicates. At the meeting of the Education
Exhibitions Committee held on 16 May, 1899, he was given 'full
discretionary power for the exhibit in Zoology, Physiology, Botany,
Physics and Pathology in accordance with schemes of experimental
instruction or examination to be drawn up by the superintendents of these
studies.' This exhibit was part of the University's contribution to the large
exhibition held in London as a preliminary to the 1900 Paris exhibition.
About 250 pieces of apparatus manufactured by the Company were
shown, some being made especially for the occasion. Records show letters
to Professor Marshall Ward, Professor J. J. Thomson, Professor Michael
Foster, Professor Alex MacAlister and Professor Sims Woodhead in this
connection.

In 1903 Darwin was elected a Fellow of the Royal Society and in
1919 he was appointed as one of the Commissioners of the Royal
Commission set up to enquire into the administration of the Universities
of Oxford and Cambridge, under the chairmanship of Herbert Asquith
(the former Prime Minister and later the Earl of Oxford and Asquith).

All his life Darwin was interested in seismological work and in
1892 he was appointed as a member of the Seismological Committee of
the British Association. With his brother, George, Darwin designed a

bifilar pendulum form of seismograph which could be used to record very small seismic disturbances. In April 1899 he also began measurements on a geological fault on some ground near Upwey, in Dorset, on part of the Bincombe Estate, owned by Caius College, Cambridge. Assisted by his son Erasmus, Darwin recorded the movement of the slip there over a number of years.

The topics on which Darwin's advice were sought were often unusual. In 1902 Somers Clarke, the surveyor at St Paul's Cathedral, approached Darwin for confidential advice as to whether raising Great Paul at St Paul's would enable the bell to be heard over a wider area. Great Paul was considered to be superior to Big Ben at Westminster in that it was bigger, weighing 17 tons compared to Big Ben's 13 tons, and it was swung and received a more violent blow from the clapper than did Big Ben which was stationary and hit by a hammer. Also, Great Paul was sound whilst Big Ben was cracked. Yet, Big Ben was heard over a vast area while St Paul's bell was not. But, Great Paul was only 120 feet from the street and boxed in whilst Big Ben was some 200 feet from the street and in an open cage. Unfortunately, there is no record of Darwin's reply, but Great Paul was never raised, nor were any modifications made to the bell chamber.

When, in 1896, the Acts of Parliament, decreeing that power-driven road carriages must have a man walking in front with a red flag by day, or a red lamp by night, were repealed, the drivers of motor cars soon discovered that increased speed and sudden braking produced side-slip and skidding on slippery roads. The problem attracted Darwin's interest. With Dr C. V. Burton he experimented with model cars and on 24 August, 1904, they presented a joint paper entitled 'Side-slip in Motor Cars' to Section G of the British Association, expressing a hope that their considerations would be of some value to motor car builders. One of their conclusions was that a car with front wheel drive and braking would be much less likely to skid. However, they did not approve of the concept of front drive and braking applied to steerable front wheels, arguing that all power of steering would be lost if the wheels were locked or racing.[19]

In 1909 an Advisory Committee for Aeronautics was set up by Prime Minister Herbert Asquith, its purpose being to advise the government on research to further the development of aircraft and also to oversee the aeronautical work being carried out at the National Physical Laboratory. Lord Rayleigh was president of the committee and Dr R. T. Glazebrook its chairman. The other members were Rear-Admiral R. H. Bacon, Horace Darwin, Sir G. Greenhill, Major-General Sir C. F. Hadden, F. W. Lanchester, H. R. A. Mallock, Mervyn O'Gorman, Professor J. E. Petavel, Dr W. Napier Shaw and Captain Murray F. Sueter.

On 21 May, 1913, Darwin gave the first Wilbur Wright Memorial Lecture under the auspices of the Aeronautical Society of Great

Britain. The subject he chose was: 'Scientific Instruments, their design and use in Aeronautics'.[20] As in all aspects of his work, Darwin's interests in aeronautical matters were many and varied. He studied the flight of birds and on 27 November, 1913, *Nature* published his article on the migration routes which birds follow and the various geographical features used by birds to assist their navigation.[21]

During the 1914–18 war the Air Ministry took over the sponsorship of the Advisory Committee for Aeronautics and during this period Darwin devoted much of his time to considerations of the use of aircraft in war. He investigated and wrote notes on a variety of topics including the accurate laying and firing of anti-aircraft guns, aircraft height finding, bomb design and bomb dropping from aeroplanes. Mervyn O'Gorman at the Royal Aircraft Factory and a fellow member of the Advisory Committee for Aeronautics, frequently sought his advice during this period. They worked together on a number of topics and years later, in a letter to Robert Whipple written during the Second World War, O'Gorman recalled the help and encouragement which he had received from Darwin:[22]

> '. . . With Horace D's advice I evolved the first pole mooring mast for a home for airships. As it exposed the airship to 1/5 or 1/7 of the strains now imposed on it by the wind in the present method of mooring I am amazed that it is still not used for our multitudinous captive balloons.
>
> 'Also (but I'm not sure it was by Horace D's advice), I found that gelatine is astoundingly impervious to hydrogen (equal to gold-beaters-skin) and so painted the inside of rubber airships with it and economised in the ox gut outlay, which was in short supply.
>
> 'H. D. came with me in my car to test the first air speed indicator that he made for me with his own hands—it is now at South Ken. Museum. I found that the air pressure developed by a travelling car is much increased when driven between an avenue of trees (at the end of Hartford Bridge Flats—between 60 and 70 m.p.h.). He encouraged me when all the RFC flyers (and the reptile aeronautical Press) crabbed the use of an air speed instrument as being fatal to the development of any good flyer—who must, they said, depend on having "hands" like a jockey!
>
> 'H. Darwin didn't think he earned his £5.5s. per meeting on the Aeronautics Advisory Committee! so he told me—and asked in what way he could help me. I never knew any more naïve proof of his humility—of course he was always useful on the committee and indeed I thought him by far the most useful member. . .'

Darwin was also appointed Air Ministry representative to the Munitions Inventions Department of the Ministry of Munitions and, in September 1917, the Air Inventions Committee was established under his

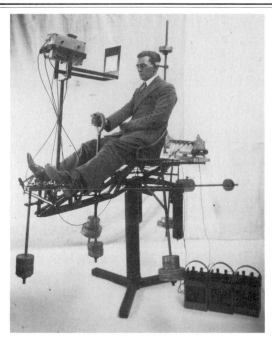

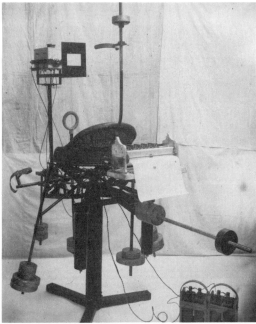

Figure 6.3 Aeroplane pilot testing apparatus c. 1928. The rear view shows the instrument to record the pilot's reactions. (Photos: C.S.I.Co., Negs. 4207 and 4209.

chairmanship. Amongst its members were Professor H. L. Callendar, Sir R. T. Glazebrook, Major A. V. Hill, Professor C. H. Lees, Professor J. E. Petavel and Brigadier-General E. M. Maitland. This latter post required considerable tact. As he remarked, only one of a thousand ideas submitted was worthy of serious consideration, and it was no easy matter to tell an inventor that his idea was worthless or impractical. In the two-year period from September 1917 to August 1919 the committee considered 7816 inventions!

On 3 June, 1918, Horace Darwin was awarded a knighthood for his 'services in connection with the War.'[23] The employees of The Cambridge Scientific Instrument Company were delighted with the news of the conferment of this honour. Many of them had worked closely with him for a number of years and felt that in a way their own efforts had also been recognized by the award. They celebrated the event by holding a garden fete in the Fellows' Grounds of Trinity College at Cambridge. Starting at two o'clock, it went on until late in the evening. During the afternoon, sports were held, followed by concert parties and dancing in the evening. In the course of the proceedings George Meaden, the senior employee, presented Sir Horace with an illuminated address, signed by every employee of the firm (*Fig.* 6.4), and congratulated him on the honour bestowed on him.

Figure 6.4 The Illuminated Address presented to Horace Darwin by the employees of The Cambridge Instrument Company on the occasion of his knighthood. (Photo: C.S.I.Co., Box 5.)

The event was reported in the *Cambridge Daily News* of 8 July, 1918, with George Meaden's speech on presenting the address. Meaden said that he had known 'Sir Horace' for thirty-nine years and that during the whole of that time he had never heard an unkind or unjust word pass his lips. They all knew the modest and retiring disposition of Sir Horace Darwin and any words of praise might be painful to a nature of that kind. But he wanted to say that there was no man connected with the Scientific Instrument Company who was more gladly welcome in the workshops than Sir Horace Darwin. This was because they had absolute faith in his honesty of purpose and strict integrity, and no man could work with him, even for a short period, without profiting thereby, not only in the mechanical sense but from the moral standpoint. They all sincerely believed that the honour had been won by merit alone. He wanted Sir Horace to feel that the address was given by the employees with goodwill, extreme affection and highest esteem.

Horace Darwin's daughter, Ruth, who had enlisted in the Red Cross during the war was also honoured. For her service with the French Red Cross she received the Medal of St Elizabeth from the King of the Belgians.

Even in his seventies Darwin continued to take an active interest in the affairs of the city in which he had lived for most of his life. In 1922, for example, he was one of the Vice-Presidents of the Cambridge YMCA. He never 'retired' in the accepted sense of the word, although during the 1920s he entrusted the running of his Shop to his managers and fellow directors. The employees of his Company, arriving for work on Monday 24 September, 1928, were therefore genuinely saddened to hear of his death the previous Saturday. *The Times* of 24 September carried a two-column obituary which began: 'By the death of Sir Horace Darwin, Cambridge has lost one of its most attractive personalities, and one who, by his devotion throughout a long life to the invention and perfection of scientific instruments, has added largely to the debt which the world of science owes to this distinguished family.'[24]

The funeral service, which was held in Trinity College Chapel, was reported in the *Cambridge Daily News*. A great many of Horace Darwin's friends were present in addition to the family mourners. Professor Sir J. J. Thomson, Master of Trinity, headed a distinguished body of representatives from the University and Colleges, whilst the Mayor, Mayoress and Town Clerk, all present in their official capacities with several other members of the City Council, showed how deeply the town felt its loss. Three directors and five other officials from the Cambridge Gas Company were present, as was also Mr W. G. Pye, an ex-employee of the Instrument Company and a successful businessman in his own right. Representatives from the Mount Pleasant Bowls Club, St Giles' Cricket Club, various city clergy and the Dean of Ely, indicated the diversity of Darwin's interests and activities. But the main body of the chapel was filled with those who were closest to him—over two hundred of the employees of his instrument company.

His body was laid to rest in St Giles' Cemetery (near the southern boundary) in Huntingdon Road, not far from his home, 'The Orchard'. Eighteen years later his wife, Ida, joined him in this other quiet, leafy, place and now the headstone reads: 'HORACE DARWIN. Born 1851, Died 1928. Son of Charles Darwin. And in memory of his only son ERASMUS, born Dec 1881, who fell near Ypres, April 1915. IDA DARWIN. Wife of Horace Darwin. Born 1854, Died 1946.'

Horace Darwin was a man who had an extraordinary breadth of scientific knowledge, yet he was remembered by his staff as a kindly, modest and gentle man; indeed the older employees regarded him with an attitude approaching veneration: 'It was almost a privilege to work for such a man.'

*　*　*　*　*

CHAPTER SEVEN

Postlude

THE positive leadership exercised by Horace Darwin over the affairs of the Company for so long was greatly missed in the years immediately following his death. Unfortunately no one person on the Board was able to lead the Company in the way that he had done. Whilst Dr Charles Darwin re-joined the Board and took on the rôle of Chairman of the Company, Cecil Mason and Robert Whipple continued as Joint Managing Directors until 1935, when Whipple handed over to Frank Wakeham. In 1938, when Charles Darwin resigned on being appointed Director of the National Physical Laboratory, Whipple succeeded him as Chairman.

William Apthorpe was made Works Director in 1932. Works Manager at the Muswell Hill works from 1919, he was a man of considerable technical ability. He had been personally involved in the development of many instruments including the Duddell oscillograph, the Galitzin seismograph and the galvanometer temperature-controller which incorporated his patented control unit. In 1933 Alan Barlow resigned from the Board when he was appointed Principal Private Secretary to Ramsay Macdonald, and Collins and Professor Blackman retired in 1934 and 1936 respectively. In 1933 Professor A. V. Hill was invited to join the Board, an invitation he would have liked to accept. However, Professor Hill was a Royal Society (Foulerton) Professor and that august body refused their permission. Industrial affiliations by their professors were at that time considered to be very definitely *infra dig*.

The recession, into which the economy of the nation had sunk after the war, continued through the late 1920s and into the 1930s. The times were difficult ones for a large percentage of the population of Britain. Short time working was common throughout the engineering industry and the employees of the Instrument Company had their share of financial difficulties. The welfare of the Company's employees—a matter on which Horace Darwin had always placed great emphasis—was of continual concern to the directors. In December 1928 a Board minute noted: 'The very poor circumstances under which some recently employed men were living was reported and a Christmas gift grant was agreed.'[1] The nature of the Christmas gifts was probably left to the discretion of the works Matron, since part of her duties was to look after the welfare of the employees.

The mining industry in particular was going through a severe slump at this time and at the same meeting of the Board the importance of offering work to married men from mining districts was considered. But not all miners could settle to a change of work and three months later it was noted that whilst one man from a mining area, employed at Muswell Hill, was 'giving satisfaction,' the men employed at Cambridge had returned to the north.

Unfortunately most of the financial problems caused by the recession were outside the scope of the Benefit Fund because of the restrictions of the Trust Deed. In view of this, Lady Ida Darwin established and maintained an unofficial fund during the 1930s and early 1940s which became known as 'Lady Darwin's Fund'. It was administered by the Benefit Fund Trustees and the money was used to alleviate cases of excessive hardship.

In those days recreation was largely home made. The Company Sports and Social Club was extremely active although, like most social clubs, it had its off years. It had begun in 1913 as the works' Amateur Dramatic Club. This developed into the Dramatic and Musical Society, later to be called the Social Club and then the Sports and Social Club. Frank Doggett was chairman from its inception in 1913 until 1938. By 1919 regular dances, socials and whist drives were being held in a wooden hut in the factory grounds, known as the 'Mess Room', the hut serving as a canteen during working hours.

During 1928–9 a further extension was made to the Cambridge works (*Fig. 7.1*), which included an addition to the stores, Shop H and a new research department.[2] The second floor of the new building provided a spacious canteen/recreation room with a modern kitchen and a stage. With these improved facilities the Social Club was able to extend its activities. The membership subscription at that time was one penny a week which also admitted an employee's wife to functions. Tickets for the monthly socials cost threepence, including refreshments. Whist drives, however, cost sixpence to cover the cost of the prizes. The Christmas party for employees' children was free, and has remained so to the present day. A weekly dancing class and an indoor games club were held in the recreation room and annual dinner dances were held at the 'Dorothy', which had the best dance hall and band in the town. The cost for these was three shillings.

In 1928 a series of film shows was organised in the Mess Room using a hired projector. These proved so popular that in January 1929 a projector was bought by the Social Club for £9.4s.0d. Robert Paul was asked to give a talk on his memories of the early days of the cinematograph. Later he presented the Club with a sound projector and Robert Whipple provided a radiogram, the latter being used to provide entertainment during the lunch hour as well as music for the dancing class.

But the Club's activities were not confined indoors. The Company's football team competed in the local league and in the Cambridge factory there was an interdepartmental cricket league with, at the end of the season, a cup (given by Cecil Mason) for the winners. There was also an annual football match and boat race against Pye Radio, with trophies for each event. Unfortunately the shield presented by Tom Robinson, a director of Pye Radio, for the winners of the football match and the cup given by Lady Ida Darwin for the victors on the river, were both usually to be found in the recreation room at Pye Radio.

During the summer the Club arranged coach trips to the seaside and the employees from the Muswell Hill factory and London Office were invited to the annual fête and sports which was held in the grounds of one of the Colleges. These later developed into an annual tennis tournament and cricket match between the two works.

Cecil Mason was a particularly enthusiastic sportsman and even when not actually playing was usually to be found acting as linesman or performing some similarly useful function. In his youth he had played rugby and during his college years he had been a keen oarsman. His son, Hugh, followed his father to Trinity Hall, and also inherited his enthusiasm for rowing. It was a proud day for father and son when Hugh rowed in the winning Cambridge boat against Oxford in 1936, Cambridge winning by five lengths. The following year Hugh again took the No. 2 oar (despite breaking his leg earlier in the season) but Oxford proved the stronger crew and won by three lengths. All in all, in the years between the wars the Sports and Social Club played a major rôle in the Company's affairs, affecting the lives of all the employees, from shop floor to Board room.

Fun was to be found at the work bench as well, and most of it was harmless enough. The new apprentices suffered most of the 'old chestnut' indignities such as being sent to the tool stores for a long rest or weight, or a left-handed screw driver! And the Company had its share of jokers willing to take advantage of those of their fellows who happened to be none too bright. Some of the stories became folklore amongst the older employees. There was, for example, the occasion when some curved glasses for indicator fronts were slightly out of shape. The person wishing to use them was advised to bend them to the required arc in very hot water. Heavy duty gloves were called into use and as glass after glass cracked his mentor advised him, with a straight face, that the water just wasn't hot enough.

Another operator needed to etch some graduations on to a piece of glass. He was advised to melt some wax on the glass, to scratch through the wax where the marks were needed, and then to run some sulphuric acid into the scratch marks to etch the glass. His efforts were, of course, unsuccessful and eventually his attention was drawn to the fact that the glass bottle containing the acid was also unaffected by its contents.

On yet another occasion a job was being done in the basement of Shop D which involved the use of a barometer. The work had to be transferred to a room two storeys higher and the person in charge was reminded by a wag that atmospheric pressure decreases as one rises above sea level and some adjustment ought to be made to allow for the fact that the work was to be finished off thirty feet higher. The worried operator applied himself to the problem and eventually sought the help of Cecil Mason, with the consequence that the joker was told not to play jokes on simple people—a two-edged rebuke.

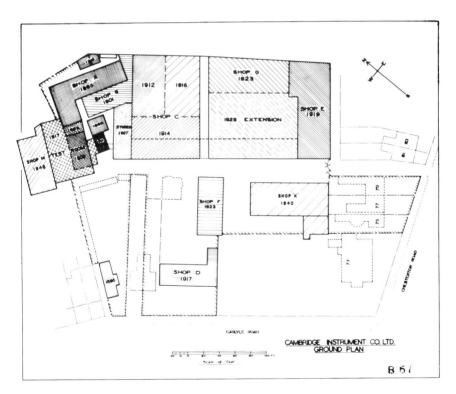

Figure 7.1 Plan of the Carlyle Road site c. 1946. (Plan: C.S.I.Co., Box 34.)

In 1932 Rawlyn R. M. Mallock approached the Company with his design for a novel type of calculating machine which he had invented. Mallock (whilst at Trinity) had been a Wrangler in 1906, and in 1908 had obtained a first in the Mechanical Sciences Tripos. After some time with a Manchester engineering company, he worked in Canada for a while, but when war broke out he returned to England and worked in the munitions department of Armstrong Whitworth and Company. After the war he joined HMS *Vernon*—the land-based Admiralty establishment at Portsmouth, responsible for the testing of undersea weapons—as an electrical expert.

About 1930 he became a part-time teacher at the Engineering Laboratories in Cambridge. He had by that time become interested in the mathematical problems associated with the determination of secondary stresses in bridges and similar structures where the solution of sets of linear simultaneous equations in several unknowns was often required. Because of the laboriousness of the calculations when more than six unknowns were involved various attempts had been made to design a machine to do this work, but none had been successful until Mallock tackled the problem. His first design of an electrical calculator working on direct current principles was not a success, but the reasons for its failure led him to design a machine using an alternating current technique, and in 1931 he successfully put together a machine which would solve six simultaneous equations in six unknowns with an accuracy better than 0·5% of the largest root—quite sufficient for most applications.[3]

At first the machine was not entirely automatic and the operator had to proceed by a series of approximations, but later, when an automatic correcting device was added, the solution was immediate, the whole operating time being that required to set the coefficients and read off the roots.

Having achieved this success Mallock applied for a patent[4] and set about designing a machine to handle ten unknowns. It was at this point that he contacted The Cambridge Instrument Company. After a lengthy discussion with Mason it was agreed that the Company would make a prototype of a ten-root machine, sharing the costs with Mallock who would receive royalties on any future sales. Robert Whipple, however, was not so enthusiastic, as the correspondence files show, and although he went along with the project his early misgivings as to its commercial viability were later proved correct.

The agreement specified that when the machine was completed it would be delivered to Mallock who was then to spend 'a considerable time proving its capabilities and developing it so that it may be used at its maximum accuracy.' In addition, Mallock was to prepare a paper for Dr Charles G. Darwin to read to the Royal Society.

By 1933 the machine was complete (*Fig.* 7.2) and it was

Figure 7.2 Mallock's calculating machine. (Photo: C.S.I.Co., Neg. 5483.)

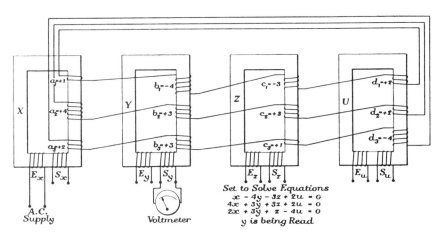

Set to Solve Equations

$$x - 4y - 3z + 2u = 0$$
$$4x + 3y + 3z + 2u = 0$$
$$2x + 3y + z - 4u = 0$$

y is being Read

Figure 7.3 Principle of operation of Mallock's calculating machine, showing the method of solution of 3 equations with 3 unknowns, x, y, and z. The number of turns in the three 'coefficient windings' on each transformer (a_1, a_2, a_3; b_1, b_2, b_3 etc.) were set to match the coefficients in the equations, the direction of a winding being reversed for a negative coefficient. An a.c. voltage was then applied to E_x. Since the secondaries S_x, S_y, S_z, and S_u all had the same number of turns, by measuring the potentials on these secondaries the ratios x/u, y/u, z/u were determined and were the roots of the equations. (Diagram: Engineering, 1934, Vol. 137, p. 698.)

demonstrated at the Royal Society Conversazione on 17 May, and at the International Congress of Applied Mechanics held in Cambridge a year later in July 1934. In addition to solving ten simultaneous equations in ten unknowns, it could also be used for calculating the value of any determinant up to the eleventh order, for giving least-square solutions and for evaluating certain mathematical expressions.

The calculator consisted of a set of transformers each with a number of windings, the numbers of turns on the windings being made proportional to the coefficients in the equations (*Fig.* 7.3). Whole number values, between -1000 and $+1000$, of the 110 coefficients could be set into the machine using push button switches, the value set appearing on a three-digit dial. The fluxes in the transformers, which were wound on mumetal cores, were then proportional to the unknowns, which could be read off directly on a five-figure dial using a null balance potentiometric technique. The error in any root was not greater than 0.1% of the largest root.[5]

The solution of sets of simultaneous equations was not confined to the analysis of bridge structures. Aircraft engineers were also faced with many hours of laborious computations whilst analysing airframe structures. Nevil Shute in his autobiography *Slide Rule* has graphically recounted his own experiences as a calculating engineer, determining the stresses on the frame of the R100 airship, an exercise which took a team of engineers many months' work. Usually the calculators worked in pairs, checking each other's work. An arithmetical mistake by one tired engineer could necessitate hours of rework, but when the final solution was proved correct by summating horizontal and vertical components Shute comments that it produced 'a satisfaction almost amounting to a religious experience.[6]

During 1936–7 Mallock's machine was transported to the Royal Aircraft Establishment at Farnborough and used for a while by the airframe engineers there. This trial does not seem to have been a success, the errors in the solutions being regarded as unacceptably large, particularly when the equations were ill-conditioned. With such equations minor variations in the equation coefficients caused large variations in the solutions and the effect of the resistance of the transformer windings became much more significant. Also the inherent instability of an ill-conditioned system magnified the effect of feedback between the transformers, causing the transformer cores to resonate and the machine to emit a whistle which worsened to a shriek if the equations were interdependent.

As Whipple had predicted, the machine did not attract the commercial interest which Mallock and Mason had hoped for, although as early as 1933 the Massachusetts Institute of Technology (where Dr V. Bush and Dr J. B. Wilbur were also designing calculating machines)[7,8] did enquire its price.

In 1937 Cambridge University announced that a computing laboratory was to be established in the mathematical faculty, the immediate intention being to purchase a Bush Integrating Machine and the Mallock problem solver.[9] The University purchased the prototype Mallock calculator from The Cambridge Instrument Company for £1750, Mallock receiving £313 of the purchase price. When the machine had been built Mallock had contributed £200 towards the expenses incurred by the Company. In 1940 M. V. Wilkes in the Mathematical Laboratory successfully applied the calculator to solve pairs of simultaneous differential equations[10] and, with the wartime need for computing power, the capabilities of the machine attracted considerable attention. De Havillands, the Royal Aircraft Establishment and the National Physical Laboratory all sent staff to Cambridge to make use of it.[11,12]

The Cambridge Instrument Company received two enquiries for Mallock calculators during the war. The first was from G.E.C. Schenectady in 1940 and the second from the Royal Aircraft Establishment in 1944. The Company declined to quote against either because of pressure of war work. In 1947 the Oscillations Sub-Committee of the Aeronautical Research Council became interested and the Council deliberated for some months on the possibility of purchasing a machine. However, by that time the Instrument Company was unwilling even to consider manufacture. Mallock tentatively looked for other makers but, although his prototype had been extensively rewired in 1946–7, its design was obsolescent. The machine had been overtaken by the development of a new generation of calculating machines—the first true computers—and in the mid-1950s Mallock's machine was dismantled.

Those members of the Cambridge University Engineering Laboratories and the Computing Laboratory who remember Mallock recall him as a short stocky man who wore plus fours and was invariably accompanied by his dog. To some degree he fitted the conventional image of the eccentric inventor. In reality his thinking was ahead of his time and the prime reason his machine was not a commercial success in the 1930s was essentially that only others of a similar calibre to Mallock himself could appreciate its capabilities.

Over the years many unusual applications were found for the products of the Company but surely one of the most unexpected was their use in the investigation of apparently paraphysical phenomena. In 1933 the Society for Psychical Research purchased two Moll galvanometers, a linear thermopile and a large surface thermopile. These instruments were soon put to use by the members of the Society who were at that time investigating the mediumship of Rudi Schneider. Schneider claimed that when he was in a trance his *alter ego*, Olga, could cause some of the energy in an infra-red beam to be absorbed. The members of the Society carried out a series of tests in the autumn of 1933 and into the following spring using the thermopiles in an effort to detect these energy changes, but the instruments stubbornly refused to confirm Schneider's assertions.[13] Not even a sensitive Einthoven galvanometer could detect any change in the energy received.

On 18 July, 1934, the Mersey Tunnel connecting Liverpool with Birkenhead was opened to road traffic. It was nearly three miles long and had taken nine years to complete, and it was claimed to be the largest sub-aqueous tunnel in the world. The ventilating fans—some as large as twenty-eight feet in diameter—in the six ventilation stations were capable of pumping 2 500 000 cubic feet of fresh air per minute through the tunnel. With the high volume of traffic which was expected to use the tunnel it was essential to monitor the carbon monoxide levels and The Cambridge Instrument Company equipped each ventilation station with two automatic analysers.[14,15]

A continuous sample of air from the tunnel was drawn through each analyser by an electric pump, extracting at the rate of one cubic foot per minute. The analysers made use of Dr Katz's technique to determine the carbon monoxide content of the air. The sample was first dried by passing it through one of two silica gel dryers. Each dryer was used for 24 hours and while one was in use the other was regenerated by blowing hot air through it. Having chemically cleaned the air sample to remove other unwanted impurities it was passed through a catalyst chamber containing hopcalite. This chamber was maintained at a constant temperature by immersing it in a steam bath. At this elevated temperature hopcalite promotes the oxidation of carbon monoxide to carbon dioxide, the reaction being exothermic. The temperature rise of the gas stream, which was monitored using forty-eight differential thermocouples, mounted on mica cards, was thus directly proportional to the concentration of carbon monoxide present. The analysis technique was extremely sensitive and the measuring system could detect a change of 10 p.p.m. in the carbon monoxide level. If the level rose excessively in any section of the tunnel an alarm sounded although in practice it was found that the pollution levels were quite low.

The scale range of the indicators and recorders for this first Katz installation was 0–600 p.p.m. carbon monoxide in air. By the 1960s the maximum safe tolerance level was generally regarded as 400 p.p.m. for one hour and in London the increased volume of motorised traffic was such that the average levels of carbon monoxide in the open streets were causing considerable concern to various medical men.

The early sixties was a period of extensive road building and a number of the in-city schemes involved underpasses, whilst on the continent several road tunnels were under construction. To meet the resulting market for analysis equipment the design of the Katz analyser was updated and refined.[16] Field trials were carried out in the old Blackwall Tunnel under the Thames. It was found that at times of peak traffic flow the carbon monoxide level in the tunnel, whilst not regarded as dangerous, was often so high that the Company technician working on the equipment complained of headaches and nausea. As a precaution he was instructed to take frequent breaks outside the tunnel. The new design of analyser was later supplied for both the Strand and Hyde Park underpasses in London.

In 1939 Professor Eric Keightley Rideal was elected to the Cambridge Board to fill the vacancy caused by Dr Darwin's resignation after his appointment as Director of the NPL. Professor Rideal, a Fellow of Trinity Hall and a notable electro-chemist was responsible for establishing an outstanding Research School in the Physical Chemistry Laboratories in Free School Lane in Cambridge during the 1920s and 1930s. As an 'outside director' of The Cambridge Instrument Company he did not take part in the day-to-day running of the Company. Alan Barlow, although no longer a director, still represented the interests of the surviving members of Horace Darwin's family and so continued to attend the meetings of the Board. He was sometimes accompanied by Frank Edward Smith. In 1920, when the NPL was transferred to the Department of Scientific and Industrial Research, Smith had moved to the Admiralty as Director of Scientific Research at the Experimental Department (reporting to the Third Sea Lord). He held this post until 1929 when he was appointed Secretary to the DSIR. However, the associations he had formed at the Cambridge Company during the war held firm and he remained a friend and confidante of the members of the Board. Indeed, in 1938 he was offered a seat on the Board although he declined this because of his public duties.

It may well have been on the advice of Barlow and Smith that the Cambridge Board purchased 12 500 of the ordinary shares of Adam Hilger at £2 each during the summer of 1937. Clearly an eventual merger was in the minds of the Cambridge directors. Relations were good between the two companies and both were highly respected traditional instrument makers with apparently compatible product lines. The purchase must have been about half the total number of shares as in July 1937 Cecil Mason and Frank Wakeham took seats on the Adam Hilger Board. In 1938 they were joined by Robert Whipple. The October edition of the *Cambridge Bulletin*† sent to all of the Company's sales force, noted that the Company had entered into a 'close business relationship' with Adam Hilger, but made no mention of the possible fusion of the two companies which the Board clearly had in mind. Instead, the *Bulletin* continued, in the genteel phraseology of the day: 'Each Company is retaining its distinct identity and organisation but representatives are asked to bear in mind

---

† Cambridge Bulletin: *The Company house journal published from April 1931 until October 1957 and intended essentially as a confidential marketing aid for field sales personnel.*

the desirability of recommending Hilger instruments where enquiries for optical instruments are encountered.'[17]

Adam Hilger was an old-established firm. It had been founded in 1874 by the instrument maker whose name it bore, Adam Hilger's father having been Master of the Mint at Darmstadt. Adam died in 1897 and control passed to his brother Otto, who was also a trained mechanic. In 1898 Otto took on an assistant, Frank Twyman, who had studied electrical engineering at the Finsbury Technical College in the early 1890s under Sylvanus Thompson, Perry and Meldola. (Twyman learnt of Otto Hilger's vacancy for an assistant through his fellow student at the College—E. W. Marchant.) Within three years of Twyman joining the firm Otto also died and Twyman in turn took over control. In 1904 the company was incorporated under the name Adam Hilger Ltd, with Twyman as managing director, a position he held until 1946.

The full amalgamation with Adam Hilger proved difficult to attain. Frank Twyman, although reasonably happy with the existing liaison, was adamantly opposed to the concept of a full merger and could not be persuaded to change his views, which were, no doubt, sincerely held, as it was largely his own labours over a period of forty years which had achieved the high reputation held by the company at that time. When war broke out, however, the Cambridge directors found themselves with an unexpected ally—the British Government—as during 1940–41 it attempted to improve the efficiency of the multifarious instrument industry in the United Kingdom by encouraging mergers.

Alan Barlow appears to have been one of the main exponents of the government's policy for rationalisation within the instrument industry, as a letter from Paul to Whipple, dated 21 July, 1941, and referring to a recent Board meeting, shows:[18]

> '. . . I feel a bit hazy about the discussion on post-war "rationa-lisation" of the instrument industry and wonder if you can help me to understand Barlow's view; do you think he wants to see extensive amalgamations? F.E.S. thinks that the continuation of the C.I.Co. with Hilger on the present lines is sufficient from the government point of view, and this seems to me to be the attitude of our directorate. . . .'

On the outbreak of war Frank Edward Smith had been 'drafted' to the Ministry of Supply as Director of Instrument Production. For a brief period from September 1939 until March 1940 Robert Whipple worked under him as Deputy Director but he then resigned this post, probably because of his poor health.

Notwithstanding the views of the British Government, Twyman refused to modify his own opinions and three more years passed with no change in the situation. Then, in September 1944, the Board of E. R. Watts and Son (manufacturers of surveying instruments since about

1855) surprised the Cambridge Board by offering to purchase their shareholding in Adam Hilger. The Cambridge directors refused to sell and decided instead to bring matters to a head by formally asking Twyman to resign in six months time, on 31 March, 1945. Twyman stood firm and refused and on 9 January, 1945, the Cambridge Board capitulated. They decided to sell their shareholding. Twyman personally purchased the 12 500 shares in March 1945 at £4.12s.0d. each. Three years later, in a move which had Twyman's blessing, E. R. Watts and Son merged with Adam Hilger to form Hilger and Watts. Twyman remained on the Board of the new company until 1952 and then continued as Technical Adviser until his death in 1959.

The managing director of E. R. Watts when the merger took place was George A. Whipple, Robert Whipple's son. Whilst at Trinity in 1927 George Whipple gained first class honours in Part 1 of the Mathematics Tripos. After two years with E. R. Watts and Son as a student mechanic he joined the Muswell Hill factory of The Cambridge Instrument Company in 1931 as an assistant in the Test Room. He then worked in Germany for a while before rejoining E. R. Watts and Son where he became Managing Director in 1938, a post he retained after the company amalgamated with Adam Hilger in 1948.

Another ex-Cambridge employee to become a director of Hilger and Watts was Richard Stanley. Stanley was an apprentice at the Cambridge works and when his apprenticeship was completed he was given a job in the Test Room there. Then, in 1931, he went out to India as an overseas representative to assist in setting up an agency for the Company (Messrs Balmer Lawrie & Co. Ltd in Calcutta). Eight years later he returned to England with eye trouble but as no suitable sales post was available he went to work for Adam Hilger and in due course achieved a seat on the Board of Hilger and Watts as Sales Director.

In 1959 Elliott Automation attempted to take over Hilger and Watts. In order to stave off this unwelcome bid the Hilger and Watts Board turned to their earlier suitors, The Cambridge Instrument Company, and suggested a tripartite union with Evershed and Vignoles as the third member. Negotiations continued for a few months but agreement could not be reached, basically because the Cambridge Board felt that the other two companies were not being sufficiently realistic in their financial assessments. Although the bid by Elliott Automation was turned away, nine years later the long held fears of the Hilger and Watts Board were realised. When the Cambridge Board defeated a take-over bid by the Rank Oganisation, the Rank Board looked for an alternative source of instrument-making skills and assimilated the Hilger and Watts Group.

The Mason–Wakeham partnership as joint managing directors of the Cambridge Company from 1935 cannot have been an easy one. Wakeham, a salesman throughout his career, had a very strong, domi-

neering personality which Mason could not match. At the same time
Mason had become the technical brains of the Company and had to
withstand all the responsibilities and pressures that this function entailed.
There was considerable friction between the two men and the outbreak of
war brought extra burdens for Mason. Additional output had to be
achieved with fewer skilled staff. These factors, combined with the
continual bickering with Wakeham, eventually took their toll and on 10
July, 1941, the rest of the Board were horrified to hear that Mason had
had a nervous breakdown and had been admitted to a mental hospital.
To those of his colleagues who knew that he was also frequently to be seen
on his allotment at 6.00 a.m. in the morning, supporting the Nation's
'Dig-for-Victory' campaign, the news was no great surprise.

Letters exchanged between Paul and Whipple during the next
few months show that they, in particular, were very well aware of the
extremely serious problems which Mason's illness created. Whilst
Apthorpe, with his technical knowledge of the Company's products, was
the obvious person to take over from Mason, the two elder statesmen were
concerned at the shortage of scientific talent amongst the younger men in
the firm, and the impossibility of recruiting such people during wartime.
Whipple had more patience than Paul, as is shown by his letter to Paul
dated 28 July, 1941:[19]

> '. . . *Everything is difficult just now and we must wait until the
> end of the war before making important decisions as to the staff.
> I do not think it is the question of strengthening the outside
> directorate. It is the inside that without Mason will be weak
> scientifically. I wish I could see a man with good scientific
> knowledge and a man who can handle people in the firm, who
> could be promoted to the higher position. Here again, I am
> afraid we must wait; it is going to be difficult and indeed, quite
> impossible without F.W.'s and W.H.A.'s co-operation to intro-
> duce such a man. It must be our aim to persuade them of the
> need of such a person. . . .'*

For about nine months the management of the Company was
in some disarray. Whipple was ill for a large part of this time with
thrombosis, unable to attend Board meetings, and he struggled by means
of letters from his sickbed to control Wakeham's, at times, high-handed
personality and actions.

Whipple's thrombosis prevented him from attending the Board
meeting held during the week before Christmas, 1941, and Paul took the
chair. He was not at ease. At previous meetings he had expressed his
opinions of the need for new young blood on the Board and for whatever
reason, but possibly because of his manner of speech, Apthorpe and
Wakeham had misinterpreted his concern as criticism of their personal
abilities. Although he had worked harmoniously with the two men during
the previous twenty years Paul could sense their present antagonism.

Perhaps because he was on the defensive, Paul's control of the meeting lacked the tact the more experienced and patient Whipple would have exercised. At one point Wakeham, to emphasise a particular argument, commented '. . . the Board must . . .'. Paul declared the remark out of order and reminded Wakeham that the duty of a managing director was not to give the Board instructions but to carry out its wishes. Wakeham withdrew his remark without comment but later in the meeting, when the formal motion of the election of Apthorpe to managing directorship was discussed, Apthorpe was more rebellious. He asserted that but for the national emergency he would have hesitated to take on the duties in the face of Paul's critical attitude. When the meeting was over Paul attempted a reconciliation with the two men but his approaches only produced a vociferous flare-up. He withdrew from the meeting room with dignity, but with nothing resolved.

On Christmas Day Paul unburdened himself in a long letter to Whipple at the end of which he restated his sincere concern for the future of the Company:[20]

> '*Pardon me, please, for writing at such length on matters, some of which may be already in your mind. I think you will understand my concern about the future of the business, a small part of it being the outcome of many years of my own labour. I regard my present position as anomalous but do not press for immediate adjustment of it; I am more worried about what I think is a vulnerable position ill-adapted to cope with post-war difficulties.*'

In early February Whipple was able to resume a more active rôle in the affairs of the Company, and to effect a reconciliation between Paul and his fellow directors. Sadly, Paul had only two more years to live and his desire to see one or more younger directors on the Board remained an unfulfilled wish when he died on 28 March, 1943.

Paul had a large number of shares in the Company and in his Will he directed that this investment should be used to establish a trust, to be known as the R. W. Paul Instrument Fund, the income from which would be used to help those whose researches were impeded for want of an instrument of a new type, and for which the usual funds of a university or other institution were not available. Forty years later the trustees still actively carry out his wishes and make major financial awards towards the costs of original research.

Paul is also particularly remembered for his endowment of the Apprentices Prizes at the Physical Society. He had served the Physical Society faithfully for many years during his lifetime and had been Vice-President from 1928 to 1931. He had also been a Founder Fellow of the Institute of Physics and Vice-President of the Institute from 1927 to 1931. Many of Paul's charitable works were, however, of a personal nature and never disclosed to the public.

Dr M. C. Marsh, who had joined the Company in 1937, was appointed Head of Research on a trial basis two weeks before Paul's death in 1943 and he subsequently held this post for over twenty years. Early in the war the Company had become a controlled establishment and as well as continuing to manufacture many instruments from the standard range, for use in munitions factories, the Company also manufactured some items specifically for wartime use. These included an updated version of the sound-ranging equipment and a 'degaussing' system for ships. Dr Marsh was a member of the team of technical experts—most of the others were Admiralty men—who perfected this latter technique in an effort to combat the menace of the magnetic mine.

Steel ships become magnetised by the earth's magnetic field, both during their construction and during their passage through the oceans. To demagnetise a ship a coil of wire, or 'girdle', was placed around it and a heavy current passed through the coil so as to reduce the ship's field to a level which would not trigger a mine. As a check on the effectiveness of the degaussing, before the ship was allowed to leave port it sailed a short straight course over a set of search coils laid on the sea bed. Its residual field could then be assessed from the deflections of recording fluxmeters connected to the search coils.

Amongst the thousands of women munitions workers recruited into Britain's factories to help the war effort was Horace Darwin's niece, Gwen Raverat. She worked for a time at the Chesterton Road factory, joining in 1941 as a factory hand. Gwen Raverat is, of course, well known for her delightful wood engravings and after a few months she was transferred to the Admiralty where she worked for the remainder of the war years as a draughtswoman. Her daughter, Elizabeth Jacqueline, married Edward Hambro, a member of the Norwegian banking family, shortly after he escaped to England with the Allied Troops in 1940.

The recovery from the ravages of war took many years for both victors and vanquished and the bad winter of 1947 produced a major fuel crisis in post-war Britain. In January the weather conditions were so severe that it became virtually impossible to move coal from the mines and, in February, fuel stocks at the power stations sank to such a low level that power cuts had to be made. Many factories had to close down for weeks. Improvisation was the order of the day. It was in a way fortunate that the same freezing conditions which had brought about the fuel crisis also prevented the farmers from getting on to their land and it was therefore possible to borrow tractors. At that time a certain amount of shafting still remained in the machine shops. Belt drives were taken from the tractors to the shafting, enabling many of the lathes and other machines to be used.

To drive the stirrers on the thermometer testing baths a bicycle was fitted up with a belt drive from the back wheel to pulleys on the stirrers. The girls in the department took turns at pedalling. In the glass-blowing shop gramophone motors were pressed into service to rotate the turntables. In the Test Room numerous lead-acid accumulators were used as power supplies for the calibrating bridges and potentiometers. These had to be kept charged so a d.c. generator was driven by a belt taken round the back wheel of a jacked up car.

There were departments, however, where it was not possible to manage without an electricity supply. Fortunately, although the Company was prohibited from using the mains supply it had not been cut off. A very large tractor was therefore procured and coupled by a belt to two of the biggest electric induction motors in the factory. Using the mains to provide the excitation field for the stators these motors were used as asynchronous generators and supplied power to the factory whilst taking no power from the national grid.

Similar expedients were adopted at the Muswell Hill works and, when fuel for the boilers ran low, trees on the surrounding property were felled, cut up and burned in the furnaces. The staff at the London Office were not so fortunate, having to manage without heating or electric light. The temperature never rose above 45 °F, and usually remained near freezing point. In coats, mufflers, and rugs and by the light of guttering candles in jam jars they managed as best they could until the restrictions were lifted on 25 February.

Figure 7.4 Robert Whipple and Frank Wakeham (foreground, left and right respectively) photographed whilst attending a Sports Day at the Muswell Hill works in 1928. (Photo: C.S.I.Co., History of Muswell Hill album.)

In 1948 Alan Barlow retired from government service and returned to the Board. He had maintained an intimate knowledge of the affairs of the Company and in 1950 he succeeded Robert Whipple as Chairman. The Board was further strengthened in 1950 by the appointment of Dr Percy Dunsheath as a director. He brought with him a fund of valuable experience of the electrical engineering industry, gained as a director of W. T. Henley's Telegraph Works Co. Ltd. During the 1939–45 war he had been associated with a number of important projects (including work against the magnetic mine) and for these he was awarded the CBE. He had been President of the Institution of Electrical Engineers for the year from 1945 to 1946 and was a Member of the Senate of the University of London and also Chairman of Convocation of that University. In 1949 he had given the Christmas Lectures at the Royal Institution, choosing as his title 'Electricity: A Giant Harnessed'. He was also involved in the work of the International Electrotechnical Commission and in 1955 he became President of that organisation. In 1956 he took over as Chairman of the Company, from Alan Barlow.

Although Alan Barlow had succeeded Robert Whipple as Chairman in 1950 Whipple remained a director of the Company until his death in 1953. During his lifetime Whipple had made a considerable contribution to the instrument industry, both at home and overseas. As Horace Darwin's assistant he had taken a leading place in the development of pyrometry and its introduction in industry in this country and America, and he had become a recognized authority on temperature measuring apparatus. He had written many papers on scientific matters and particularly on instrumentation, and given many lectures in this country and in America. He had also played a significant part in the creation of the Scientific Instrument Manufacturers Association and twice served as its President.

Over the years Whipple amassed an extensive antiquarian collection of scientific instruments and books. In 1945 he gave this collection to the University of Cambridge with a sum of money to establish a Museum of the History of Science. Many of the Company's early instruments are now permanently housed in this museum, known as the Whipple Museum, in Free School Lane in Cambridge.

The post-war years brought an upsurge in the demand for instruments similar to that experienced after the First World War. This increase in demand highlighted the shortage of factory floor-space and, even more serious, the need for a larger research and design department for work on new products. The provision of additional manufacturing area was solved, in 1949, by the purchase, from Specialloid Ltd, of a 40 000 square foot factory at Finchley, for £100 000. This was about a mile and a half from the Muswell Hill works and the manufacture of mechanical thermometers and gauges was transferred entirely to this factory, relieving the congestion at both the Cambridge and Muswell Hill works.

The need for additional research and development space had been realised as early as 1944. Fortunately it had been Company policy over the years to purchase the properties adjacent to the Chesterton Road site as they came on the market, and in 1944 the directors instructed an architect to prepare plans for a new central research laboratory in Chesterton Road. The Board of Trade, however, advised that there was no immediate prospect of getting permission to build, but in 1949 a permit to develop the Cambridge works was given on condition that the County Authority approved the proposal. The County Authority did not and suggested other sites be considered. After seven years this decision was reversed and plans for a new four-storey building to house research laboratories, design workshops and a drawing office were then approved. At the same time an extensive rebuilding programme on the Muswell Hill site was embarked upon after a public enquiry had pronounced that the factory could be extended provided a belt of trees was planted to screen it from the houses and flats in the vicinity. The field originally purchased by Paul sixty years earlier had long since become encompassed by the residential sprawl of suburbia.

The new research laboratories in Cambridge were completed in 1959. The new building (*Fig.* 7.5) had clean, modern lines, with large windows running the length of each floor, producing a fine view over the river Cam and Jesus Green. A formal opening was arranged for Wednesday, 14 October, and Lord Adrian, Nobel Laureate in Medicine in 1932, Master of Trinity College and retiring Vice-Chancellor of Cambridge University, agreed to perform the opening ceremony.

Over 120 distinguished guests from all branches of science and the engineering industry were invited to attend the celebrations and, as the hour for the opening ceremony drew near, they lined the paved approach to the main entrance of the new building. Their hosts cast surreptitious, anxious glances at their watches. There was no sign of Lord Adrian, who had earlier declined the Company's offer to send a car to collect him. Then, in the distance, a lone cyclist appeared—Lord|Adrian —pedalling down Chesterton Road on an elderly, upright bicycle. As he dismounted at the foot of the steps, and bent down to remove his cycle clips, he peered over his half-moon spectacles and rather shyly greeted his perspiring hosts with an apologetic 'I do hope I'm not late.'

Whilst the Company PR men had reserved parking space for cars they had made no provision for parking bicycles. A quick-thinking porter saved the situation. He wheeled the machine away, round a corner, and leant it against the new building where it was out of sight of the photographers.

Later, with the opening ceremony safely performed and the

Figure 7.5 The new research department in Chesterton Road, Cambridge, c. 1959. (Photo: C.S.I.Co.)

door unlocked with a 'golden' key made in the design workshops, Lord Adrian talked to the waiting newsmen. Riding his bicycle was, he claimed, his favourite form of exercise, but during the previous two years as Vice-Chancellor he had found it almost impossible to use it because of the encumbrances of his robes of office. Since he lived only half a mile from the Company's premises he had taken the opportunity to ride it that morning. His eleven-year-old bike was, he assured the reporters, equipped with all the latest gadgets. It was the sort of bike on which one could go anywhere, he told them, proudly.[21]

During the celebration lunch which followed there was considerable activity behind the scenes. Eventually Dr Dunsheath rose to address the guests and during his speech he presented Lord Adrian with a compass, remarking that the Company considered the gift appropriate to a scientist who 'explored unfamiliar realms of thought alone—particularly on a bicycle.' Lord Adrian in reply commented that he felt he might be rather too old to change his method of navigation from a rule of thumb method to an instrument of precision. Looking round his audience he reminded them that it was 48 years since he had begun his researches in Cambridge—under Keith Lucas, who would sometimes take him round the Company's workshops to see the new instruments that were being made there.[22]

The late Lord Adrian was typical of those eminent Cambridge scholars who have such a casual, unassuming, approach to life that actions regarded by us lesser mortals as eccentricities are to them both natural and entirely logical. Would that there were more men of his stature in high places today.

The first Cambridge recorder to incorporate an electronic servo-amplifier was marketed in 1945. Known as the Cambridge 'Quick-acting Recorder' it was developed to display the rapidly changing output signal from an automatic infra-red spectrometer being used by Dr G. B. B. M. Sutherland in experimental work at the University. With a span of 5 mV and a pen traverse time of 2 seconds across the chart, the critically damped servosystem incorporated a galvanometer to detect the difference signal between the voltage being monitored and the potential derived from the potentiometer slidewire. A beam of light from a lamp was reflected in a mirror on the galvanometer suspension on to one or other of the two light sensitive detectors in the servoamplifier input circuit. The performance of the amplifier was thus made virtually independent of the amplifying characteristics of the valves used.

An interesting development a year later was an electronic circular-chart recorder, embodying a null balance potentiometric system and with a minimum span of 10 mV. Single pen and multipoint instruments were designed, the multipoint (*Fig.* 7.6) having a patented pen mechanism which gave a different coloured record for each point. One cycle of six points was completed every 30 seconds. This multipoint dotting record was an unusual concept to find on a circular-chart recorder although over the years it became commonplace on strip-chart recorders.

Despite these developments the overall attitude of the Company to the electronics revolution in the immediate post-war years was one of caution. The *Cambridge Bulletin* of January 1950 included an article on the advantages and disadvantages of electronic systems, for the guidance of the Company's sales representatives. The opening paragraph commenced:[23]

> '*There has been a strong tendency, in the post-war years, for many people who regularly use instruments in industry and research to have a notion that if a new instrument does not embody electronic components, or an old instrument is not redesigned to do so, then it is not progressive and is indeed regressive in some senses. This craze for the use of electronic circuits as applied to measuring and recording instruments is often illfounded and may be pressed to disadvantage for the user, ...*'

Some merits were conceded, for example the amplification of the small, rapidly-changing potentials met with in cardiography would allow a direct writing galvanometer to be used but, insisted the writer of the article, 'Such an instrument would not replace the direct photographic

*Figure 7.6 Experimental multipoint circular-chart recorder c. 1946.
(Photo: C.S.I.Co., Neg. 8099.)*

recording instrument;' (which was what the Company was manufacturing at the time) 'moreover it would be subject to the over-riding check
and standardisation against the directly operating instrument.'

The Company was, in fact, so accustomed to manufacturing
mechanical parts to the tight tolerances found in precision instrument
making that no cost savings could be envisaged from using an electronic
system in conjunction with a simple, less precise mechanism: 'When costs
are to be considered, the electronic system invariably means a considerable increase since additional apparatus is required and the saving (if
any) on the cost of manufacture of the less precise or sensitive units is often
relatively small.' In fairness it should be conceded that as this was still the
era of the valve, the statement was generally true.

Amongst the older instrument makers on the shop floor electronic systems were not at all popular. An old craftsman assembling the
loose-fitting components of an electronic recording system was quoted as

saying: 'This isn't instrument work—it's ironmongery.' The writer in the *Bulletin* concluded his article:

> '*To sum up: electronics is a great and potent means of further-ing instrumentation and enlarges the scope of the potential appli-cation of instruments for many investigations or processes. Use it if you must but never if you need not.*'

The 1950s again saw several Board Room changes. In 1950 William Edwin Lamb, manager of the London Office, became a director. Professor Rideal retired the following year and Albert Elliott Stone, who had been works manager at Cambridge for a number of years, was elected in his place. He retired in 1958. In 1954 Frank Wakeham, who had served as joint managing director for nineteen years, retired from the post, although he continued on the Board for a further six years. Sir Alan Barlow handed over chairmanship of the Company to Dr Dunsheath in March 1956 but continued on the Board until 1959. In 1958 his son, Dr Erasmus Darwin Barlow was elected to the Board, thus carrying on the family associations with the Company.

Apthorpe continued as sole managing director for a further three years after Wakeham stepped down from the post in 1954, but early in 1957 he too told his fellow directors that he wished to retire. He was then 71. His long service with the Company had begun in 1900 at a workshop bench in the Cambridge works, and had continued for over 50 years, interrupted only by a break from 1907 to 1911 when he had left the Company to work as an assistant to Professor Donnon at Liverpool University. He remained a director of the Company until he died in 1961.

The problem which Whipple and Paul had recognised in 1941—the need for new, young blood on the Board—had not been attended to in the post-war years and when Apthorpe expressed his wish to retire the Company was living on its past reputation. At that time the average age of its directors was near 70 and no significant new products had been introduced for a number of years. The Board realised that it had at last to grasp the nettle and the directors resolved to recruit a young managing director to succeed Apthorpe. They needed a man with the right background and experience to find the type of new products which the Company desperately required, as well as a knowledge of modern management and manufacturing systems in order to begin an overhaul of the Company's administration procedures. After a considerable number of candidates had been interviewed Harold C. Pritchard was offered the job. He took over from Apthorpe on 1 January, 1958.

Pritchard was then 49. He was an Oxford mathematician, having gained a first class honours in 1930 whilst at Jesus College. Most of his subsequent career had been in the civil service, as an administrator of various research projects associated with aircraft navigational systems.

For part of this time he had been based at the Royal Aircraft Establishment and in 1949 he had been loaned to the Australian government for four years to act as Chief Superintendent of the Long Range Weapons Testing Establishment at Woomera. Returning from Australia in 1953 he joined Elliott Brothers for four years where he held various management posts connected with new product introduction before applying for the managing directorship of The Cambridge Instrument Company.

In 1957 The Cambridge Instrument Company balance sheet had shown sales turnover at approximately £1·6 million with profits before taxation of £0·5 million. Expenditure on research and development was, however, very low, little higher than the £18 000 depreciation on tools and equipment. Pritchard realised that he could not hope to maintain the profit/turnover ratio at its existing unrealistic level and introduce new products. Moreover, although the Company's strength still lay in its highly skilled instrument makers, it no longer had the expertise to take on its own research and development on any major new products.

To begin with Pritchard began to look for products which could be brought in under licence. One such, in a field in which the Company was already famous, was the microtome designed by A. F. Huxley at the Engineering Laboratory in Cambridge, where it had been developed in order to cut sections of soft biological tissues, down to 10 μ thickness, for examination in an electron microscope. But what Pritchard really wanted was a new, advanced technology product which would update the Company's public image. He found it almost by chance. The Research Director of Tube Investments, Dr T. Hughes, had been one of Pritchard's colleagues at the Royal Aircraft Establishment a few years earlier and in March 1959 he invited Pritchard to the Tube Investments Research Laboratories at Hinxton Hall, just outside Cambridge, to see the X-ray microanalyser which they had just finished constructing as a research tool. Pritchard was impressed.

Castaing and Guinier had been the first workers to demonstrate the practicability of using X-ray emission as an analytical technique in 1949.[24] Its possibilities in the analysis of metals and alloys soon attracted the attention of metallurgists. For a while, during 1952–4, the Metallurgical Division of the British Iron and Steel Research Association was amongst those interested and Dr V. E. Cosslett of the Cavendish Laboratory and Dr M. E. Haine of A.E.I. Central Research Laboratories, as members of a subcommittee of the Division, were asked to assess the practicalities of constructing an instrument. Both men were interested in the project but wished to tackle it in different ways. In 1954 the subcommittee was wound up but, in October 1953, Dr Cosslett had already independently initiated action on an X-ray microanalyser, Peter Duncumb working on it as a PhD research project at the Cavendish from 1953 to 1956.

Duncumb's machine was a considerable scientific success. In it a metallurgical specimen could be scanned by a fine-focus beam of electrons and the resulting emission of X-rays spectroscopically examined to identify the distribution of selected elements in the sample. By monitoring the X-ray emission with a counter an X-ray image was displayed on a cathode ray tube scanned in synchronism with the electron beam. Alternatively, by focusing the electron beam on a particular point in the specimen a quantitative analysis of that location could be made with the spectrometer. A view of the surface topography could also be obtained, whilst scanning, by means of the reflected electrons.

In 1957, when Duncumb was in the process of writing up his thesis, he was visited by Dr D. A. Melford of Tube Investments Research Laboratory. Dr Melford was a metallurgist working on the composition of metal samples and his superior, Dr J. W. Mentor, who knew of Cosslett and Duncumb's work, had suggested he might find such a visit fruitful. After a day spent looking at his samples in the microanalyser Dr Melford returned to Hinxton Hall absolutely convinced that he needed one. The Tube Investments Board eventually agreed to finance the construction of an instrument and with Duncumb acting as consultant Melford produced about sixty or seventy design drawings from which, in 1958, the instrument makers at Tube Investments made a microanalyser.

One week after Pritchard's visit to view the instrument in March 1959, Steve Bergen, The Cambridge Instrument Company's Chief Development Engineer, also visited Hinxton. By that summer the Company was publicly declaring its intention to manufacture microanalysers. Dr Melford's design sketches were used to prepare some 700 production drawings from which the Company's design workshop made a prototype instrument in about six months—in time, in fact, to be demonstrated at a private exhibition at the Company's London Office whilst the Physical Society Exhibition was being held in January 1960. By the end of that year customers' instruments were already being delivered.

The 'Microscan', as the Company called the X-ray micro-analyser (*Fig.* 7.7), sold well, much better than the Company had expected. In the first year of production about eleven units were sold at prices around £12 000 to £15 000 each, and in the first five years sales topped 80 instruments. This success did, however, rely a great deal on the 'know-how' of Duncumb and Melford and in parallel with manufacturing Microscans the Company had to build up, virtually from scratch, its own team of engineers to work on future developments of the instrument. Furthermore, whilst Melford had 'engineered' Duncumb's design so that the instrument could be operated without a particularly detailed knowledge of its construction, the design was not suitable for large batch production. Manufacturing costs were therefore high and the profit margin lower than it could have been.

Figure 7.7 X-ray microanalyser—one of the first batch made in 1960. (Photo: C.S.I.Co., Neg. 10155.)

Notwithstanding these difficulties, the success of the Microscan stimulated the interest of Pritchard and Bergen, in 1960, in the possibility of using some of the Microscan components as a jumping off point from which to build a scanning electron microscope. The operating principle of this type of electron microscope was complementary to that of the Microscan. Whereas in the Microscan the topography of the specimen was displayed by means of reflected electrons, in the scanning electron microscope the surface of the specimen was examined using the secondary electrons emitted as a result of the electron beam striking the surface. By using a scintillation counter to collect these electrons a picture of the surface of the specimen could be displayed on a cathode ray tube scanning in synchronism with the electron beam. Moreover, the scanning electron microscope had a distinct advantage over the transmission electron microscope in that the specimen did not have to be sliced with a microtome. Solid specimens, with rough surfaces could be examined. This was the factor that subsequently prompted the use of the name 'Stereo-scan' for the instrument.

Such an instrument had already been developed and refined at the Engineering Laboratory in Cambridge by a number of PhD research students working under Professor C. W. Oatley.[25] About 1954 A.E.I. had agreed with Professor Oatley to undertake its manufacture if the instrument could be shown to be commercially viable. In fact, not only did A.E.I. have difficulty finding potential customers but they also encountered a number of technical problems whilst trying to develop a commercial instrument and in the spring of 1961 the agreement with Professor Oatley was dissolved, leaving the way clear for The Cambridge Instrument Company to take over the project. The Company realised at that time that it needed a man from the University, with experience of electron optical systems, to head-up the fast expanding electron probe work. The University staff were consulted and suggested A. D. G. Stewart, who was due to complete his postgraduate work at the Engineering Laboratory in the autumn of 1961. Early in 1962 Stewart joined the Company. From about the summer of 1963 he was put in charge of the Stereoscan project and within a few years he was given over-all technical responsibility for all the electron probe development work in the Company. His ability was publicly recognised in 1968 when he was placed third in the *New Scientist* awards for contributions to technology by younger scientists.

At about the same time that work began on the Stereoscan, Dr Long of the Department of Mineralogy and Petrology at Cambridge University contacted the Company to see if they would make some parts for him for a microanalyser he was constructing for geological applications, work the Company was quite happy to take on. In the event Dr Long's instrument did not produce the performance which he required and he subsequently asked the Company to redesign it for him, which the

Company did, marketing the finished instrument as a further member of the electron probe family of instruments. Because it was originally designed with geological and mineralogical applications in mind it was given the name 'Geoscan' but in fact it was a highly sophisticated and much more versatile version of the Microscan. When the Geoscan was launched at the end of 1963 this sophistication necessitated a higher price than the market could stand, and in consequence very few instruments were sold.

Thus, in 1962 the Company had parallel design work in hand on three major projects: an updated Microscan, the Geoscan, and the Stereoscan. These projects absorbed nearly all the Company's research and development budget—and the Geoscan and Stereoscan competed with each other for the largest share of the resources available. The Stereoscan was, however, destined to be another best seller, sales reaching one hundred per year in 1968. But the first instrument was not delivered until 1965, and by then Pritchard had left the Company. He had been unable to couple the technological breakthrough which he had achieved for the Company with an increase in profits. Despite a significant rise in the value of the sales turnover in the early 1960s the pre-tax trading profits remained persistently at or below the £0·5 million figure. In 1963 they dropped to under £0·4 million and the results for 1964 were worse still due to increased manufacturing costs and the money being spent on research and development. In 1965 the Board decided it could no longer concur with Pritchard's policies. Although he was offered the post of Executive Vice-Chairman he eventually decided to leave the Company.

During Pritchard's term as managing director a younger, more progressive Board had begun to emerge, largely as a result of the natural retirement of the older members. Leslie F. Cooke, sales manager at the London Office became a director in 1962, and in 1963 Dr Erasmus Barlow succeeded Dr Dunsheath as Chairman. Dr Barlow, a respected physician, had been educated at Marlborough and Trinity College, Cambridge, and was at that time Research Fellow, Senior Lecturer and Consultant Physician in the Departments of Medicine and Psychological Medicine at St Thomas's Hospital and Medical School. In September 1966 he gave up his medical teaching work because of the increasing demands placed on his time by the affairs of the Company.

One of Dr Barlow's first actions as Chairman was to bring on to the Board a much needed financial expert. The man appointed, Leonard Pearce, came from outside the Company. He joined the Board in 1964 after thirty-seven years with the Bank of England (where his final position had been Assistant Chief Cashier) and five years as Finance Director of Bowater Europe. When Pritchard resigned Lamb and Cooke were appointed temporary joint managing directors until, in November 1966, Edmund E. Webster joined the Company from the Plessey organisation and took over from them as managing director.

Figure 7.8 Harold Pritchard, Sir Hamilton Kerr and Dr Erasmus Barlow, photographed during a visit by Sir Hamilton Kerr to the Chesterton Road works in October 1963, when he was Member of Parliament for Cambridge. (Photo: C.S.I.Co., Neg. M/246.)

As well as looking for new products to bring into the Company's factories, Pritchard, when he was appointed Managing Director in 1958, had also hoped to expand and update the Company's range of products by taking over suitable small companies with specialist, complementary product ranges. Many of the smaller instrument companies were going through a lean period at that time and some were openly seeking the financial support of larger organisations, provided the terms were reasonably attractive. In addition to the talks with the Foster Instrument Company, and Hilger and Watts, preliminary discussions were also held with Land Pyrometers, The Drayton Regulator and Instrument Company, Pullin, Muirhead, Elcontrol, Negretti and Zambra and H. Tinsley and Company but all proved abortive. However, in 1960 the Company did acquire Electronic Instruments Ltd, of Richmond, and with it a range of modern pH measuring and control equipment. E.I.L. had been founded after the war by Paul Goudime who was still managing director. Goudime joined the Cambridge Board after the merger and in 1965 took over responsibility for research and development within the Group. In 1967 H. W. Sullivan, the Orpington-based manufacturers of precision electrical instruments, were also brought into the Group.

During the late 1950s there were at least two bids to take over the Instrument Company. One was an anonymous enquiry through solicitors on behalf of a client who was interested in acquiring control of an instrument manufacturing company. The Board was unanimous in opposing this bid and discouraging further approaches from the unknown client. The second was a tentative approach made late in 1957 through William R. Darwin, a stockbroker and nephew of Horace Darwin. The offer came from W. G. Pye. It was repeated some months later at which time the Darwin family, who owned about 30% of the Company's shares, firmly squashed the proposal.

But ten years later a more positive takeover bid was made—one which the family were unable to fight off unaided. It came from the Rank Organisation during the afternoon of Tuesday 9 April, 1968. The offer was not liked at all by the Cambridge Board who felt that not only had the two companies very little in common but also that the Cambridge Company would lose its identity as part of a large conglomerate.

The Rank Board had, in fact, had their eyes on The Cambridge Instrument Company for about four years prior to the bid, i.e. from the years of disastrously low profits in the early 1960s. In May 1965 John Davis, chairman of Rank, had hosted a dinner party at which he had hinted to his main guest, Dr Erasmus Barlow, that he was interested in acquiring the Cambridge Company. For his part Dr Barlow was not at all interested in selling. He believed that the Company would recover and his convictions proved to be correct.

That is not to say that the Board was completely against the concept of joining forces with a larger company as a progressive move. Indeed, at the time that the Rank bid was made, tentative negotiations with another company were being nurtured by the government's Industrial Reorganisation Council, set up in January 1966 to promote rationalisation and hence increased efficiency in British industry.

Right from the start the I.R.C. was interested in the instrument industry. The Second World War proposals for amalgamations in the industry had virtually come to naught and there were still many small and medium-sized companies, a large number of which were not operating efficiently. By April 1968 the I.R.C. was fostering discussions between several companies, including talks between the Boards of E.M.I. and The Cambridge Instrument Company. The bid from Rank brought an abrupt end to these discussions and the Cambridge Board was faced with the impossible task of fighting the giant Rank Organisation alone. They looked for a more compatible partner and quietly approached Rodney Kent, chairman of the George Kent Group.

On 15 May, the Kent Group Board made their first bid, the Cambridge Board immediately issuing a statement recommending the bid to its shareholders. The I.R.C., too, favoured the proposed Kent-

Cambridge link-up and, in an endeavour to dissuade the Rank Organisation from making a counter bid, suggested a compromise in which the Rank instrument division, Taylor–Hobson, would be part of the alliance. This peace move was rejected by John Davis who could see little point in a settlement in which he would not have overall control of the Cambridge Company. On 30 May, Rank put out an improved offer. A second bid by Kent on 5 June was followed by a third bid by Rank on 12 June. On 13 June the I.R.C. decided to show its muscle power and stepped firmly into the market place where it purchased some 20% of the Cambridge shareholding to support a Kent–Cambridge merger.

On 14 June, 1968, the George Kent Board, with the I.R.C. solidly behind them, made a final and successful bid—and Horace Darwin's Shop was sold.

* * * * *

Supplement

An outline of the history of The Cambridge Instrument Company after the merger with George Kent Ltd.

At the time of the merger The Cambridge Instrument Company was organised as four divisions:

Cambridge Industrial Instruments Ltd (instruments for industrial applications).

Cambridge Scientific Instruments Ltd (scientific and medical instruments).

Electronic Instruments Ltd (analytical instruments).

H. W. Sullivan Ltd (instruments for precise electrical measurements).

1970 George Kent Electronic Products Ltd was formed, in its own premises in Cambridge, to manufacture the 'Cambridge' range of gas analysis equipment.

1971 A marketing link was established between Cambridge Scientific Instruments Ltd and Image Analysing Computers Ltd (a subsidiary of Metals Research Ltd).

1971 The Foster Instrument Company Ltd was merged with Cambridge Industrial Instruments Ltd to form Foster Cambridge Ltd based at the Muswell Hill and Finchley factories.

1972 George Kent Ltd bought Elmed Ltd and Kent–Cambridge Medical Ltd was established.

1974 Brown Boveri and Company Ltd. took over George Kent Ltd, creating a new holding company Brown Boveri–Kent Ltd. As part of this deal the 'Cambridge' scientific and medical divisions were given independence as Scientific and Medical Instruments Ltd (a holding company for Cambridge Scientific Instruments Ltd and Kent–Cambridge Medical Ltd).

1975 Scientific and Medical Instruments Ltd merged with Metals Research Ltd, the new company assuming the name The Cambridge Instrument Company Ltd. The wholly owned subsidiaries included Cambridge Analysing Instruments Ltd, Cambridge Medical Instruments Ltd, Cambridge Scientific Instruments Ltd, Metals Research Ltd and Image Analysing Computers Ltd.

1979 The subsidiaries of The Cambridge Instrument Company were sold to Gladecrown Ltd, Gladecrown assuming the name 'The Cambridge Instrument Company' and the existing 'The Cambridge Instrument Company' becoming CIC Investment Holdings Ltd.

1980 Cambridge Medical Instruments Ltd was sold to Picker International Holdings Inc. (a company formed by G.E.C. Ltd) and a new medical instrumentation company was formed combining Cambridge Medical Instruments, the medical equipment group of G.E.C. Ltd and the American Picker Corporation, which was acquired by G.E.C.

1984 The Cambridge Instrument Company Ltd and CIC Investment Holdings Ltd re-registered as plc's.

1985 CIC Investment Holdings plc. was wound up, the minority shareholders receiving a cash payment and loan stock in The Cambridge Instrument Company plc.

Note: In the interests of conciseness this outline does not include details of the various subsidiary British and foreign companies formed or acquired by The Cambridge Instrument Company plc. since 1979.

Part 2

Introduction

The instruments and topics examined in the following chapters highlight significant facets of the Company's product range during the period covered by this book.

As the *raison d'être* for the Company was the manufacture of physiological instruments it is fitting that the first chapter in this section should cover the history of the automatic microtome; a particularly good example of the reduction of a complex design to a simple, reliable and inexpensive instrument, by the application of sound mechanical engineering. Three decades later Wilson's original cloud chambers were one-off pieces of research apparatus, laboriously constructed, yet here again, by 1926 the Company had produced a simplified design—the school's cloud chamber—which could be mass-produced in large numbers.

In contrast, Ewing's seismographs and Duddell's oscillograph were specialised research instruments, requiring skilled workmanship for successful manufacture on a commercial basis. Duddell's oscillograph in particular represented a major technological advance enabling workers in the field of alternating current electrical engineering to see circuit waveforms virtually at a glance. In a completely different field the electrocardiograph was of even greater importance, representing as it did a major breakthrough in medical diagnostic technique.

The wide-scale introduction of temperature measurement and recording in industrial processes at the turn of the century, rapidly followed by the development of alarm and control systems, brought about major advances in industrial technology and productivity. The Cambridge Scientific Instrument Company was one of the pioneers in industrial temperature measurement and Callendar's recorder was the first of generations of paper chart recorders. Paul's Unipivot galvanometer also played an important role in taking instruments out of the laboratory and into industrial applications.

Finally, Shakespear's katharometer is included because of the revolution it created in gas analysis. A relatively simple, mass-produced analyser, it enabled continuous, on-line analysis and control to be introduced into chemical plants.

Each chapter commences with a brief historical account in order to put the instruments into context.

CHAPTER EIGHT

The invention of the automatic microtome

1879–80 Robert Fulcher's sliding Microtome
1881 Roy's freezing microtome
1882 Roy's improved freezing microtome
1883 Caldwell and Threlfall's automatic microtome
1885 Darwin's rocking microtome

ZACHARIAS Janssen is credited with the invention of the compound microscope about 1590 but the magnifying properties of the single convex lens were known centuries before this date. Indeed, it is usually accepted that ancient craftsmen used beads of glass to magnify fine ornamental carving well before the first recorded comment on the optical properties of lenses by Roger Bacon in 1268.

Janssen's microscope, which had a convex objective and concave eyepiece, did not give a very clear image and during the next two centuries improvements in the optical system were made by various men, notably Johann Kepler who suggested using a convex lens for the eyepiece, and Christiaan Huygens who made an instrument with a two-lens eyepiece. But it was not until 1830 that Joseph Jackson Lister (the father of Lord Lister, the surgeon) made the significant advance of combining achromatic lenses to balance their spherical aberrations.

In the meantime, although the novelty of the microscope tended to attract the attention of amateur dilettantes, some serious work in the biological sciences began to be accomplished with the relatively crude instruments then available and also with single-lens microscopes, such as Anton von Leeuwenhoek's, which often produced a clearer image.

A natural result of this progress in microscopy was the need to be able to produce extremely thin sections of a specimen for study under the microscope by transmitted instead of reflected light. To cut a thin slice of uniform thickness from vegetable matter or tissue, with a razor held in the hand, is a virtually impossible task and in the late eighteenth century the first instruments designed to cut thin sections, so-called 'cutting engines', were invented.

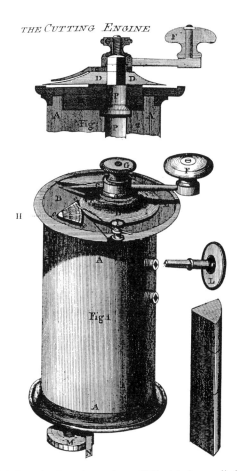

Figure 8.1 Cummings' cutting engine c. 1760. AA, ivory cylinder; BB, bell-metal top plate; C, brass base plate; DD, rotary cutter; F, cutter handle; G, handle retaining nut; H, timber specimen; KK, specimen clamping screws; L, key to tighten clamp screws K; M, micrometer screw to raise specimen; N, micrometer index; ee, index pointer; coo, sector-shaped hole through cylinder for specimen. (Photo. Hill J 1770 The Construction of Timber, Plate 1.)

In the 1760s Dr John Hill was greatly interested in the structure and growth of trees and the earliest recorded cutting engine was made to cut thin transverse slices of wood. He may well have commissioned the design, although all that he says in his book, *The Construction of Timber*, published in 1770 is:[1]

> *The Cutting Engine is an invention of the ingenious*
> *Mr Cummings. The two or three first were perfected under his*
> *own hand; and they are now made for general use by Mr*
> *Ramsden.*

In the early forms of Cummings' cutting engine (*Fig.* 8.1) the cylindrical body was of ivory, the bottom plate of brass and the top plate of 'bell-metal'. The wedge-shaped specimen was held lightly in place by screws tightened by the key L, and the specimen was raised to protrude through the top plate by the calibrated screw M, which had 40 threads to the inch. Slices were cut by rotating the spiral cutter. Dr Hill records that slices 1/1000th of an inch thick could be readily cut but that to obtain slices 1/2000th of an inch thick required 'management much depending on the force with which the screws KK pinch the wood.'

Cummings also designed a refined version of this section cutter with a feature which did not come into general use on microtomes until a century later: automatic advance of the specimen as each slice was cut. Dr Hill was not overly impressed by this refinement:

> *It performed extremely well, but was judged less fit*
> *for general use than that which has already been described, it*
> *being more complex, and liable to disorder, as well as more*
> *difficult to manage.*

George Adams, 'the elder', and his son, George Adams, 'the younger', were eighteenth century instrument makers with a family business at 'Tycho Brahe's Head', at the corner of Raquet Court, No. 60 Fleet Street. Both men wrote books to help promote the sales of their instruments. In 1787 Adams the younger published his *Essays on the Microscope*—a detailed discussion on its use, the preparation of specimens and a catalogue of 'interesting objects for observation'.[2] In this book Adams refers to Dr Hill's treatise on *The Construction of Timber* and remarks that at about the same time as it was published his father had also invented an instrument for cutting transverse sections of wood, the instrument afterwards being improved by Mr Cumming. He does not describe this section cutter but instead goes on to describe 'another instrument for the same purpose, more certain in its effects and more easily managed,' but he does not positively name his father as the inventor of this later instrument. Although this instrument is not included in the price list at the end of the book, in the second edition, published posthumously in 1798 by W. & S. Jones, there is included in the list of instruments made by Messrs Jones, Holborn, London: 'Cutting Engine for slices of vegetable objects £3.3s.0d.'[3]

Essentially, Adams' second section cutter consisted of a rectangular brass plate with a triangular hole towards one end, four ornamental brass pillars being used to mount the plate on a wooden plinth. The specimen was clamped in a vertical tube under the triangular hole and by using a micrometer screw the top of the specimen could be advanced through the hole. Sections were cut by sliding a guillotine-shaped knife manually along the top surface of the brass plate, the base of the knife fitting in grooves running longitudinally along the plate and the cutting edge of the knife being in contact with the surface of the plate.

There was a refinement for those experimenters who wished to obtain sections of repeatable thickness. A triangular brass plate, standing on three legs, had a screw through its centre with a brass disc attached to the lower end of the screw and a knob on the top end. The height of the disc could thus be adjusted by rotating the screw. With the triangular plate standing on the brass bed of the section cutter, the specimen would be advanced until it contacted the disc before each section was cut.

One other maker of section cutters during this period deserves mention—Custance, a carpenter living in Ipswich. He used the cutters he had designed to produce what were generally acknowledged as the finest sections of vegetable matter available at that time.

In action his cutter was very similar to the instrument described by George Adams but being made from a solid lump of wood it was a much more rigid construction and it also had a better knife action. Comparing the two instruments one might postulate that Adams' instrument was an optical instrument maker's version of Custance's design. Indeed, Teyler's Museum, Haarlem, possesses one of Adams' instruments (known to have been bought from Adams in 1789) in which the guillotine knife has been replaced by a long sliding blade, with a very similar action to Custance's instrument.

Whether Custance imparted the principles of his design to Adams is speculation. What is known is that when Custance died in 1799, Dr R. J. Thornton, a lecturer in medical botany at Guy's Hospital, who had earlier tried several times to persuade Custance to sell him the secrets of his design, bought both of Custance's cutters at the auction of his effects. Thornton then described the cutter in a paper to the *Philosophical Magazine*, 'fearful that a monopoly might be made of the art of preparing vegetable cuttings.'[4]

During the first half of the nineteenth century numerous types of section cutter were made, many being described in the pages of the *Journal of the Royal Microscopical Society*. All were designed around the same basic principle. In the simplest and most compact form the specimen was contained in a vertical brass tube beneath a central hole in a glass disc. It was advanced by a micrometer screw thread and sections cut with an ordinary cut-throat razor pressed against the surface of the glass disc. The

Zeiss instrument, included in the first price lists of The Cambridge Scientific Instrument Company, and sold by them for many years was typical of these simple 'microtomes'—the name adopted about 1840 in preference to the earlier 'cutting engines'.

Although the early microtomes were designed for cutting sections from timber, ways were soon found of using them to cut animal tissue. Usually the tissue was embedded in paraffin wax for this purpose but an alternative technique was to reduce the temperature of the specimen to near freezing. This had the advantage of making the fresh tissue firm for cutting without the chemical and microscopic structure changes frequently caused by embedding in wax. Although freezing was first used about 1825 by Raspail[5] and 'rediscovered' by Stilling in 1842,[6] it did not become popular until the 1870s when several experimenters made freezing microtomes. Freezing was accomplished either by surrounding the specimen with a box containing a freezing mixture (e.g. William Rutherford's microtome of 1873)[7,8] or by means of an ether spray directed at the knife and specimen—the method adopted by Professor Roy.[9,10] As mentioned in Chapter 2, Professor Roy's designs were made and sold by The Cambridge Scientific Instrument Company for a number of years.

The first sliding microtome was made by Rivet in 1868.[11,12] A fundamental feature of this type of section cutter was the method of raising the specimen by causing it to advance up an inclined plane. The knife was mounted on a block which slid in a V-shaped runnel alongside the inclined plane. Rivet's instrument was made in hardwood but two years later Brandt translated the design into metal with the aid of the university mechanic at Leipzig.[13] It was, however, Professor R. Thoma of the University of Heidelberg who made the sliding microtome (*Fig. 8.2*)

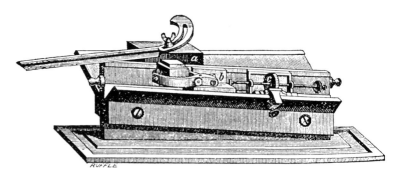

Figure 8.2 Thoma's sliding microtome c. 1880 a, knife carriage; b, specimen carrier; c, micrometer screw. (Photo: Journal of the Royal Microscopical Society, 1883, p 298.)

into a precision instrument in about 1879, the instruments being made by Herr Jung (of Heidelberg) under his instructions and, in consequence, often referred to as 'Jung' microtomes.[14] Thoma described his microtome in detail in a communication to the *Journal of the Royal Microscopical Society* in 1883. On one side of the central web of the stand (which was made of cast iron) the specimen was moved up the inclined plane by a micrometer screw, thus enabling extremely thin sections to be cut. On the opposite side the carriage for the knife slid in a trough, but with five raised bearing points on the carriage in contact with the sides of the trough—i.e. a kinematic design.[15]

Comparatively speaking the sliding microtome made by Robert Fulcher about 1879–80 (one of which is now in the collection of early microtomes in the Zoological Laboratory in Cambridge) was a crude design. It was made of brass, with a simple sliding carriage and vernier scales to indicate the advancement of the specimen (*Fig.* 8.3). The calibration of the vernier scale, 'EACH DIVN = 1 MM', was usually engraved at one end on the top surface of the central dividing plate, with 'R. FULCHER CAMBRIDGE' at the far end. The gradient of the incline was 1 : 10. The instrument was clearly based on Rivet's and Brandt's simple designs.[16]

Figure 8.3 Robert Fulcher's microtome c. 1879–80. (Photo: C.S.I.Co., Box 34.)

Darwin and Dew-Smith continued to manufacture this microtome after the dissolution of the Robert Fulcher partnership. The description in the handwritten, priced list of products sent to Professor J. D. Munsen of Eastern Michigan Asylum by Dew-Smith, on 17 February, 1881, read:[17]

> 'Section Cutter': *Balfour's modification of Rivet's Instrument. It is so arranged that each division corresponds to ·1 mm and the Vernier attached permits sections to be cut to ·01 mm in thickness for each division. Suitable flat knives are supplied with the Instrument.   £6.6s.0d.*

This wording is very similar to that appearing in Fulcher's advertisements in the *Journal of Physiology* from December 1879. Unfortunately the nature of Professor Balfour's modification cannot be traced. It is somewhat surprising that the microtome remained in the Company's price lists for a further ten years as the design of the sliding carriage would not have pleased Darwin.

William Hay Caldwell and Richard Threlfall were jointly responsible for the invention of the automatic microtome. They were both students at Cambridge although Threlfall was three years junior to Caldwell. Caldwell went up to Gonville and Caius in 1877, obtained a first in the Natural Sciences Tripos of 1881 and stayed on to do research under Francis Maitland Balfour. After Professor Balfour's death in the Alps in July 1882 Caldwell became a demonstrator under the new head of the Department of Comparative Anatomy, Adam Sedgwick. Many years later Dr G. P. Bidder, in his obituary, recalled attending Caldwell's lectures and being faced by 'an attractive young man, on the tall side of middle height with finely cut features, fair wavy hair and a carefully twisted little fair moustache.'[18] Threlfall must also have attended these lectures, since he was a student under Caldwell, having gone up to Caius in 1880.

The published accounts of the events leading up to the invention of the automatic microtome are by no means consistent. There was obviously some contention between teacher and pupil, but with the aid of notes made by Robert Whipple during a conversation with Caldwell in 1928 it is possible to piece together the likely course of events.[19]

On 10 January, 1881, The Cambridge Scientific Instrument Company sold Caldwell a simple Zeiss microtome—price in walnut cabinet, complete, £2.17s.6d. Caldwell subsequently used this microtome to prepare sections for his researches. One day, whilst he was cutting sections on the microtome, Caldwell discovered that if paraffin of the right consistency was used and cut at the optimum temperature, the section would adhere to the sharp edge of the razor. By cutting a second section without removing the first from the razor the second would then weld itself to the first and push it across the blade. This was probably about February 1882.[†]

Caldwell conceived the idea of trying to make a ribbon of sections so that, for example, one might have a whole larva in one strip. Probably, after a few preliminary experiments, he put the work on one side until he might have time to experiment further, or until he had a suitable student to give the work to as a research project. And there was also the perpetual problem of how to cut sections of a repeatable thickness. A small difference in the pressure on the blade during cutting would cause it to flex so that successive sections were not the same thickness.

One evening during the early summer of 1882 Caldwell and Threlfall had supper together in hall and afterwards the two men walked out to the old windmill at Madingley—an energetic, uphill, stroll, known as the 'Madingley Grind'. Not surprisingly, their conversation turned to the work in the laboratory. Threlfall takes up the story in his account which he published in *Biological Reviews* in 1930:[20]

> '*Some time towards the end of May or the beginning of June, in the course of a stroll after hall, Caldwell told me of his discovery in regard to the welding of successive sections, and remarked (or I did—I forget who said it first, but most probably Caldwell[‡]) that this discovery made the construction of a section-cutting machine a possibility. We discussed in general terms the sort of machine that should be made, and decided that it should be a block of metal bored so that a metal rod or tube could be screwed up or down through the block by means of a micrometer screw. The amount through which the tube or rod should be raised at each stroke could be adjusted by the motion of the block itself. This general idea was mainly or perhaps entirely due to Caldwell.*'

Despite Caldwell's ideas, at some point around this time Threlfall appears to have experimented with a crank fitted to a Jung (Thoma) sliding microtome. This was not a success. So, instead, it was agreed that during the long vacation Threlfall would design a machine based on Caldwell's principle with a fixed knife and moving specimen. Somewhat peevishly Threlfall continues his account of the work:

> '*. . . This I proceeded to do, keeping Caldwell informed of what I proposed, but on no occasion did he reply to my letters, so that I received no assistance from him. I proceeded to get out drawings showing the machine substantially as con-*

[†] *In Robert Whipple's notes of his conversation with Caldwell in 1928, Caldwell placed this discovery as February 1881, but this seems a year too early and likely to be an error of memory.*

[‡] *Robert Whipple has noted that Caldwell told him that he had no doubt but that he, Caldwell, had made the remark.*

*structed, though, as I was (and still am) a very poor draughts-
man, the drawings were redrawn in Professor Stuart's workshop,
where I had arranged that the machine was to be constructed at
my expense. The machine was put in hand during the Michaelmas term, 1882, and completed during the Easter term, 1883. I
took the machine to the Cavendish Laboratory and put it through
preliminary trials, driving it by a small water motor that happened to be available. During the time that the machine was
under construction I met with a good deal of criticism, particularly from Dew-Smith, of The Cambridge Scientific Instrument
Company, and Caldwell himself. I remember particularly that
Dew-Smith's view was that I had once seen a horizontal engine
and could not get it out of my head, while Caldwell claimed that
he had nothing to do with the construction, that he was not in
any way responsible for the machine, and that when it failed, as
he expected it to do, it would be my affair entirely. This was
perfectly just, because Caldwell had nothing whatever to do with
the construction of the machine, for which I was also at that
time financially responsible.*

*'As it happened the machine succeeded from the first
trial, and I sent over to the Department of Comparative Anatomy, where Caldwell was working, for him to bring over some
embedded specimen to cut, as, of course, I had begun by cutting
paraffin only. It succeeded beyond expectation, and was then
taken over by the Comparative Anatomy Laboratory, which was
then under Adam Sedgwick, Professor F. M. Balfour having
been killed in Switzerland in July 1882, while I was at work on
the design. The machine remained at work in the Laboratory for
many years. It was to the best of my recollection still at work in
1898 when I came back from Australia, though in the meantime
variations had been brought out. The only biological work I ever
did with it at Cambridge was to cut an Amphioxus into sections
from end to end, making a ribbon some yards long. These
sections all being of the desired equality in thickness, which if I
remember rightly was about 1/4000 of an inch, satisfied me that
the machine was satisfactory so far as the mechanics and construction were concerned.'*

Credit for the microtome thus belongs evenly to both men;
Caldwell saw what might be achieved but Threlfall converted Caldwell's
ideas into a practical machine.

The work on the most suitable paraffin for embedding, so as to
produce long welded ribbons, was also done by Threlfall as a research
project, in the autumn of 1883. In the archive in the Cambridge
University Library there is a signed typed copy of Threlfall's report,
which was dated 16 January, 1884.[21] Unfortunately, Robert Whipple
returned the original handwritten manuscript to Threlfall in 1929.

The original microtome made to Threlfall's design in 1883 is
now preserved as a scientific treasure in the Department of Zoology in
Cambridge. Despite regular use for many years the only restoration work

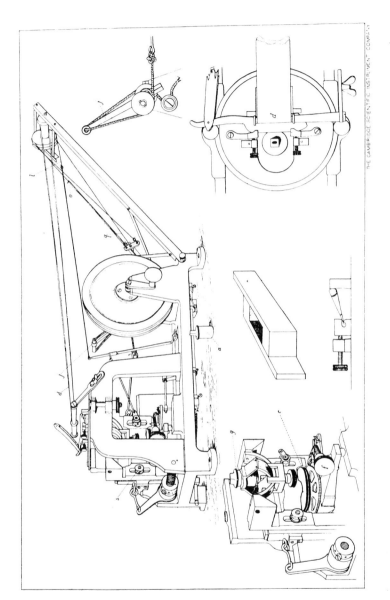

Figure 8.4 Caldwell–Threlfall automatic microtome c. 1883–4. a., paraffin container; c, milled knob to raise or lower specimen; d, belt of black ribbon; f, section thickness adjustment; g, specimen in socket; j, arm to adjust length of traverse; l, string; o, elastic band; q, string; s, carriage lock nuts (tightened so that carriage just fell under its own weight). (Photo: C.S.I.Co. Price Lists 1882–90.)

which seems to have been necessary was to fit a new belt to carry the ribbon of sections. In accordance with the original design this has been fashioned from the strings of a B.A. gown.

The Cambridge Scientific Instrument Company made about twenty microtomes based on Threlfall's design during 1883–4. *Fig.* 8.4 shows the general construction.[22] Turning the crank caused the carriage carrying the specimen to be pulled forward beneath the fixed razor. A strong spring then pulled it back ready for the next pass. The specimen holder was mounted on a micrometer screw and a ratchet system automatically raised the object by a small increment each time the carriage returned. The magnitude of this increment could be varied, thus changing the thickness of the sections. Sections down to 1/10 000th of an inch in thickness could be cut. Rotating the crank also caused the 2 inch wide band, which carried the ribbon of sections, to advance by the width of one section each time the carriage passed beneath the razor and once the first few sections had been fed on to the band by means of a needle or the tip of a scalpel the action of the machine was entirely automatic.

Commercially, Threlfall's design was not a success. The complexities of the mechanics were such that it had to be relatively highly priced. But it was the first of its kind and Darwin was therefore quite justified in putting it into production. However, within two years Darwin had designed a better microtome—his now famous 'Darwin Rocker'. Altogether simpler in construction, and based on kinematic design principles, it could be made for a fraction of the cost of the Threlfall machine. The classical simplicity of the design can be seen in *Fig.* 8.5, the illustration which was printed in the 1885 sales leaflet.[23]

The embedded object to be sectioned was cemented into a brass tube using paraffin wax. This tube was made to be a tight sliding fit on the end of a cast iron lever which was pivoted, in V-shaped grooves, at a point about 7·5 cm from the end of the tube. By sliding the specimen tube along the lever the embedded object could be brought up to the clamped razor, ready for sectioning. A cord attached to the other end of the lever was used to pull it down, against a return spring, thus imparting the rocking motion. The section was cut on the return stroke of the lever.

The horizontal arm supporting the rocking lever in turn pivoted on a second pair of inverted V grooves, which were cast into its lower face immediately beneath the upper grooves. From *Fig.* 8.5 it can be seen that by raising the far end of this lower arm, using a micrometer screw, the object to be sectioned could be moved a minute amount towards the razor. Incremental movement was obtained by means of a pawl and ratchet, the cord from the rocking lever being taken round a pulley and attached to the short radial arm which carried the pawl.

Thus, when the radial arm was pulled towards the user the pawl engaged with the ratchet and fed the embedded object forward. At the same time the string pulled the rocking lever down, raising the object past

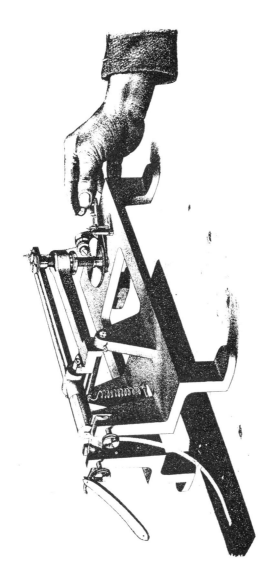

Figure 8.5 Darwin 'Rocker' c. 1885. (Photo: C.S.I.Co. Price Lists 1882–90.)

the razor and stretching the return spring. When the radial arm was released the spring drew the embedded object across the edge of the razor and a section was cut. The magnitude of the incremental feed could be varied and the practical minimum thickness of sections obtainable with a good razor was 1/40000th of an inch (i.e. 0·0006 mm).

It was essential that the rocking lever should rotate with great precision about the same axis every time it rocked and, in 1900, a knife edge bearing was introduced comprising four knife edges in line. These rested on four flat surfaces forming the two V's. *Fig.* 8.6, showing the construction principle of this bearing, is a reproduction of drawings used by Darwin to illustrate the point in his lecture to the Aeronautical Society in 1913.

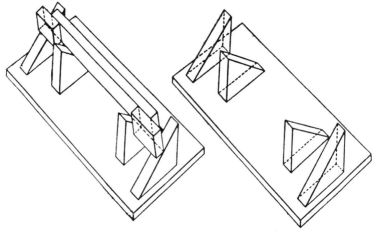

Figure 8.6 The design principle of the rocking arm of Darwin's Microtome after 1900. (Diagram: C.S.I.Co., Neg. 1643.)

Whilst Caldwell and Threlfall's automatic microtome represented a breakthrough to a new concept of microtome function and action, in contrast, Darwin illustrated how good engineering could both simplify the design and at the same time maximise the performance of such an instrument. In the years which have followed many other microtomes have been designed by many other manufacturers but surely none have enjoyed the reputation achieved by the 'Darwin Rocker'.

*   *   *   *   *

CHAPTER NINE

The early development of the seismograph

1888 Ewing's horizontal pendulum seismograph
1888 Ewing's vertical motion seismograph
1888 Ewing's duplex pendulum seismograph

IN very simple terms the prime aim when designing a seismometer is to arrange that during an earthquake some point of the apparatus will remain stationary and provide a reference against which the motion of the ground may be observed and, in the case of a seismograph, recorded. The motion of the ground may, of course, take place in three dimensions and different forms of seismographs have been developed to record horizontal movements and vertical movements.

Earthquakes, like eclipses, comets, volcanic eruptions and other natural phenomena traditionally associated with witchcraft and superstition, have been of particular interest to mankind for a long time and the first attempts to record movements of the ground were made many centuries ago. One of the earliest recorded seismoscopes was set up in China by Chang Heng in AD 132. It consisted of a circle of ornamental, open-mouthed dragons, each with a ball balanced in its mouth. Beneath each dragon a carved toad squatted, head up, mouth open, waiting to catch the ball from the dragon's mouth if an earth tremor dislodged it.[1] How effective this particular seismoscope was in practice is not recorded, but a similar, if more refined version was later used for many years by Cacciatore at the Palermo Observatory in Sicily. This consisted of a wooden circular dish about ten inches in diameter, with eight small notches cut in the rim at the cardinal points of the compass. The dish was carefully levelled and filled to the base of the notches with mercury. Beneath each notch was a small cup and any displacement or oscillation of the ground caused mercury to be thrown out into one or more of the cups. Some indication of the direction of the shock was given by which cups received mercury and, by measuring the volume of mercury, an estimate could be made of the magnitude of the earthquake shock.

Several other variations of this apparatus were proposed. In one a cylindrical tub with a whitewashed interior was partially filled with a coloured liquid. More sophisticated versions incorporated L- or U-shaped tubes of mercury with marking indices on the surfaces.[2]

However, the pendulum was the instrument most frequently used to detect ground movement and many observers in Italy and other Southern European countries particularly prone to earthquakes used pendulums to measure the horizontal motion of the ground. A typical pendulum seismometer as used during the early nineteenth century would have a heavy bob on a long suspension, the bob being free to move in any direction. Beneath the bob would be a concave dish with a thin covering of fine dry sand. A stylus on the underside of the bob traced the pattern of the ground movement in the sand. It was supposed that the stylus would mark a straight line in the direction of the shock. In fact, because of the inherent oscillatory characteristics of a pendulum, the trace was usually a pattern of elongated ellipses.

An alternative form of the pendulum seismometer was that used at Santi. This consisted of two pendulums suspended close to the faces of two walls, one North–South, the other East–West. The pendulums were free to oscillate in those planes only and the bobs recorded ground movements by making chalk marks on the walls.

The inverted pendulum was much in favour about the middle of the nineteenth century. The bob was supported by a springy rod and a chalk or pencil attached to the top of the bob registered ground movement on the inside of a concave dish supported over the pendulum.[†]

In 1858 Robert Mallett (President of the Geological Society of Ireland) reporting to the British Association on the 'Facts and Theory of Earthquake Phenomena' claimed to have invented the first truly self-registering seismometer. His proposed design consisted essentially of six fluid pendulums—glass tubes partially filled with mercury, four for the horizontal components and one for the vertical element of the shock. Displacement of a mercury column would temporarily break a circuit and cause a pencil to trace a line on a chart wrapped round a drum-driven by clockwork, the length of the line being proportional to the amplitude of the earthquake. The time the earthquake occurred could be obtained from the timing lines on the chart.[3,4] Mallett received a grant from the British Association to construct a seismograph to his design during the 1840s but although the work was started the instrument does not appear to have been completed.[5,6]

[†] *In 1900 Wiechert developed the inverted pendulum into a very effective instrument and during the next twenty years many seismographs of this type, with bobs weighing between 200 lbs and 17 tons were made. The 17-ton instrument at Tacubaya near Mexico City is still in use.*

James Ewing went to Japan in 1878 as Professor of Mechanical Engineering at the University of Tokio, initially on a three-year engagement which was subsequently extended to five years at the invitation of the Japanese authorities. He wrote in the preface to his book of papers, *An Engineer's Outlook*, that he had 'an instant attraction to earthquakes as a subject of experimental study, and no little satisfaction in devising instruments which would make the earthquake itself write, if not the story of its birth, at least a complete account of the components of its motion, in all phases of the disturbance from start to finish.'[7] Ewing was to lay the foundations for the design of effective seismographs and in 1883, just before his return to Scotland, he published a summary of his work in the *Memoirs of the Science Department, University of Tokio.*[8]

During his time in Japan Ewing established a seismological observatory in the lowest part of the vale of Gedo. His first seismograph, designed in 1879, was a conventional long pendulum but with a pair of multiplying levers added. The two components of the horizontal ground motion were recorded by these levers on two smoked glass plates, which were continuously rotated by a clock. This was one of the earliest continuously recording seismographs.

In order to achieve a good steady-point with a simple pendulum its period had to be long compared to the periodic time of the disturbance and very long suspensions were commonly used in order to achieve periods of 10–60 seconds. Such long suspensions were obviously inconvenient, and in 1880 Ewing devised a modification to the simple pendulum which had the effect of lengthening the period whilst at the same time reducing the overall size of the apparatus. The duplex pendulum (*Fig. 9.1*), as this was known, incorporated a simple pendulum mounted above, and coupled to, an inverted pendulum, both pendulums being free to move in any direction. The coupling took the form of a ball on the end of a rod projecting down from the suspended pendulum, and fitting into a cylindrical hole in the centre of the inverted pendulum, so that the pendulums could move quite freely together. The relative masses of the two bobs were chosen to give nearly neutral equilibrium and the degree of stability could be adjusted by raising or lowering the upper bob. A recording pen was attached horizontally to the top of a vertical multiplying lever, which was supported by a gimbal joint above the hanging bob and geared into the bob by a ball and tube joint. The pen thus traced a magnified record of the total horizontal ground movement.

To obtain a steady-point with respect to movements in one horizontal direction only was a simpler problem, the solution being the horizontal pendulum. In principle this consisted of a vertical rod with pivots top and bottom and with a second, but horizontal, rod securely fastened to the centre of the vertical rod and carrying a weight at its extremity. By tilting the vertical rod very slightly through a small angle θ

the component of gravitational force causing the weight to return to its equilibrium position became $g \sin \theta$. Although the earliest attempt to use a horizontal pendulum to measure earthquake motion was made by Professor Chaplin of the University of Tokio in 1878, this apparatus was soon abandoned, probably because of friction at the joints in the structure. Ewing designed the first successful horizontal pendulum seismograph in 1880. It consisted of two pendulums mounted at right angles to each other. Each was fitted with a long multiplying lever and stylus providing permanent records of the ground motion on a rotating smoked glass plate. Ewing's first earthquake records, obtained in 1880, were made using this instrument.

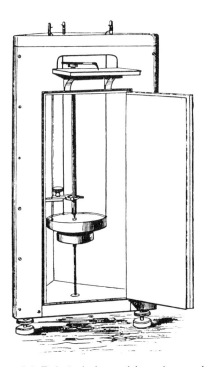

Figure 9.1 Ewing's duplex pendulum seismograph as manufactured by the Cambridge Scientific Instrument Company c. 1889. (Photo: C.S.I.Co. Price Lists 1882–90.)

Little effort was made by early observers to monitor the vertical motion of the ground. One of the first vertical motion seismographs was that mentioned by the British Association Committee which was appointed in 1841 to register shocks of earthquakes in Great Britain. In their report of 1842 they referred to 'a horizontal bar, fixed to a solid wall by means of a strong flat watch-spring and loaded at the opposite end.'

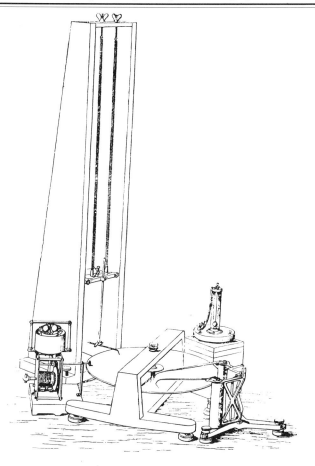

Figure 9.2 Ewing's vertical motion seismograph and horizontal pendulums seismograph as manufactured by the Cambridge Scientific Instrument Company c. 1889. On the left is the clock which drove the smoked glass recording plate at a uniform speed by a projecting friction roller. The clock was started when an electric circuit was closed by a sensitive seismoscope (shown in the right background). This seismograph consisted of a short pendulum with a multiplying lever surrounded by a platinum contact ring. (Photo: C.S.I.Co. Price Lists 1882–90.)

The report went on to say that an instrument of that kind, set up at Comrie in Scotland, had given a vertical movement of half an inch on one occasion.[9]

This type of construction would have been too stable to work well as a seismometer. The arrangement used by later observers was a boom, hinged at one end to a fixed support, with a heavy mass attached to the far end of the boom. The weight of this mass was supported by means of a spiral spring attached to the boom near the hinge. To achieve neutral equilibrium Thomas Gray, in 1881, used a tube containing a liquid, the tube being linked to the horizontal boom in such a manner that when the bar was depressed the tube tilted and the liquid moved so as to increase the load on the boom and vice versa.[10] Ewing pointed out that there was a much simpler way to obtain neutral equilibrium: by changing the leverage exerted by the spring. If the spring support was attached to the end of a vertical strut projecting below the boom, as the boom was depressed the vertical line through the point of attachment of the spring would move slightly towards the fulcrum, thus decreasing the moment.

Ewing designed a vertical motion seismograph on this plan and installed it in his observatory. A multiplying lever projecting vertically downwards from the top of the boom, near the bob, carried a stylus to record ground movement on a smoked glass plate. Ewing observed that whereas horizontal pendulums were extremely stable and one might keep the recording plates continuously rotating in anticipation of earth movements, the vertical pendulum was much less stable, due to the effects of temperature variation on the supporting springs. He therefore recommended that a small seismoscope be used to detect the first earth tremors and that this should close an electrical circuit and start the recording plate revolving.

Thus by 1880 Ewing had established the basic designs for seismographs of quite small dimensions but which had very long periodic times. During the next few years he made many detailed refinements to his designs. In 1883 he returned to Scotland to become Professor of Engineering at Dundee. Three years later, when his seismographs were exhibited at the Edinburgh International Exhibition, he was awarded a gold medal for 'masterly execution of complicated scientific apparatus.'[11]

The Cambridge Scientific Instrument Company began making seismographs to Ewing's designs about 1888,[12] (*Fig.* 9.2) the sensitive seismoscope used to start the clock driving the recording plate being based on a design by Professor Palmieri.

The Company continued to manufacture these seismographs until about 1907. By that time Ewing's designs had become outmoded. His former associates, Milne and Gray, had continued his work in Japan. During the next few years major advances in the design of seismographic equipment were also made by other workers, including Wiechert, Shaw, Omori and Galitzin, but the foundation for all of this work had been laid by Ewing during his five years at the University of Tokio.

CHAPTER TEN

The advent of industrial temperature measurement

IT is perhaps fitting that Horace Darwin's great-grandfather, Josiah Wedgwood, should have been one of the first industrialists to attempt to use an instrument to measure the temperature of his furnaces when, in 1782, he designed and made a pyrometer for use in his potteries (*Fig.* 10.1). The operating principle was very simple, being based on the amount of shrinkage of a clay cylinder during firing. The higher the firing temperature, the smaller the final size of the clay cylinder. The measuring device consisted of two tapered grooves, each six inches long, one being a continuation of the other. Each inch of the groove was divided into twenty equal parts, making a total of 240 divisions, arbitrarily called 'degrees' by Wedgwood. Before firing, the cylinders of special clay would just fit into the wide end of the groove, with the lower end of each cylinder opposite the zero mark. After firing (which only took a few minutes) the cylinders were allowed to cool and again inserted in the grooves. They would now slide down the groove and the mark opposite the lower end of each cylinder was a rough indication of the temperature of the furnace in which it had been baked. Whilst this crude technique inevitably suffered from errors resulting from variations in the composition of the clay, Wedgwood found that it did help to produce better repeatability in firing temperatures than could be obtained by relying on the visual judgement of his workmen.[1]

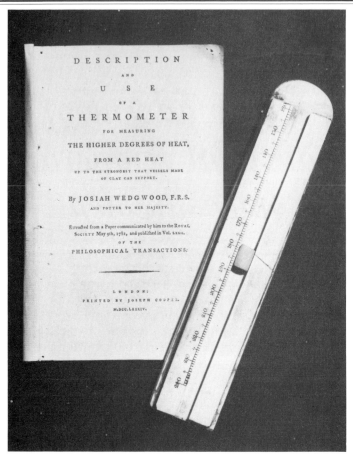

Figure 10.1 Josiah Wedgwood's pyrometer c. 1782 and the title page of his pamphlet describing its use (extracted from the paper Wedgwood communicated to the Royal Society on 9 May 1782). (Photo: By courtesy of the Trustees of the Wedgwood Museum, Barlaston, Staffordshire; Neg. 2285–1.)

In 1822 John Daniell published a description of a pyrometer based on the expansion of a platinum rod enclosed in a plumbago tube. This was a significant advance in thermometry, being the first pyrometer to provide a continuous indication of temperature. One end of the rod pressed against the end of the tube whilst the other was free to move and was connected to a multiplying linkage which converted the expansion of the rod into movement of a pointer on a circular scale. Using this thermometer Daniell measured the melting points of various metals including silver and iron. Although the results he obtained were considerably higher than the correct figures, they were much closer than those which had been obtained by experimenters using Wedgwood's technique.

Also in 1822 Seebeck discovered thermoelectricity[2] and some four or five years later Becquerel (senior) conceived the idea of using thermoelectricity as a method of measuring high temperatures. He experimented with a platinum–palladium couple and used it, albeit not very successfully, in an attempt to measure the temperature of an alcohol lamp, obtaining a figure of 1350 °C.[3] Pouillet also endeavoured to use the technique to measure temperatures in a furnace, employing an iron–platinum couple, but, like other experimenters at that time, his results were inconsistent.[4,5] Their failures were due to a combination of factors: the unsuitability of the junction materials used, the unreliability of the galvanometers, and a lack of appreciation of the importance of using a high resistance galvanometer so that changes in the resistance of the couple would be small in comparison with the total circuit resistance. After a while the method was abandoned until, in 1886, Le Châtelier published his researches and showed that, using a d'Arsonval moving coil galvanometer as an indicator, reliable results could be obtained with a junction of pure platinum against platinum–10% rhodium alloy. Le Châtelier thus laid the basis for thermocouple pyrometry as it exists today.[6,7]

In 1871 Sir William Siemens had put forward the idea of a thermometer based on the variation in resistance with temperature of platinum wire.[8] Coincidentally, a year later Sir William Barrett observed that when iron or steel was allowed to cool from white heat a transition point was reached when heat was given out as a result of internal molecular change (recalescence) and the temperature of the metal increased temporarily. It was very soon realised that to produce hardened steel it should be quenched whilst its temperature was just above the transition point. This stimulated a demand for accurate pyrometers from those blast furnace operators who were interested in improving their product and cutting down wastage. Siemens attempted to make resistance thermometers for furnace temperature measurement in response to this demand, but it was soon found that measurements made using his thermometers could not be relied upon. The matter attracted so much attention that a committee of the British Association was appointed to carry out tests on some of Siemens' thermometers. The chairman was Professor G. Carey Foster, Professor J. J. Thomson and Sir William Siemens being amongst the members of the committee. The unreliability of Siemens' thermometers was confirmed in a report presented to the 1874 meeting of the Association in Belfast.[9] Although the committee did put forward suggestions as to how the reliability might be improved, as a consequence of this report the resistance thermometer came to be regarded with considerable distrust.

It was left to Callendar to show, in 1887, that the resistance thermometer was capable of high accuracy.[10] Siemens' thermometers had failed because of contamination of the platinum element, which was wound on a fireclay cylinder, the whole unit being enclosed in an iron cylinder. In the reducing atmosphere present in the iron cylinder as the temperature was raised, not only was the wire attacked by silica impurities in the clay mandrel, but impurities in the iron sheath, typically copper, tin and zinc, further contaminated the element causing a permanent and continual change in its characteristics. Although Callendar used a hard glass tube as a mandrel for the elements in his early experimental thermometers, he soon adopted mica as the best support for the element with mica discs to keep the platinum lead-in wires separated.[11] As mentioned in Chapter 3, the idea for the well-known cruciform former, with serrated edges, is attributed to E. H. Griffiths. The whole thermometer was enclosed in a porcelain tube. To eliminate errors from the unknown and varying temperatures of the copper connecting leads and platinum lead-in wires, a thick platinum wire compensating lead was run alongside the lead-in wires to the sensing element and this compensating wire was connected by copper leads to the opposite arm of the measuring bridge.

The porcelain tube was considered by some users to be both costly and not sufficiently robust for industrial use. In a lecture to the Iron and Steel Institute in 1892 Callendar firmly disposed of this latter criticism. He remarked that he had only had the misfortune to break one tube and that was with a hammer! The pyrometer in question had been in use for some six months at the Mint when it suddenly ceased to operate. As the exterior of the porcelain tube had been attacked by lead oxide, alumina and cast iron, as well as being subjected to rough treatment whilst adhering metal and slag had been scraped off, he had assumed that some metal must have found its way through the walls of the tube. 'A post-mortem examination was accordingly performed with a hammer.' The post-mortem disclosed that there was nothing wrong with the resistance thermometer—the fault was a short circuit in the external connections.[12]

The Cambridge Scientific Instrument Company obtained sole manufacturing rights for Callendar's resistance thermometer in 1891 and this was the beginning of a long and profitable association with Callendar. Initially the resistance thermometer was used with a special Wheatstone bridge. The scale alongside the bridge wire was divided into equal divisions and the temperature could be read directly from this scale.[13] It was soon realised that this was not a very suitable piece of equipment for industrial use and in 1893 the Company began to manufacture Callendar's 'Patent Electrical Pyrometer' (*Fig.* 10.2). This was a portable instrument, with a battery included in the case.[14] The design was protected by two patents.[15]

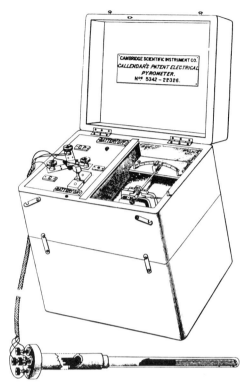

Figure 10.2 Callendar's patent electrical pyrometer c. 1893. (Photo: C.S.I.Co. Catalogues 1889–1901, Callendar's Platinum Thermometers and Pyrometers.)

Patent 5342 (1891) covered the use of the compensating leads, connected in the opposite arm of the measuring bridge. But the pyrometer also incorporated a special galvanometer with two coils, their axes being at right angles, and this galvanometer was protected by the second patent, 22326 (1891). One coil on the galvanometer was connected so as to monitor the out of balance current in the bridge in the normal way. A proportion of the battery current to the bridge passed through the second (field) coil, compensating the bridge so that the out of balance deflection was independent of the battery voltage. The temperature of the thermometer could be read directly from the deflection of the galvanometer pointer on a calibrated scale.

Whilst this instrument was simpler to use than the original calibrated bridge, the use of a special galvanometer which required careful adjustment in order to achieve accurate compensation meant that the instrument was not cheap to manufacture.

Figure 10.3 Temperature indicator c. 1901. (Photo: C.S.I.Co., Neg. 37.)

About 1900 Callendar's pyrometer was superseded by the temperature indicator shown in *Fig.* 10.3. Although one of its advantages was claimed to be its portability, it was 8 inches in diameter, 10 inches high and weighed 11 pounds (plus a battery). The instrument design reverted to the straightforward Wheatstone bridge technique, with a built-in null balance galvanometer. (The pointer is visible at the front of the small window at the top.) One of the two concentric knobs on the top of the instrument operated a switch, to switch in fixed resistors, and the second adjusted the position of the sliding contact on the bridge wire to achieve null balance, the temperature being read directly from the calibrated dial.[16]

In 1902 Whipple designed a much simpler temperature indicator (*Fig.* 10.4). The instrument was again portable, and contained a Wheatstone bridge circuit; one arm of the bridge comprising a calibrated resistance wire wound on a cylindrical former. By rotating the knurled knob on the end of a shaft which passed down the centre of this former, a contact was moved along the calibrated resistance wire, the galvanometer showing when balance was obtained. The temperature could then be read directly from the cylindrical scale, mounted on the same shaft as the sliding contact. The Company claimed in their 1904 catalogue that: 'By means of this instrument any workman, without electrical knowledge, can

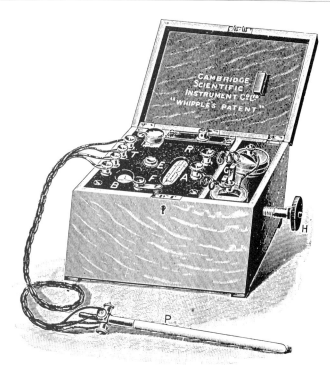

Figure 10.4 Whipple's patent temperature indicator c. 1906. With the contact key F depressed, the milled knob H was rotated to make the resistance of the indicator equal to that of the thermometer P. Balance was shown by galvanometer B and the temperature read from scale A. (Photo: C.S.I.Co. Catalogues 1905–11, List No. 39.)

learn the temperature of his furnace or source of heat in two or three minutes.'[17]

With its exceptionally long equivalent scale length, this instrument was later widely used as a sub-standard to check the accuracy of resistance thermometers in large installations where many thermometers were in constant use. The instrument was still being manufactured in 1950 and the model then in production had an equivalent scale length of 5·5 m, for a span of 1200 °C; i.e. 1 °C = 4·5 mm.

Although Le Châtelier had shown in 1886 that reliable thermocouples could be constructed, The Cambridge Scientific Instrument Company was late in exploiting this method of measuring temperature. Other companies were manufacturing thermocouples before 1902 when the Company first included thermocouples in its catalogue. Even then the sales approach was somewhat half-hearted as the Company considered the thermocouple to be inferior to the resistance thermometer in reliability. As it happened this was unfortunately true, for all the early thermocouples sold by the Company were platinum against platinum–10% iridium alloy, since the e.m.f. given by this couple was greater than that from platinum against platinum–rhodium and allowed the use of a slightly more open scale on the indicator. Platinum–iridium was also less expensive. However, the decision to use it was a mistake since it was later found that iridium was apt to volatilise from the alloy side of the couple and combine with the pure platinum side, thus contaminating the couple, reducing the e.m.f., and giving erroneous results.

To eliminate variability in characteristics resulting from different batches of thermocouple material, the Company used only wire drawn from one particular ingot held by Johnson and Matthey, the suppliers. The thermoelectric characteristics for this ingot were determined by the National Physical Laboratory.

Compensating leads were first used with thermocouples about 1909.[18] They were the invention of W. S. Peake who was employed by the Company at that time.[19] Because of the cost of thermocouple wire, in most installations copper wire was used to link the couple to the indicator, thus leaving the cold junction in a location where the temperature was likely to vary considerably, producing a significant error in the individual readings. With the invention of compensating leads it was no longer necessary to link the couple to the indicator with the expensive thermocouple wire in order to eliminate this error. Instead, the connection could be made with a cheap combination of materials (usually copper against a copper–nickel alloy) having the same low temperature characteristics as the thermocouple. Peake also patented a 'Scale Control Board'[20] which was manufactured by the Company about 1910/11.[21] By means of this device the zero of the indicator or recorder could be electrically suppressed and the scale thus expanded to enable the temperature to be read more accurately.

Becquerel's son, Edmond, was the first researcher to suggest that a measurement of the temperature of a hot body might be obtained by measuring the intensity of the radiations from that body.[22,23] This was in 1862–3 and it was another twenty years before the subject of heat radiation was properly understood and the Stefan–Boltzmann fourth power law theoretically postulated. Becquerel's ideas were thus not successfully developed until 1892 when Le Châtelier devised his photometric pyrometer. In this instrument an iris diaphragm was used to reduce the quantity of light entering the telescope from the heat source until the brightness of the source matched that of the standard lamp. A temperature scale corresponding to the diameter of the opening was computed, using Wien's Law.[24,25]

This class of instrument was developed by other workers into a convenient instrument for industrial use where occasional readings of high temperatures were required. It was not, however, capable of giving a continuous measurement for record purposes.

In 1902 Féry demonstrated his experimental design for a total radiation pyrometer in which the radiation from a hot body was focused on to a small blackened thermocouple junction.[26,27] The technique was a breakthrough in non-contact continuous measurement of temperature. In his first design Féry used a lens to focus the radiation from the hot body but the lens had the disadvantage of absorbing some of the radiation and Féry soon replaced it with a concave mirror.

The Cambridge Scientific Instrument Company began manu- facturing Féry's pyrometer in 1905, at first making both designs. After a few months the lens design was discontinued. The pyrometer was used with a calibrated d'Arsonval galvanometer or a thread recorder. The beauty of the technique lay in the simplicity of the design of the pyrometer, as can be seen from *Fig.* 10.5. The copper–constantan thermocouple junction was located on the optical axis and electrically connected via the brass supporting strips R and D and the terminals *b* and *b'* to the calibrated galvanometer or recorder.[28]

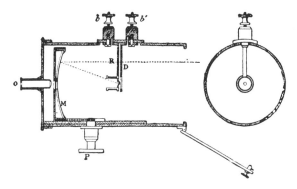

Figure 10.5 Féry's total radiation pyrometer c. 1905. b,b', terminals for galvanometer connection; D, R, thermocouple supports and electrical con- nections; O, eyepiece; M, mirror mounted on rack; P, focusing knob with pinion. (Diagram: C.S.I.Co. Catalogues 1902–5, List No. 36.)

In use the operator sighted on a hole in the wall of the furnace through the eyepiece O, adjusting the position of the pyrometer so that the image of the hole slightly overlapped the blackened disc attached to the thermocouple junction. When measuring high temperatures a dia- phragm with a smaller aperture could be fitted in front of the pyro- meter, to reduce the amount of radiation reaching the thermocouple, the temperature then being read on a second precalibrated scale on the galvanometer or recorder.

Strictly speaking, the instrument calibration was only correct for true black body sources of radiation, but usually a sighting tube, closed at the far end, was inserted into the furnace and then, provided the temperature of the furnace was reasonably uniform and the diameter of the open end of the tube was small in proportion to its length, the far end of the tube behaved as a black body radiator. In any case, for industrial purposes the measurement of absolute temperature was invariably of less importance than the attainment of repeatable conditions over a period of time.

The vast majority of temperature measurements in industry today are still made using thermocouple or resistance thermometer sensors. Although improved combinations of thermocouple materials are now available, with some seven or eight couple combinations in common use, the basic design of both types of thermometer has changed little over the years. In contrast, since Féry designed his radiation pyrometer the techniques for the detection and measurement of heat radiation have advanced enormously but, it should be said, in association with an increased complexity in the design and cost of the instruments, which accounts for the continuing popularity of thermocouples and resistance thermometers for many industrial applications.

*   *   *   *   *

CHAPTER ELEVEN

Temperature control and temperature alarms

IN 1882, at the request of the Board of Trade, the Royal Society appointed a committee to advise on methods by which the comparison of standards of length at the Standards Office might be improved. One of the Committee's recommendations in their report was that action should be taken to reduce the variations in temperature of the bars under comparison. Consequently, The Cambridge Scientific Instrument Company was asked to investigate the subject of temperature regulation and also to consider the general design of a comparison apparatus. In the latter part of the nineteenth century the automatic control of temperature was a scientific exercise and the system which Darwin designed gives an interesting insight into the imaginative methods which were adopted during that era.

Darwin based his technique on that already in use at the Bureau International des Poids et Mesures at Sèvres, i.e. immersion of the standard bars in a bath of water maintained at a constant temperature.[1] Indeed, Darwin visited Sèvres before constructing his own temperature regulator.

The regulator utilised the variation in pressure with temperature of a volatile liquid in a glass bulb. This pressure variation was used to control the flow of gas to the coal gas burners which heated the water bath. So far, this was essentially the Sèvres system, but Darwin then incorporated a novel feature of his own invention: a compensation system for variations in atmospheric pressure. One of the unusual aspects of this

195

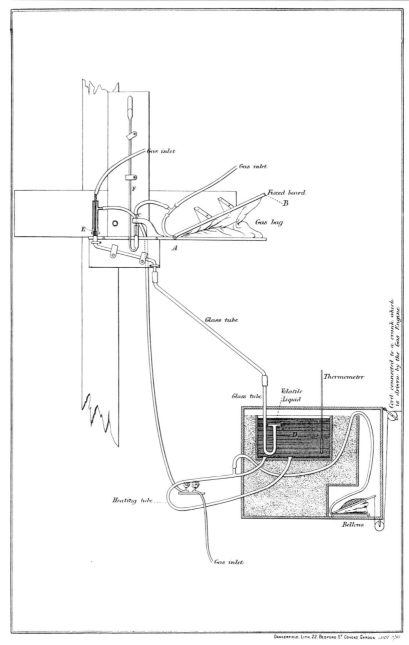

Figure 11.1 *Temperature regulator for the Standards Department of the Board of Trade. The diagram is taken from the pamphlet published by the Company in 1885. A, pivot for pressure compensating board; B, fixed board with gas bag; C, gas valve; D, water bath with volatile liquid temperature regulator; E, gas regulator; F, barometer. (Diagram: C.S.I.Co. Box 3.)*

latter system was that the pressure of the gas supply was used to provide power to control the position of the pressure compensating mechanism.

The following extracts from an account of the work published by the Company in 1885 provide an interesting commentary on Darwin's apparatus (*Fig. 11.1*):[2]

The action of the regulator used at Sèvres[†] depends on the variation of pressure of a saturated vapour, caused by a change of temperature. The pressure on the volatile liquid and vapour is due to a column of mercury, as well as to the atmosphere; consequently the regulated temperature will vary with any change in the atmospheric pressure, amount of this variation depending on the initial pressure. In the following experiments, in which the volatile liquid was under a head of about 1,240 mm. of mercury, the corresponding change of temperature, for one inch alteration of the barometer was about 0·37° C. The accuracy of the regulator, therefore depends on the constancy of the atmospheric pressure, and to overcome this serious disadvantage, the Company have now devised an arrangement for maintaining a constant pressure on the volatile liquid notwithstanding the variations of the atmospheric pressure.

Description of Apparatus

Heating.—*A cast-iron bath D, containing about 7 gallons of water was placed in a wooden box and the intermediate space filled with saw-dust; this was done in order to minimise the unequal cooling due to the varying temperature of the room. The two ends of a U-shaped tube were fixed into the bottom of the iron bath and passed through holes in the side of the wooden box. The water was kept warm by means of two gas flames placed under a part of this tube. One of the gas flames was connected to the regulator and the other direct to the gas main. The object of the second flame was to re-light the regulated gas-jet in case it should have been completely extinguished by the regulator.*

Stirring.—*The water in the bath was kept thoroughly stirred by air forced through it by means of bellows. These were placed entirely inside the box containing the bath, in order to keep them warm, and also for the more important reason of avoiding the currents of air which would otherwise be produced at each stroke. Had the bellows been outside the box and the air merely drawn from the inside, obviously the same volume of cold air from the room must find its way into the box to replace that drawn out, and the reverse must happen on the return stroke. This would be most objectionable, as not only would there be a constant cooling at the surface of the water, but also the air used for stirring would be slightly cooler than the required temperature; and as it would not be saturated with aqueous vapour, it would by absorbing moisture cool the water in the bath. From the nozzle of the bellows an india-rubber pipe was led through the sawdust in the box, and connected to the U-shaped tube by a branch inserted just above the point where the gas flame was applied. The air thus pumped through the upper part of the U tube caused a rapid circulation of water through it. This method has the advantage of applying the heat in a manner which does not tend to make the water in one part of the bath perceptibly hotter than the rest. Even when the bellows were not working there was still a slow circulation of water through the U tube. This was sufficient to keep the water in the bath at a fairly uniform temperature through the night when it was inconvenient to work the bellows. Through the day the bellows were driven by a system of cords connected with the gas engine which supplies power to the Company's Works.*

Regulator.—*The volatile liquid in the regulator was a mixture of methyl-chloride and ethylchloride, boiling at about $2\frac{1}{2}$ °C. under the normal atmospheric pressure, similar to that used at the Bureau International.*

[†] *See Travaux et Mémoires du Bureau International des Poids et Mesures, Tome I., p. C. 10.*

It was contained in a flat bulb, D, blown at the end of a glass tube, and was under a head of about 1240 mm. of mercury. The glass tubes containing the mercury were connected by short lengths of canvas-lined india-rubber tube.

The use of india-rubber was, however, avoided as far as possible on account of the error which may be introduced by its stretching, as mentioned in the Travaux et Mémoires du Bureau International des Poids et Mesures.

A double brass tube was secured to the open end of the regulator, E. The gas entered by the inner tube, which passed down to the surface of the mercury, and the outer tube was connected with the gas burner placed under the U-shaped heating tube. Thus a rise of mercury in the regulator reduced the supply of gas to the burner.

The cross section of the flat glass bulb at the common surface of the mercury and volatile liquid was large compared with the cross section at the upper end of the regulator; thus nearly all the increase in height due to expansion of the volatile liquid and vapour takes place at the upper or gas inlet end of regulator, and the level of the common surface of the mercury and volatile liquid remains nearly constant.

Compensating Barometer.—The object of the compensating barometer is to maintain a constant pressure on the volatile liquid, however the atmospheric pressure may vary.

Let us suppose that the barometer rises an inch, then it is necessary, in order to maintain a constant pressure, that the surface of mercury which closes the gas inlet should fall an inch, since the level of the mercury in the flat bulb does not vary perceptibly.

The barometer employed consisted of a bent tube as shown at F; thus the exposed surface of the mercury falls half an inch for an increase of atmospheric pressure corresponding to 1 inch of mercury. Therefore if the upper end of the regulator is caused to rise or fall twice the height of the exposed surface of the mercury in the barometer, the required object is accomplished. In order to do this the upper part of the regulator and the inlet gas tube were attached to a board turning about a horizontal axis, A. A gas bag was placed between the projecting end of this board and a fixed board, B. The board turning about A was so weighted as to tend to close the bag. The nozzle of the bag was connected to the gas-main and a branch pipe led to a small tube, C, passing down the open end of the barometer. This small tube was fixed by a bracket to the movable board at half the distance of the gas inlet tube from the pivot A. Now if the mercury rises in the open end of the barometer it closes the tube C, and the gas from the main passes into the bag, forces the boards apart, and raises both the gas inlet tube and the tube C, until the escape restores the equilibrium. Thus the rise and fall of the gas inlet tube will be twice that of the tube C, that is, twice the rise and fall of the mercury in the open end of the barometer. The flexible india-rubber joints allow the necessary movement to take place. This arrangement is of some interest, as it is probably the first occasion in which the pressure of the gas supply has been the motive power for automatically moving a piece of mechanism in a required manner.

Gas Pressure Regulator.—The gas supply was connected with a Stott's Regulator, and the pressure was thus maintained fairly constant notwithstanding the variation of pressure in the main.

The Stott's pressure regulator, which was connected to the gas main, did its work well, but when a water gauge was arranged to measure the pressure, each explosion in the gas engine became evident, although the only connexion between the gas engine and the Stott's regulator was through the street mains. The mean pressure varied very slightly, and the sudden fall of pressure at each explosion was probably not an important matter. It would perhaps be advisable in future apparatus to have a more delicate regulator for the gas supply

A brief summary of the experimental results was included in the report and these show that even with the limited technology of the period

Darwin was able to control the temperature variations to no more than 0·04 °C during a test period of 14 days, despite quite large changes in barometric pressure.

The first step towards the automatic control of industrial processes was taken during the early 1900s when alarm contacts were fitted to temperature indicators, so that the operator (and the manager of the plant) would know if the process temperature was outside the prescribed limits. One such system, designed by Robert Paul and fitted inside the medium and large Unipivot indicators, is shown in *Fig.* 11.2.[3]

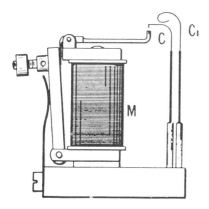

Figure 11.2 Alarm relay for use with a Unipivot galvanometer c. 1914. C_1C_1, contacts; M, solenoid. (Diagram: C.S.I.Co.—Robert Paul's Catalogue, c. 1914.)

The current to the solenoid M, which was normally energised, was interrupted at regular intervals using a clock mechanism. The tip of the solenoid armature was fork-shaped and above it were mounted two light platinum–iridium contacts, C and C_1. The system was so arranged that the galvanometer pointer passed between the forked armature and the lower contact C. When the pointer was above the fork, de-energising the solenoid caused the pointer to press contact C onto contact C_1, thus completing a bell or regulating circuit. If required, two such units could be fitted to give maximum and minimum alarm indication.

Sometimes self-contained alarm units were supplied, the alarms working in conjunction with a resistance thermometer or thermocouple. One of the techniques employed is illustrated in *Fig.* 11.3. When the temperature at which the alarm was set to act was reached a light arm on the galvanometer coil was deflected on to the toothed surface of wheel W. The wheel carried the arm towards the two contacts L thus completing the bell circuit.[4]

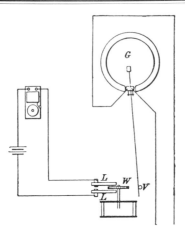

Figure 11.3 Circuit diagram for temperature alarm c. 1906. G, galvanometer; L, contact; W, toothed wheel; V, pointer stop. (Diagram:
C.S.I.Co. Catalogues 1905–11, List No. 39.)

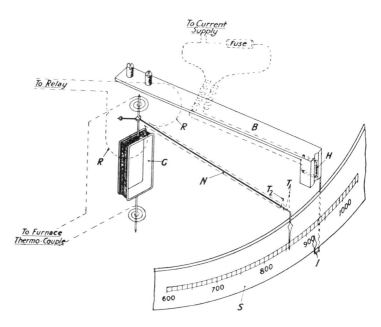

Figure 11.4 The operating principle of Apthorpe's control unit. B,
preset arm; G, galvanometer coil; H, heater; I, index pointer; N,
indicating pointer; R, connections to relay coil; S, scale; $T_1, \backslash T_2$, thermocouple junctions. (Diagram: C.S.I.Co. Catalogues 1921–26, List
No. 150.

By the 1920s, galvanometer indication of the temperature of industrial processes was commonplace. Such indicators were normally contained in robust metal cases for wall or panel mounting and fitted with horizontal edgewise scales. In 1923 W. H. Apthorpe patented the operating principle of his process controller which fitted inside such an indicator.[5] The movement of the galvanometer indicating pointer past a control or 'index' pointer caused a sensitive, moving coil relay to break the electrical heating circuit of the furnace which was being monitored. The operating principle is shown diagrammatically in *Fig.* 11.4.[6]

The galvanometer indicating pointer N carried at its extremity a differential thermocouple T_1, T_2, which was connected electrically to a moving coil relay. The index pointer I could be set to the desired control point by adjusting the position of the movable arm B through the top of the case. Arm B also carried a small electrical heater H. When the indicating pointer N was in line with the index pointer I the thermocouple T_2 was at its closest point to the heater H and the e.m.f. generated by this thermocouple was sufficient to actuate the moving coil relay, thus reducing the power to the furnace. As the furnace cooled the indicating pointer N moved downscale, the e.m.f. generated by thermocouple T_2 diminished and thermocouple T_1 in turn approached heater H. Since the e.m.f. generated by T_1 was in the reverse polarity to that generated by T_2, the moving coil relay would be forced to break contact if, by any mischance, the contact was sticking, and power to the furnace would then be restored.

Apthorpe's ingenious instrument was the first of several generations of galvanometer indicator-controllers manufactured by the Company over a period of half a century, until, eventually, the advent of servo-operated systems in the 1970s, made the technique of galvanometer indication obsolete.

*   *   *   *   *

CHAPTER TWELVE

The first paper chart recorders

1898 Callendar's recorder
1906 Darwin's thread recorder

LTHOUGH Callendar is usually remembered for his work on the platinum resistance thermometer, his invention of the 'Callendar' recorder around 1897 was equally important.[1] It was to be the next firm step in raising temperature control in industry to a higher standard than the plant operator's eye. Not unnaturally the industrial workforce of that time needed to be convinced that such apparatus could be of benefit to them. They regarded all such innovations with suspicion, seeing the recorder only as a means whereby the manager could keep an eye on their activities in his absence.

In marketing the Callendar recorder (*Fig.* 12.1) The Cambridge Scientific Instrument Company was very aware of this antagonism. In their 1906 catalogue they recommended the introduction of a bonus system (devised by Robert Whipple) as a way not only of improving the quality of the plant product but also of selling the merits of the instrument to the plant operator.[2]

> '*We believe that the Temperature Recorder should be placed near the man who is responsible for the particular operation the instrument is recording; and the man should be paid directly for the success of his efforts. A form of bonus system lends itself very readily to this. If, for example, a constant temperature (say 700 °C) has to be maintained, the Works or Furnace Manager tells the man that a bonus of $\frac{1}{2}$d. per hour will be paid to him for every hour in which the record is inside given limits, say $\pm$ 20 °C, i.e. between 680 ° and 720 °C.*
>
> *In important processes the system could be still further extended by holding out a larger inducement for more efficient control, a bonus of 1d. per hour being paid for every hour the*

*record is inside the limits of say ± 10 °C, that is, between 690 °
and 710 °C.*

*Before putting the paper on to the recorder drum the
Manager rules a black line down the sheet at the particular
temperature at which he wishes the apparatus kept, ruling two
red lines for the inner limits and two blue lines for the outer
ones. The fireman who may be quite uneducated and knows
nothing whatever about degrees Centigrade appreciates the fact
that if the pen of the instrument has been kept between the two
red lines he obtains a penny extra for every hour it was inside
them.*

*As an additional incentive to efficiency an extra bonus
of 6d. might be paid if the pen has been kept inside the narrow
limits for the whole of the shift.'*

In case the plant manager might regard payment of an extra 6d.
for a night's work as extravagant the Company hastened to add:

*'Experience shows that it is very difficult to avoid one lapse
during a night's shift, and this additional bonus might very
likely prevent it.'*

Essentially Callendar's recorder consisted of a Wheatstone
bridge or a potentiometer, the movement of the slider along the bridge
wire being automatically effected by relays actuated by the galvanometer
connected between the bridge arms. As the galvanometer deflected in one
direction or the other, so a relay circuit was completed through the
appropriate electromagnet to release the brake on one or other of two
mechanical clocks. Driving through epicyclic gearing on to a common
output shaft, the clock mechanism then pulled the bridge slider along the
slidewire in the appropriate direction to return the galvanometer to its
rest position, when the electromagnet was de-energised and the brake
re-applied to the clock mechanism. The movement of the bridge slider
was recorded by a corresponding movement of the pen on the chart.[3]

The main difficulty in designing a satisfactory instrument to
work on this basis lay in obtaining a sufficiently sensitive and reliable
relay. The total operating current available was necessarily very small,
and in such cases the contacts were very liable to stick. Callendar
overcame this problem by mounting one contact piece on the arbor of
another clock movement. Metallic spring contacts, one pressing on each
side of the contact disc, polished the disc as it was rotated by the clock.
Two light platinum wires on the galvanometer boom formed 'fork'
contacts at its tip, one on either side of the disc, and the electromagnet
circuits were completed when one or other of the wires touched the disc. A
high-resistance shunt across the electromagnets prevented sparking at the
contact discs which might have damaged the surfaces of the discs. A
cut-out was arranged at each end of the travel of the pen carriage to break
the electromagnet circuits and prevent the pen running off the chart.

General view

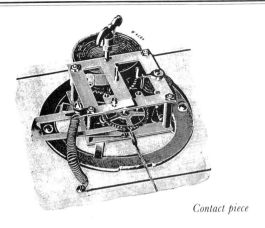

Contact piece

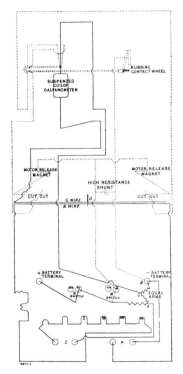

Circuit diagram

Figure 12.1 Callendar's recorder c. 1899. (Photo: C.S.I.Co., Neg. 656.)

Inside the chart drum was yet another clock mechanism. The drum could be coupled to either the minute arbor or the hour arbor of this clock by clamping the appropriate end of the axial spindle to its support bracket, thus giving one drum revolution per hour or 12 hours respectively.

In the Company's catalogue the recorder was offered for use in a number of different applications including temperature measurement by resistance thermometer or thermocouple, recording electrical parameters i.e. resistance, voltage, current or power, meteorological recording such as sunshine intensity, humidity, wind velocity and direction, and barometric pressure, steam temperature and pressure, tide level recording etc. But perhaps the most significant feature was that the recorder could be fitted with a simple regulator and thus act as a recorder-controller. To quote from the 1901 catalogue: 'The cord which moves the recording pen is made to work a small balanced valve which admits or shuts off the pressure one side or the other of a piston according as the temperature or pressure is too high or too low. The piston works the damper or gas cock as the case may be.[4]

Some five or six years after The Cambridge Scientific Instrument Company began making Callendar's recorder it became clear that there was also a need for a simpler, and cheaper, recorder; one that would also be suitable for use with the low e.m.f. thermocouples available at that time. It was this that prompted Darwin to design his well-known 'thread recorder'.[5]

The thread recorder was, in concept, an extremely simple instrument and because of this simplicity it proved over the years to be an

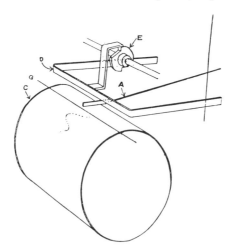

Figure 12.2 Operating principle of the thread recorder. A, galvanometer pointer; C, chart; D, chopper bar; E, cam; G, inked thread. (Diagram: C.S.I.Co., Neg. 621.)

extremely reliable instrument. Basically it consisted of a galvanometer with a long hinged pointer or 'boom' ('A' in *Fig.* 12.2) which pressed an inked thread G against a paper chart C at minute or half-minute intervals. The chopper bar D which performed this action was raised and lowered by a cam E driven by a clockwork motor. This motor also caused the inked thread to traverse slowly from a spool on one side of the instrument to a take-up spool on the opposite side. A second motor powered the mechanism which rotated the drum carrying the paper chart. In later models of the instrument both motors were replaced by synchronous electric motors.

Because the galvanometer pointer was only in contact with the chopper bar for a small portion of each dotting cycle, the accuracy of indication was very good, there being no frictional drag as is inherent in continuous writing systems where the pen is constantly in contact with the chart paper. A further advantage of the recorder was that the method of recording gave rectangular co-ordinates, like the record from Callendar's recorder, which made the records much easier to understand. The fact that the record consisted of a series of dots and not a continuous line was not a significant disadvantage, since most industrial processes have long time constants and the dots thus tended to produce a continuous record.

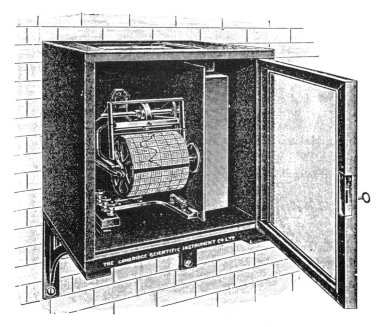

Figure 12.3 Thread recorder c. 1906. (Photo: C.S.I.Co. Catalogues 1905–11, List No. 39.)

Fig. 12.3 shows an early thread recorder, *c.* 1906. Double thread recorders, which were fitted with two independent galvanometers, recording side by side on a common double width chart, were also made. Later models of the instrument included multipoint recorders with thread frames for two or three different coloured inked threads. The threads were brought sequentially under the galvanometer boom by a rocking mechanism, driven by the 'chopping' motor. The mechanism also operated a signal selector switch. Four or six distinct records could thus be obtained on a double width chart.

The galvanometer thread recorder continued in production for about sixty years until, about 1970, it became obsolescent with the introduction of cheap electronic servo-systems.

*   *   *   *   *

CHAPTER THIRTEEN

A portable industrial galvanometer

1903 Robert Paul's Unipivot galvanometer

IT was during the winter of 1819–20 that Hans Christian Oersted made his discovery that a magnetic needle was deflected by the current in an adjacent wire—a finding which laid the foundation for the electromagnetic detection and measurement of electrical current. According to tradition the original discovery was made by chance at one of Oersted's lectures for advanced students at the University of Copenhagen. As part of a demonstration he closed a battery circuit and happened to notice a small deflection in a magnetic needle nearby. Excitedly he announced the result to the class and invited the students to make the experiment for themselves. The long sought after secret of the connection between electricity and magnetism had been uncovered.[1]

Oersted commenced a series of experiments to confirm the effects he had observed, and to test the effect on the movement of a magnetic needle of interposing a variety of materials between it and the wire. None of those that he tested had any appreciable effect. He published the results of his experiments (in Latin) in July 1820.[2] They immediately attracted widespread interest and stimulated much further experimenting amongst his contemporaries, one of whom was André Marie Ampère. Building on Oersted's experimental results Ampère established the relationship between the current in the wire and its magnetic field.[3] But equally important from the point of view of the history of electrical instrumentation, although not so well known, was the work done by a German chemist named Schweigger after hearing of Oersted's experiments.

The first movements of the magnetic needle observed by

Oersted in front of his class had been minute and his reaction was to make a bigger battery for use in his experiments but, in September 1820, a bare two months after the publication of Oersted's original paper, Schweigger announced his own method of increasing the deflection of the magnetic needle. Observing that the deflection produced by a current flowing in a wire over a needle was the same as that for a reverse current in the wire under the needle, he wound the wire in a complete loop and obtained, as he expected, twice the effect. By increasing the number of turns the effect was further magnified, in direct proportion to the number of turns.

Using this principle Schweigger constructed an instrument consisting of a small compass box around which was coiled several turns of copper wire in a direction parallel to the meridian line of the card. He called this first crude instrument a 'multiplier' but before long it was being referred to by other experimenters as a 'galvanometer'.[4]

In Schweigger's simple instrument the deflecting force produced by the current was balanced by the restoring force from terrestrial magnetism. Ampère realised that if the effect of terrestrial magnetism could be neutralised, or at least greatly reduced, the deflection of the needle would be much increased. In his memoir of 1821 he proposed the concept of astatic control in which two magnetic needles, magnetised in opposite directions, were mounted on a common shaft, one above the coil of wire carrying the current, and the other below it. The magnetic field from the current in the wire would then produce a turning force on both needles in the same direction whilst the restoring force from the earth's magnetic field was effectively neutralised. This technique was later refined by the Italian physicist Leopaldo Nobili.

For a number of years galvanometers were only used to detect current, or to give a very approximate indication of magnitude. In these early instruments the deflection of the magnetic needle was not proportional to the current, mainly because for large deflections the poles of the magnet emerged from the coil. In 1837 Pouillet constructed a galvanometer with a short magnet and in this instrument the tangent of the angle of deflection (or its sine, depending on the method of use) was directly proportional to the current in the coil.[5]

However, a few years before this, Sturgeon conceived the idea of turning the system inside out and he designed the first galvanometer with a moving coil.[6] Highton used this device in 1856 as a telegraphic receiver and in 1867 Sir William Thomson (Lord Kelvin) significantly improved the design, and then used it in his syphon recorder which replaced the mirror telegraph receivers.[7] Thomson's improvement consisted of placing a cylindrical iron core inside the coil so as to concentrate the magnetic field in which the coil rotated. In 1882 d'Arsonval further refined this system in his sensitive dead-beat mirror galvanometer.[8,9]

Although suitably modified galvanometers, such as d'Arsonval's, could be used as direct reading current meters, their use was restricted to laboratory conditions and the first practical ammeters were moving iron meters. Kohlrausch, in 1876, invented a moving iron meter in which an iron core was drawn into a solenoid[10] and in 1879 Ayrton and Perry made a portable ammeter in which a light magnetic needle, suspended between the poles of a magnet, was deflected by the current passed through a fixed coil adjacent to the magnetic gap.

The first pivoted moving coil ammeter was designed by Weston of New Jersey in 1888. His work has formed the basis for the design of general purpose voltmeters and ammeters to the present day. The pivoted system had several advantages over the suspended movement. The latter required accurate levelling in use; suspensions were fragile and easily broken so that the instrument could only be used under vibration-free conditions in a laboratory. But a suspended system did have a high sensitivity, whereas a pivoted movement required much greater power for full-scale deflection and its sensitivity was limited by pivot friction. Even with the coil clamped for transit the pivots were still in contact with the jewelled bearings and easily damaged by accidental shock.

In 1903 Robert Paul overcame many of these drawbacks in his design of the Unipivot galvanometer, which combined the high sensitivity of the d'Arsonval movement with a robustness even greater than that of the double pivot type of Weston meter.[11] The coil was supported on a single pivot resting in a jewel cup at the centre of a spherical iron core (made in two halves and bolted together). A cylindrical spiral spring attached to the top of the coil provided the controlling force without taking any of the weight of the coil assembly and the current feed was via this spring and a flexible ligament at the lower end of the coil.

The instrument did not require levelling before use as the centre of gravity of the moving coil assembly coincided with the pivot and the control spring provided sufficient force to keep the coil assembly in the normal position even when the instrument was tilted. It was also claimed that this system of neutral equilibrium made the instrument suitable for use where considerable mechanical vibration was present e.g. on board ship or in a tube train. At the same time the instrument could be made very sensitive electrically: down to $0.2\,\mu A$ f.s.d. (with a 1000-ohm coil) or $20\,mV$ f.s.d. (with a 10-ohm coil). Dynamometer Unipivots were also made, with the magnet replaced by a pair of fixed coils.[12]

Paul made his instrument portable by fitting a simple and efficient locking device which held the coil away from the pivot jewel during transit. It was a system of which he was very proud, as Robert Whipple recalled after Paul's death in 1943: '... He (Paul) was fond of demonstrating the efficiency of the clamping device by throwing the

Figure 13.1 *Movement from large Unipivot galvanometer with one polepiece removed, c. 1955. H, spring defining movement sensitivity; K, coil lift for transit use; L, phosphor-bronze current ligament; P, pointer; S, spherical iron core; Z, zero adjust; l_1, l_2, lugs engaging with zero adjust control in case. (Photo: C.S.I.Co., Neg. 8965.)*

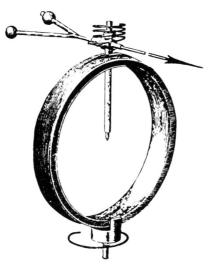

Figure 13.2 *Unipivot coil assembly. (Photo: C.S.I.Co.—Robert Paul's Catalogue, c. 1914.)*

galvanometer in its leather case downstairs, or even using it as a football.'[13]

Paul designed an extensive range of Unipivot instruments—indeed, 126 pages in his 1914 catalogue were devoted to them. In a clever piece of advertising he also adopted 'Unipivot London' as the telegraphic address for his New Southgate works. Manufacture of many of the Unipivot instruments continued when Paul's business was amalgamated with The Cambridge Scientific Instrument Company and the 'Pattern L' indicators continued in production until about 1968.

* * * * *

CHAPTER FOURTEEN

The recording of alternating current waveforms

1897 Duddell's oscillograph

THE key event which made possible the mechanical generation of electricity was Faraday's discovery of the principles of electromagnetic induction—principles which he demonstrated before the Royal Society on 24 November, 1831.[1] Within a matter of only two or three years of the publication of his work simple electromagnetic generators were being made commercially. All of these early generators produced alternating current electricity, which was at the time considered to be a serious disadvantage, so a commutator was usually employed to convert the output to direct current.

For about half a century the mechanical generation of electricity was largely only of interest to scientists but during the latter part of the nineteenth century a series of inventions caused a major expansion in the new field of electrical engineering. Swan's demonstration of a practical incandescent filament lamp in 1878 produced an immediate demand for electric lighting, and the provision of public electricity supplies. The telegraph was by that time firmly established but demonstrations of a new invention called the telephone were attracting world-wide interest. There was a need for improved specialised educational facilities for electrical engineers in Great Britain and on 1 November, 1879, the City and Guilds of London Institute at Finsbury was established. The post of Professor was given to Ayrton (a former pupil of Lord Kelvin) who, with his colleague Perry, had been instrumental in the setting up of the college.

By the 1890s the merits of alternating current electricity were becoming increasingly recognised. It began to be appreciated that for long-distance transmission, power losses were much lower with high voltages than with low voltages, whilst the conversion of high-voltage alternating current to low voltage for domestic use was easily accomplished with a transformer. But the science of alternating current engineering was still very much in its infancy and the study of alternating current waveforms still required the slow, laborious plotting of individual points—the method first used by Wheatstone about 1860 and by Joubert in 1880[2]—since there was no method of displaying a complete waveform.

William du Bois Duddell's association with the Finsbury Technical College has already been mentioned. During the late years of the nineteenth century the college under Professor Ayrton became a power house of instrument design for the fast expanding electricity supply industry. Both Robert Paul and Duddell were stimulated to make their own contributions to instrument design as a result of their association with the work going on there.

During 1896–7 Duddell and E. W. Marchant (later appointed Professor of Electrical Engineering at the University of Liverpool, but at that time a fellow student at the college) were plotting voltage and current waveforms of various types of alternating current arcs, point by point, using a modified form of reflecting quadrant electrometer. Each curve took at least an hour to plot, even when the experiments went well, which frequently they did not, as the phosphor-bronze spring contacts were continually fracturing. The frustrations of the technique spurred Duddell to consider possible designs for a galvanometer which would have a sufficiently fast response to follow the alternating current waveforms.

Duddell's idea was not a new one and several other experimenters were trying to achieve the same end by various methods. Before deciding on his own approach Duddell meticulously reviewed their work.[3] That of Blondel, the French scientist, seemed to Duddell to hold the most promise and he was attracted by Blondel's idea that a skeleton d'Arsonval galvanometer, reduced to only its bifilar suspension, might be used as an oscillograph, even though Blondel's own attempt to make such an instrument had failed because of the difficulty of damping the loop of wire effectively.[4,5,6] Furthermore, Ayrton and Mather had been experimenting along these lines with one and two wires in a stong magnetic field during 1895–6 and their data was freely available to Duddell.

Despite the thoroughness of his survey Duddell did overlook the work of Ewing, who, in 1892, had already described what was in effect a 'string' galvanometer with the conducting fibre attached to a small pivoted mirror. Ewing had used this instrument for tracing magnetisation curves which may account for it escaping notice as a reflecting mirror galvanometer.[7,8]

In his laboratory and workshop at the top of his house at Hans Place, Duddell began to make experimental fast-response galvanometers, often working late into the night. At times his friend, Marchant, helped him with the work and, some fifty years later Professor Marchant related his memories of that time:[9]

> '*Duddell started to use flat phosphor-bronze strips specially rolled for him by Johnson and Matthey. These were arranged between the poles of a strong electromagnet, and in the first instrument the strip was kept taut by weights, hung on a wire, passing over a pulley at the end of the base of the instrument. This cumbrous arrangement was soon replaced by a spring balance. The next problem was to find a mirror that could be attached to the strips, to indicate their deflection. The mirror had to be as light as possible and the glass surface absolutely flat and even, to give regular reflection. The thinnest glass we could think of was the cover glass for a microscope slide. The cover glasses were tested for flatness and equal thinness over their whole area by examining the interference fringes produced by a monochromatic sodium light, a method now used universally by the makers of flat mirrors and lenses; but, at that time, a novel means of testing. Having found a suitable glass, it was next silvered, and Duddell took endless trouble to find the best and most adherent silvering solution to employ; then the mirror had to be attached to the strips and this again was carefully thought out. If the mirror was stuck to the strips by resin, it would almost inevitably be twisted and distorted in the process, so four tiny dots of resin were first put on the strip, and the glass carefully placed in position on them. In this way a perfectly flat mirror was obtained and a definite spot observed when a beam of light was reflected from the surface.*
>   *The problem of getting enough light to make the instrument of any practical use was difficult. The mirror could not be too large or its weight would reduce the periodic time of the strips and mirror too much. I had fortunately been working on the solution of the equation of motion of a stretched wire with a load attached at its centre, and was able to give some help in calculating the most suitable distribution of weight and thus determining the largest mirror that could be used, without altering the periodic time too much. After that part of the instrument had been completed, the question of the best light system was discussed, and this again involved much careful study. Such details as the choice of a damping oil which had nearly the same refractive index as glass was carefully considered, and the use of a mixture of castor oil and clock oil provided the immediate solution.*'

In the autumn of 1897 Duddell presented a paper at the British Association Meeting in Toronto in which he announced the results of his work. He was able to describe not only the design of a successful oscillograph galvanometer but also the dual unit which he had recently constructed, with two 'vibrator' systems, one to record current and the other potential.[10]

Fig. 14.1 shows the construction principle of Duddell's vibrating

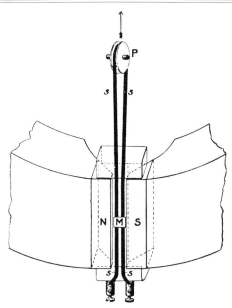

Figure 14.1 Principal components of the vibrating system in a Duddell oscillograph. M, mirror; P, pulley; s, strip. (Diagram: C.S.I.Co. Catalogues 1902–05, List No. 20.)

system.[11] The pulley *P* at the upper end of the loop *s* was supported by a light spring balance, enabling the period of the instrument to be varied by changing the tension in the loop. Typical dimensions for the strip *s* were width 0·18 mm and thickness 0·008 mm. The vibrating system was mounted between the poles of a specially designed horseshoe electromagnet. Each leg of the loop *s* passed through a slot in a soft iron armature (with a clearance of only 0·04 mm) and the system was damped by filling these slots with oil.

The electromagnet was energised by a series of toroidal coils, the magnetic circuit being saturated by a relatively small energising current. Duddell paid particular attention to the shape of the pole pieces so as to ensure that the magnetic flux was concentrated at exactly the desired point. The coils, too, were wound on special formers, wide at the base and tapering towards the top. When the coils had been impregnated with wax or thin shellac these formers were removed and the coils were then slid on to the magnet, oiled silk insulation being used to wedge them firmly in position. *Fig.* 14.2 shows a dual system galvanometer *c.* 1900.

Duddell succeeded in obtaining an extremely fast response from his vibrator: a periodic time of the order of 0·1 milliseconds. With a loop resistance of 4 ohms and a normal working current of 50 to 100 mA the galvanometer would produce a deflection of 290 mm per ampere on a

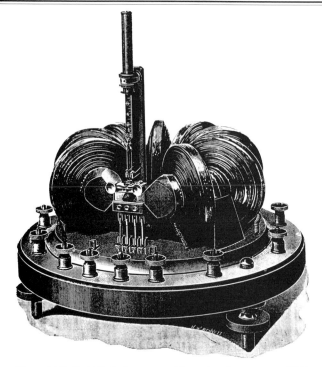

Figure 14.2 Duddell dual system oscillograph galvanometer c. 1900.
(Photo: Engineering, 1900, Vol. 69, p 583.)

scale 500 mm from the vibrator.[12] A complete oscillograph system, *c.* 1902
is shown in *Fig.* 14.3. A beam of light from the lantern was reflected from
the galvanometer mirror on to a rocking mirror driven by a synchronous
motor. This latter mirror reflected the waveform upwards on to the
translucent tracing desk.

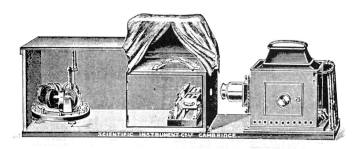

Figure 14.3 Cut-away illustration showing double oscillograph, syn-
chronous motor, tracing desk and lantern all mounted on baseboard
c. 1902. (Photo: C.S.I.Co. Catalogues 1902–05, List No. 20.)

The Cambridge Scientific Instrument Company began to manufacture these oscillographs in 1898 and Duddell's original drawings for their construction are preserved in the Cambridge University Library.[13] Many design improvements were made during the next fifty years, while the instrument remained in the Company's sales catalogue—the vibrator, in particular, becoming a compact, replaceable unit as new magnetic materials were developed—but the basic design changed little from Duddell's original concept.

*   *   *   *   *

CHAPTER FIFTEEN

The history of the electrocardiograph

IN 1855, five years before Willem Einthoven was born, Kölliker and Müller first demonstrated the presence of an action current in the heart.[1] In addition, by laying a frog's nerve muscle preparation in contact with the heart, they were able to show two distinct electrical discharges at each beat of the ventricle. Their observations were continued by a number of workers, and in particular by Burdon Sanderson in the early 1880s, who used early types of rheotomes and galvanometers as detectors.[2,3] In 1887 Dr A. D. Waller, using a Lippman capillary electrometer, became the first person to record photographically the changing electrical potentials associated with each beat of the human heart[4,5,6] and although Bayliss and Starling are credited with obtaining the first true electrocardiograms, in 1892,[7] the term 'electrocardiogram' is believed to have been originated by Waller.

Neither the Lippman capillary electrometer nor the Thomson galvanometer, sometimes used by Waller, were anything like ideal instruments for monitoring heart currents. It was this need for an instrument better suited to the problem which attracted Einthoven's attention during the late 1890s, at about the same time as William Duddell was working on the design of his oscillograph. In many respects the problems which the two men faced were very similar, although they do not seem initially to have been aware of each other's work.

Einthoven began his experiments by attempting to develop a highly sensitive d'Arsonval moving coil galvanometer. By decreasing the number of turns on the coil he minimised the moment of inertia and shortened the response time until eventually, like Duddell, he had reduced the galvanometer to a single turn system. Einthoven was not satisfied. The next step was to discard the bifilar loop and instead stretch a single fibre in a strong magnetic field. This was not a new concept. Ayrton and Perry had experimented with single wire galvanometers in 1895–6 and in 1897 Ader had published a paper describing a single wire detector for use in cable telegraphy. Again, Einthoven was not aware of this work and, in any case, Ader's detector was relatively insensitive, although it did have a short period.[8]

Ideally, Einthoven needed an instrument with a high internal resistance, a dead-beat fast response, and high sensitivity coupled with good stability to allow accurate calibration. As sensitivity was normally obtained with a sacrifice of period and stability this presented a considerable problem, but, by 1903, using a silver-plated quartz fibre, Einthoven had an experimental instrument which worked well. The shadow of the fibre or 'string' was projected by a specially designed microscope system, the movement of the shadow being photographed on a falling photographic plate. Einthoven published his work in a paper entitled 'Ein neues Galvanometer'[9] and a year later, in 1904, this paper was followed by another in which Einthoven compared the results obtained by Waller, using a capillary electrometer, with his own 'electrocardiograms' using a string galvanometer. Einthoven was able to show that without a doubt the string galvanometer did produce highly accurate records of heart currents and effectively made the use of the capillary electrometer obsolete.[10]

Einthoven's instrument (*Fig.* 15.1) was extremely bulky and unwieldy. The massive electromagnet was surrounded by a water jacket for cooling and the whole equipment was very much an experimental system. But having designed a functional detector Einthoven had no great interest in refining his design. Instead he wished to concentrate on using his instrument to develop techniques for taking electrocardiograms. He therefore approached both The Cambridge Scientific Instrument Company and Edelmann in Germany, suggesting to each company that they should design 'electrocardiographs' based on his experimental design and market them under royalty agreements whilst he concentrated on using his own instrument to develop techniques for taking electrocardiograms. Edelmann agreed and initially made what was virtually a copy of the Einthoven instrument. Later they introduced many design improvements until an unfortunate dispute occurred between Edelmann and Einthoven. The German company discovered the earlier publications of Ader and decided to consider their agreement on royalties void. The acrimony of

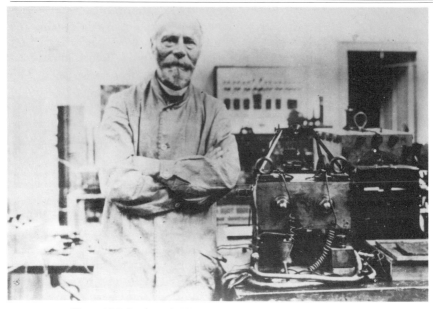

Figure 15.1 Professor Willem Einthoven in his laboratory at Leiden University with his original string galvanometer. (Photo: C.S.I.Co., Neg. 8478.)

this dispute had a great effect on Einthoven. For many years he distrusted commercial enterprises, particularly German companies, and contact with him became very difficult, Einthoven insisting on secrecy and confidentiality in almost all communications until he had himself published the subject matter.

Horace Darwin's reaction to Einthoven's approach was much more cautious than Edelmann's. Robert Whipple went to Leiden to look at the equipment. At first sight Einthoven's experimental electrocardiograph did not appear to be a commercial proposition. It occupied two rooms and required five people to operate it. In fact it was not until the publication of Einthoven's later paper in 1908, 'Weiteres uber das Elektrokardiogram', that the full significance of the invention as a diagnostic tool became apparent.[11]

Initially, therefore, Darwin concentrated on the string galvanometer as a marketable item on its own. With Einthoven's approval he commissioned Duddell to redesign it so as to obtain a more manufacturable product. This Duddell did very successfully in 1905, receiving a fee of £10.10s.0d, and a royalty of 5% on the list price of all string galvanometers sold.[12] Hardly a princely sum when one considers the amount of work Duddell had to do.

The heat dissipated by the powerful electromagnet had been a major problem in Einthoven's prototype. Since the quartz fibre and its metal mount had different coefficients of expansion any significant rise in temperature caused the tension in the fibre to increase and, thus, changed the sensitivity. Einthoven had minimised temperature variations by surrounding the electromagnet with a continuous-flow water jacket, but this was a cumbrous solution. Duddell attacked the problem at its source. He redesigned the magnetic circuit, improving its efficiency by making the field in the string gap more concentrated and by reducing magnetic leakage. In this way he was able to use an electromagnet which was considerably smaller whilst maintaining the field strength at 20 000 gauss compared to Einthoven's original 22 000 gauss. Keeping the smaller electromagnet, with its reduced heat dissipation, well away from the quartz fibre and utilising the inherent thermal capacity of the iron magnet castings, Duddell was then able to dispense with the water-cooled jacket. As a final refinement he proposed a 'carrier' for the fibre so that it would be completely enclosed during use, thus eliminating the effects of draughts and any residual convection currents. The overall result of his work was an extremely robust and stable system.

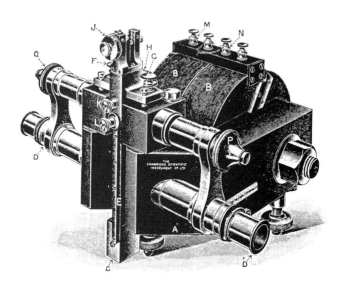

Figure 15.2 Einthoven string galvanometer c. 1908. A electromagnet; B field coil; C fibre carrier; D microscope; E fibre; F, G fibre carrier clamping screws; H fibre carrier position adjusting screw; J fibre tension adjustment; K, L terminal connections to fibre; M, N field coil terminals. (Photo: C.S.I.Co. Catalogues 1905–11, List No. 53.)

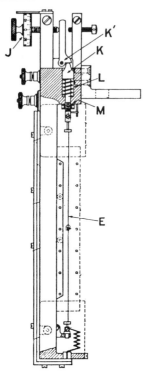

*Figure 15.3 Sectioned diagram of fibre carrier c. 1908. E, fibre; J,
fibre tension adjustment; K, spring-loaded piston; K′, bell-crank lever;
L, spring; M, collar to limit fibre tension. (Diagram C.S.I.Co.,
Neg. 730.)*

The first string galvanometer to be produced by The Cambridge Scientific Instrument Company was made about 1907. An early
instrument is shown in *Fig.* 15.2, with a sectioned diagram of the string
carrier in *Fig.* 15.3. The operating principle is shown in *Fig.* 15.4. The
movement of the fibre in the intense magnetic field could either be viewed
through the microscope D or an enlarged image could be projected on to
a screen. Adjusting the tension of the fibre changed its period and
sensitivity. This was effected by means of the micrometer screw J (*Figs.*
15.2 and 15.3), the screw adjusting the position of the spring-loaded bell
crank lever K′. The fibre carrier was supported at three points, one
bearing point being adjustable by screw H so that the fibre (visible
through the mica window shown dashed in *Fig.* 15.3) could be aligned in
the field of view of the microscope.

The sensitivity of the galvanometer was very high; a current of
only 0·1 μA would cause the fibre to deflect 1 mm. Since the mass of the

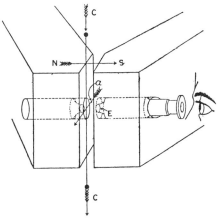

Figure 15.4 Operating principle of the string galvanometer. a, direction of fibre deflection; C, C, direction of current through fibre; E, microscope. (Diagram: C.S.I.Co., Neg. 741.)

fibre was only about 1 microgramme it had a very low moment of inertia and the period was about 0·005 seconds. Typically the resistance of the plated fibre would be about 4 000 ohms but detectors with various characteristics could be produced by changing the amount of plating.[13]

Although the entry in the 1908 edition of the Company's catalogue of electrical instruments pointed out that the galvanometer had originally been developed for physiological work, and gave examples of Einthoven's electrocardiograms, it was stressed that the instrument might be used wherever records of small alternating or pulsating currents were required. In particular its use during shipboard insulation testing of submarine cables was postulated, because of its mechanical stability. Whether the instrument was ever used for this purpose is not known but a few years later, during the 1914–18 war, it was used to register the microphone signals in the sound-ranging equipment.

The first Cambridge Electrocardiograph was completed in 1911 and supplied 'on hire' with right to purchase to Dr Thomas Lewis. It was installed in his laboratory in the basement of University College Hospital, London. Over the years Dr Lewis made great advances in the science of electrocardiography as a clinical and diagnostic tool and he and The Cambridge Scientific Instrument Company worked closely together to this end. Indeed, for many years the Company would not market any new piece of cardiographic equipment until it had been thoroughly tested and approved by Dr Lewis.

By the time Dr Lewis retired from cardiographic work, about 1930, his laboratory contained a considerable amount of experimental equipment from the Company. When the time came for the hospital administration to resume responsibility for the laboratory and to take inventory of the equipment it was discovered that, by accident, the rent for his original cardiograph had never been paid, nor had the right to purchase been exercised. Over the years the amount of indebtedness had reached quite a high figure. The matter was raised somewhat jokingly with Dr Lewis who, horrified, at once insisted that the Medical Research Council should make a nominal payment to the Company. In return the Company then formally gave all the apparatus in the laboratory to University College Medical School.

During the three years between 1911, when Dr Lewis' instrument was delivered, and the outbreak of war in 1914, the Company manufactured about thirty-five cardiographs, ten of which were for orders from the USA. This was quite a good performance when one considers the complexity of the equipment at that time.

The operating principles of the cardiograph are shown in *Fig.* 15.5. An arc lantern with condensing lenses was used to strongly illuminate the fibre. The field of the objective was projected on to a cylindrical lens which focused part of it into an intensely bright band of light in the plane of the photographic plate (or paper). The fibre appeared in front of the lens as a long vertical shadow about a millimetre wide, the part striking the cylindrical lens becoming a dark spot in the band of light falling on the photographic plate. Thus when the plate was moved vertically downwards behind the cylindrical lens all the plate was exposed except for the portion hidden by the shadow of the fibre, which moved horizontally, parallel to the length of the cylindrical lens. The unexposed portion of the photograph thus formed the cardiographic record.

A horizontal slit, whose vertical aperture was adjustable, was placed between the cylindrical lens and the photographic plate. This enabled maximum detail in the record to be obtained, consistent with a good level of illumination. Vertical lines engraved at precise intervals on the cylindrical lens produced amplitude lines along the photograph whilst a time marker interrupted the light at regular intervals to produce time lines on the record.

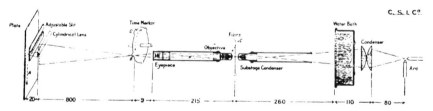

Figure 15.5 Operating principle of the electrocardiograph. The distances between the components are given in millimetres. (Diagram: C.S.I.Co., Neg. B601.)

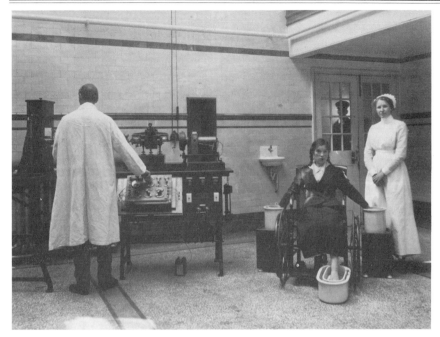

Figure 15.6 Cardiograph in use with immersion electrodes c. 1922.
(Photo: C.S.I.Co.)

All the controls, including the lead selector switch, standardising switch and a skin current compensator were mounted on a control board. Skin current was balanced out by an equal and opposite current from a tapped potential slidewire which had its centre point at zero volts. Standardisation of the instrument was effected by injecting a one-millivolt signal into the patient circuit and adjusting the fibre tension to obtain a deflection of 10 mm on the camera scale.[14]

The quartz 'strings' in the Company's early galvanometers were made using Professor C. V. Boys' method, which was to shoot a light arrow from a tightly strung bow, a filament of fused quartz being attached to the tail of the arrow.[15] The stretched filament, usually about twenty feet long, was collected by winding it on a sticky wooden frame. Selection of suitable portions of fibre for use was a long and tedious process and, about 1913, Keith Lucas designed a process to make strings from hard glass using a small electric furnace. A glass rod was first drawn out by hand in a Bunsen flame to about 0·2 mm in diameter and short lengths were then hung vertically in the cylindrical cavities in the furnace. Each length was weighted with a glass bead. When the heater was switched on the glass slowly became plastic and the descending weight drew out a glass fibre. A fair amount of skill was required to determine the exact moment when the furnace should be switched off: too soon, and the resulting string would be too thick; too late, and the glass would become too plastic so that the weight would fall to the ground.

Selected strings of about 0·003 mm in diameter were mounted with shellac on a wooden frame and chemically plated with silver. The plating operation was also difficult to control, the silver deposit varying greatly for no apparent reason. Sometimes it was thin and practically non-existent; at other times thick and spongy. The optimum string resistance was about 3 000 ohms and these strings were selected to be soldered into carriers using low melting point solder. When each string was mounted its tension was roughly checked by lightly blowing on it and observing the magnitude and frequency of movement. The last, and most delicate, operation was to clean and burnish the string by gently stroking it with a thin polished wire. If the string survived this process the carrier was closed and final adjustments made in the galvanometer. Perhaps surprisingly, the finished result was often very durable and in some cases a single string would give over twenty years' service.

Einthoven must himself have experienced difficulties in obtaining an evenly-deposited covering of silver on the fibre by chemical plating. As early as 1910 he was experimenting with cathodic bombardment of quartz fibres with silver ions. By 1911 he was successfully coating fibres in this way and details of the process were confidentially communicated to The Cambridge Scientific Instrument Company. This process was not in fact used by the Company, although Hindle in the USA adopted the technique some years afterwards. However, the Cambridge Company in England did later coat hard glass fibres with gold by ionic bombardment, a process which remained in use for many years.

Although actual string breakage in the instrument was rare, fractures in the silver coating were quite common, the string then becoming open-circuit. These fractures usually occurred at the ends where the string was soldered to its support, or in the centre if the string tension had been relaxed too far so that it floated to the side of the carrier and rubbed. With Duddell's design it was a relatively easy matter to insert a spare string, which was supplied in its carrier as a replaceable unit. However, locating the image of a new string, or finding one from a string that had been excessively loosened, could cause considerable exasperation. With a very short focus objective and a string only 0·003 mm in diameter it is not difficult to imagine how easily the image could be lost. A displacement of the string carrier of only 0·1 mm or a slight change in the tension of the retaining spring on the displacement adjustment for the string would take the string completely out of the field of view. To find it again, and to re-centre it, was an operation that required considerable practice and patience. A distracted physician would often spend fruitless hours searching for the image before finally, in desperation, calling on the

Company for assistance. As might be expected reactions were often somewhat mixed when the Company technician arrived, after travelling a considerable distance, and showed that the adjustment only took a matter of minutes if tackled systematically.

Heat generated by the arc lamp was also a source of trouble, since the microscope focused the beam on to the string and concentrated heat at this point. To reduce this effect a water bath with two windows was placed between the arc lamp and the microscope. Much of the infra-red radiation was absorbed—but nurtured the growth of fungi and other organisms which in time absorbed much of the illuminating power of the 15-ampere arc lamp. About 1921 the water bath was dispensed with when the arc lamp was replaced by the 'point-o-lite' lamp, which was also a much more stable source of light than the flickering arc lamp.

To provide a time-base for his records Einthoven had used a bicycle wheel with specially spaced spokes. The spokes cut the optical beam each 1/25th of a second, thus ruling a line on the photographic record. The early commercial instruments had electrically-maintained, tuned, vibrating reeds which marked either across the record or along the fringe.[16] Later small synchronous electric motors, controlled by a bar vibrating at a constant frequency, came into use.[17] These marked each 1/25th of a second, with a thicker line each 1/5th of a second. To get one of these motors to run satisfactorily it often had to be started manually by spinning the wheel steadily at exactly the synchronous speed. The process required a certain knack and was another source of frustration to many physicians, especially as it was possible for the motor to run at exactly double speed. The advantage of the system was its constant speed of rotation, locked into the natural frequency of the vibrating bar.

The standard three-lead electrocardiogram from right arm/left arm; right arm/left leg and left arm/left leg (named leads 1, 2 and 3) was established by Einthoven in his 1908 paper. In the same paper he also showed the true nature of the extra systole and gave examples of many of the more common abnormal rhythms. Einthoven also devoted considerable time to electrode design in order to obtain the best results. To eliminate polarisation effects his electrodes consisted of large earthenware baths containing a zinc electrode and an inner porous porcelain pot (*Fig. 15.6*). The inner vessel was filled with a 20% salt solution and the outer with zinc sulphate solution. The limb was immersed in the inner vessel and an electrical connection taken from the electrode in the outer.[18] The inner porous pots were often difficult to obtain and frequently caused a production bottleneck. By 1914 electrodes in the form of zinc trays each containing two pads, one saturated in zinc sulphate and the other in salt solution, were also in use. The palm of the hand or the base of the foot would be pressed in contact with the salt pad. Although not as good as the pot electrodes they were used for bedridden patients and were generally

Figure 15.7 Cardiograph with non-immersion tray electrodes c. 1914.
The third (leg) electrode is shown on a low stand in front of the
cardiograph. (Photo: C.S.I.Co., Neg. 1542.)

deemed more suitable for consulting room work (*Fig.* 15.7). In the 1920s strap electrodes began to be used in the United Kingdom and the USA, but the earthenware jars continued to be standard equipment until direct contact strap-on electrodes were introduced in 1929.

The growing use of AC power supplies in Great Britain in the 1920s introduced one of the most serious difficulties in the use of electrocardiographs—that of 50 Hz interference on the cardiograph records. Unfortunately the 50 Hz wave also corresponds very nearly to the somatic waves and physicians frequently mistook somatic waves for AC interference and vice versa. Careful insulation and earthing of the apparatus and the patient often eliminated the trouble. Sometimes, in extreme cases, it was found necessary to enclose the patient in a silk covering containing a metallized net fabric that could be connected to earth. Eventually it was discovered that the most effective solution was to connect to earth an unused additional electrode attached to the right leg of the patient.

The early cardiographs were all fixed installations, often in basements with reinforced concrete floors, as it was mistakenly believed that such a delicate instrument must be abnormally sensitive to vibration. This was not at all the case and, later, almost identical outfits were satisfactorily installed in rickety conditions in the upper rooms of older houses so often occupied by consultants. In hospitals it was often not practical to take the patient to the electrocardiograph room, so in many instances connecting wires were run from the ward to the instrument with a telephone link between the patient's nurse and the person operating the instrument. Einthoven pioneered this technique as early as 1905/6 when a link-up between his laboratory and Leiden Hospital created great excitement. In Cambridge in 1916 a similar link was made between the University Pathology Laboratory and Addenbrooke's Hospital, the connecting leads being carried on post office telephone poles. Satisfactory records were only obtained with difficulty and the connection was soon abandoned. Mobile outfits, mounted on wheels, were later introduced for hospital use.

Figure 15.8 Transportable cardiograph c. 1929. (Photo: C.S.I.Co., Neg. 4288.)

In 1929 a transportable design for consultancy use was produced,[19] (*Figs.* 15.8, 15.9) some time after its American counterpart. New magnet steels had made it possible to manufacture a permanent magnet

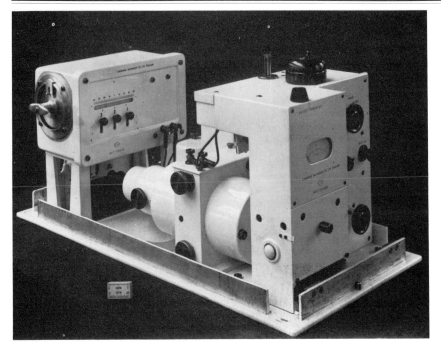

Figure 15.9 Transportable cardiograph with cover removed c. 1929.
(Photo: C.S.I.Co., Neg. 4380B.)

galvanometer which was only a fraction of the size and weight of the electromagnet model, but having similar characteristics. The fibre was shortened from 10 cm to 4 cm and the point-o-lite lamp replaced by a high intensity filament lamp. The time marker was clock driven and a new camera enabled films wrapped round a drum to be used and exposed in three sections. A portable developing tank was later introduced which allowed films to be processed at a patient's house. The weight of this new equipment was only 63 lb compared to the 336 lb of the old cardiograph, and its size only 2 ft by 1 ft. The whole outfit was driven from a 12-volt battery. When mounted on a trolley the unit formed a convenient mobile outfit and a large number of these equipments were made, the early instrument being discontinued.

The delay in marketing a transportable unit in this country was in part due to Dr Thomas Lewis's lack of enthusiasm for the project. He had doubts as to the practicability of attaining a performance equal to that of the larger instrument and would not be associated with anything that might be regarded as a retrograde step. The Cambridge Company therefore delayed production until extended tests of a prototype convinced Dr Lewis that the design was entirely satisfactory.

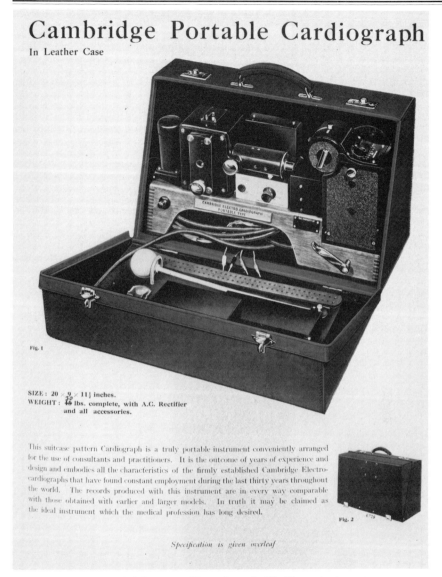

Cambridge Portable Cardiograph

In Leather Case

Fig. 1

SIZE : 20 × 9 × 11½ inches.
WEIGHT : 45 lbs. complete, with A.C. Rectifier
and all accessories.

This suitcase pattern Cardiograph is a truly portable instrument conveniently arranged
for the use of consultants and practitioners. It is the outcome of years of experience and
design and embodies all the characteristics of the firmly established Cambridge Electrocardiographs that have found constant employment during the last thirty years throughout
the world. The records produced with this instrument are in every way comparable
with those obtained with earlier and larger models. In truth it may be claimed as
the ideal instrument which the medical profession has long desired.

Fig. 2

Specification is given overleaf

*Figure 15.10 Suitcase portable cardiograph. The illustration is a repro-
duction of the front page of the 1944 publicity leaflet. (Photo:
C.S.I.Co. Catalogues 1944–52, Sheet 263.)*

Siemens and Halske in Germany were probably the first company to produce a portable electrocardiograph incorporating a valve
amplifier and oscillograph. With the advent of electronics a large number
of companies, not previously interested in cardiographs, but with elec-

tronics expertise, entered the market, particularly in the USA. Various advantages were claimed for these portable electronic instruments but for several years the Company was able to demonstrate that the Cambridge transportable provided adequate competition. The Company was also trading with the advantage of a good reputation established over a long period.

Valve instruments also appeared to be more prone to AC interference, and deterioration in the valve characteristics during use could distort the records obtained. Here the Company was on firm ground. Indeed, examination of some electrocardiograms taken on electronic instruments showed marked differences from those obtained with the Einthoven system, which was believed to be capable of accurately responding to the whole range of frequencies met with in the clinical electrocardiograms.

Figure 15.11 Electrite cardiograph c. 1952. (Photo: C.S.I.Co.,
Neg. 8517.)

Nevertheless, by the late 1930s, a new instrument was needed. The Second World War dictated other priorities. When the situation was reviewed towards the end of the war the management of the Company was reluctant to embark on a radical redesign using unfamiliar techniques. Furthermore, a careful design assessment showed that a much smaller and less expensive instrument using the Einthoven technique could be made. This instrument, the 'Cambridge Suitcase Portable' (*Fig.* 15.10), was put in production in 1944.[20] It was sold in the USA as the 'Simpli-trol' model. It was compact, weighed only 32 lb complete with all accessories and electrodes, simple to operate and produced records as good as those obtained from the earlier larger models.

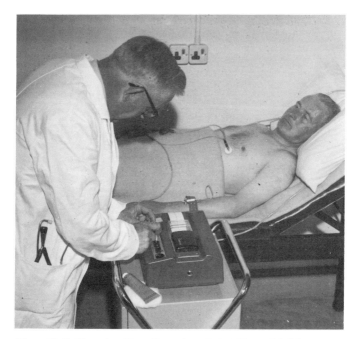

Figure 15.12 Transrite III cardiograph c. 1963. (Photo: C.S.I.Co.)

So far photographic recording had been used in all the Cambridge cardiographs. This had the obvious disadvantage that the photographs had to be processed before a diagnosis could be made, a situation which was found increasingly irksome in consultancy work away from the consulting room. In 1952 the first Cambridge direct-writing cardiograph, the 'Electrite', was produced[21] (sold in the USA as the 'Simpli-scribe') (*Fig.*15.11). And, equally significant, this was also the first Cambridge cardiograph to have a valve amplifier. The galvanometer had a heated stylus which 'wrote' on wax-coated recording paper. Gliding easily over this surface, with very little friction, the stylus produced a clear, permanent, black record as the wax was volatilised. About seven or eight years later the valve amplifier was replaced by a transistorised amplifier, the instrument being renamed the 'Transrite'.[22]

The Transrite was robustly housed in a light alloy case. Its performance was very good but it was strictly functional in appearance and after a relatively short period it was completely re-styled as the 'Transrite III' (*Fig.* 15.12). First marketed in 1963 the elegant appearance of this instrument matched the quality of its performance and, justifiably, the Transrite III proved to be exceptionally popular with medical users all over the world. Weighing only 20 lb, even when in a carrying case with accessories, it was a far cry from Einthoven's first instrument which occupied two rooms.[23]

The Transrite III was succeeded by the IIIA in 1965, with an improved amplifier.[24] The Mark IV, a restyled suitcase version without a separate carrying case was brought out in 1968. But it is the Transrite III that stands out as providing the greatest contrast with its predecessors. It was the product of a continuing evolutionary process, over a great many years, from teams of designers who all operated on the sound premise that no design change should ever be made unless the new instrument was at least as good as that which it was to replace.

*   *   *   *   *

CHAPTER SIXTEEN

The thermal conductivity method of gas analysis

1916 Shakespear's katharometer

IN his book *An Experimental Inquiry into the Nature and Properties of Heat* John Leslie described how, in the spring and summer of 1801, he retired to the 'calm seclusion' of his native Fifeshire to carry out a series of experiments to 'discover the nature, and ascertain the properties, of what is termed Radiant Heat'.[1] This was a subject which was attracting the attentions of a number of experimenters at that time, notable amongst them being John Dalton and Sir Benjamin Thompson (Count Rumford).[2,3] Leslie, however, appears to have been the first to experiment with different gases and, in his book, published in 1804 (and dedicated to his friend Thomas Wedgwood) he comments on the variation in cooling properties of these gases:[4]

> *The permanent gases differ as much from common air, perhaps, by their disposition to conduct heat, as by their density or other properties. The azotic and the oxygenous, indeed, seem to possess it nearly in the same degree. But carbonic gas abstracts the heat from a vitreous surface about an eighth part slower, and from a surface of metal one-fourth slower, than common air. By progressive rarefaction, that property is also reduced on a similar scale. Hydrogenous gas, however, is the most distinguished by its affection for heat, which it conducts with unusual energy.*

In making these observations Leslie unwittingly laid the foundations for the thermal conductivity method of gas analysis.

A few years later, in 1817, Sir Humphry Davy published the results of his experiments to determine the time taken for a heated thermometer to cool from a pre-defined temperature in various gases. In his memoir he commented on his experiments:[5]

*It appears from these experiments that the powers of elastic
fluids to abstract or conduct away heat from solid surfaces is in
some inverse ratio to their density, and that there is something in
the constitution of the light gases which enables them to carry off
heat from solid surfaces in a different manner from that in which
they would abstract it in gaseous mixtures, depending probably
upon the mobility of their parts.*

It was, however, Dr Thomas Andrews who took the next
significant step towards the design of the present-day gas analyser, when,
some twenty years later, he set out to improve on the inconsistencies in the
results of the earlier experimenters by using an electrically heated wire. In
a paper presented to the Royal Irish Academy in 1840 he described how,
with the wire at red heat in air, he first noted the changes in colour of the
conductor when immersed in various other gases. For each gas he then
measured the current flowing through a fixed length of the heated wire.
The higher the current, the greater the cooling power of the gas.[6] At the
time of Andrews' work, Pouillet and Sturgeon were still experimenting
with their newly invented electromagnetic instruments for current measurement, and Andrews had to use the conventional means of measuring
current of that era. This was to collect the hydrogen evolved in a small
electrolytic cell, connected in series with the wire, for a given period, in his
case, two minutes.

Similar experiments by Professor W. R. Grove during the next
few years confirmed Andrews' results,[7] but it was not until 1860 that
Magnus showed that even when convection cooling was virtually eliminated (by containing the gas within a tube of 1 mm diameter around the
wire) hydrogen produced a much more marked cooling effect than other
gases.[8,9]

During the 1880s both Bottomley and Schleiermacher carried
out series of experiments with electrically heated wires.[10,11,12,13] The
main aim of these experiments was the determination of the emissivities of
various wire surfaces, but during 1888–9 Schleiermacher also used the
method to determine the thermal conductivity of air, hydrogen, carbon
dioxide and mercury vapour. For his experiments he used a platinum wire
stretched along the axis of a glass tube which was immersed in a water
bath to provide a constant temperature heat sink. Its resistance (and thus
its temperature) was determined by measuring the potential drop along
the conductor and also across a fixed resistance in series with the wire,
using a high resistance galvanometer. End corrections were eliminated by
making potential measurements from two light auxiliary wires attached
to the hot platinum filament at a distance from the current input leads—a
new technique at that time.

Goldschmidt, in 1902, further improved the experimental
method by using a massive brass block as a heat sink and by using two

wires of different lengths, enclosed in silver capillary tubes and electrically connected in adjacent arms of a Wheatstone bridge network, to eliminate the effects of end resistance.[14,15]

The first suggestion that change in thermal conductivity might be used as a means of gas analysis is reputed to have been made about 1880 by Leon Somzée, a Belgian aristocrat and mining engineer. His proposal is said to have been noted in the Report of the 1880s Prussian Commission on Explosive Atmospheres, but, unfortunately without any details of the proposed method.[16] No other references to his idea are known but some twenty years later a German company, the Vereinigte Maschinenfabrik of Augsburg, took out the first patents on the thermal conductivity method of gas analysis, in both Germany and England.[17] These 1904 patents covered several different devices utilising variation in thermal conductivity as a means of determining the hydrogen content of producer gas and water gas. One involved the measurement of the resistance of an electrically heated wire in a closed tube but the company does not appear to have been able to follow up its patent by developing the idea into a practical technique.

However, four years later Koepsel did develop such a device for producer gas analysis. He claimed that he could easily detect 0·001% of hydrogen and also proposed the further use of his analyser for flue gas analysis (for carbon dioxide content) and for methane in mines. His analyser consisted of four electrically heated wires, connected as a Wheatstone bridge, the opposite arms being paired and exposed respectively to air and the gas to be analysed, i.e. a differential configuration. A relatively high gas flow was used and in order to prevent errors from forced convection the detecting wires were surrounded by thin mica cylinders with the ends closed by fine gauze. In addition, to ensure matched conditions, an equal flow of air was passed through the cells containing the reference arms exposed to air.[18,19]

Although Koepsel's apparatus did have the disadvantage that the two pairs of cells, reference and measuring, were mounted separately, and the measurement was thus susceptible to ambient temperature differences between the two pairs of cells, Koepsel foresaw a number of the chemical techniques which were subsequently to be made use of in this method of analysis. For example, he suggested the use of a gas other than air as a reference standard and the determination of one particular constituent in a complex mixture of gases by comparing the mixture with the residual gases after that constituent had been removed.

The German company, Siemens and Halske, refined Koepsel's experimental apparatus, eliminating the special housings for the wires, and in 1913 the company took out a German patent for this design.[20] The analyser incorporated one reference and one measuring cell, connected in series to ensure identical currents through each. To compare cell resistances the cells could either be connected in a bridge network or a differential galvanometer could be used, in which case each galvanometer coil was connected in parallel with a cell through a suitable resistance. The reference cell normally contained air, but provision was made for the gas being analysed to be passed through one cell, oxidised by a catalyst, and then passed back through the second cell in the analyser. One significant advance over Koepsel's design was the mounting of both cells in a single metal block to equalise their temperatures, but, like Koepsel's apparatus, the analyser was flow sensitive and the flow through both cells had to be equalised.

This was the state of the analysis technique when war was declared in Europe in 1914. In the early years of the war there arose the same need in both England and Germany to measure hydrogen leakage through balloon materials. In Germany the Siemens and Halske instrument was developed for this purpose. In England the Board of Inventions and Research turned to Dr Gilbert Shakespear at Birmingham University for help (no doubt because of his work early in the war on a chlorine meter for use in the trenches). A few years later, in an introductory note to H. A. Daynes' paper on the 'Theory of the Katharometer', presented at the Royal Society in 1920, Shakespear described the development of his hydrogen detector:[21]

> '*In September, 1915, at the request of a member of the Board of Invention and Research of the Admiralty, I undertook to devise an instrument capable of giving automatic indication of the presence of hydrogen in small quantities (e.g., 1 or 2 per cent) in air. The well-known surface-action of palladium and platinum wires suggested itself as a phenomenon obviously adapted to the purpose. The wire was used as two arms of a Wheatstone bridge, one of these arms being protected from the gas by a thin glass tube, the other being exposed. When a sufficiently great current of electricity was passed through the bridge, the exposed arm rapidly increased in temperature owing to surface combustion. The temperature, however, was liable to rise dangerously high if the hydrogen were present in suitable quantity, and, as safety from explosion was indispensable, this method was abandoned. The same apparatus was then applied with a much lower current, and with the wires consequently at a much lower temperature, to make use of the increase in thermal conductivity of the gas due to the admixture of hydrogen. This arrangement was found to be unexpectedly sensitive, and the method was adopted for the desired purpose. As the instrument was primarily intended to measure the purity of the air, the name 'katharometer' was given to it.*'

In its final form Shakespear's katharometer consisted of two small helices of thin platinum wire, about 0·001 inch in diameter, each enclosed in a cell in a copper block (*Fig.* 16.1). Each helix was mounted in a small frame, made from a loop of copper wire soldered to a ring of

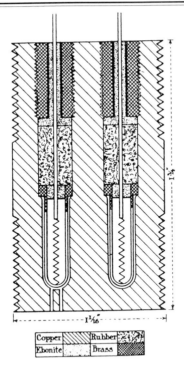

Figure 16.1 Diagram showing the construction of Shakespear's original katharometer c. 1916. (Diagram: Proceedings of the Royal Society, 1920, A, 97, p 274.)

copper. This ring was fitted with an insulating plug through which the copper lead-in wire passed. One extremity of the helix was soldered to this lead and the other to the far end of the loop. A gas-tight rubber seal was pressed around the outer length of lead-in wire where it passed through the copper block. One gas cell was completely sealed whilst gas could enter the other through three small holes in the end adjacent to the loop in the copper wire. The resistance of each platinum helix was about 8 ohms when cold, and the working current in the bridge was normally 100 mA, which heated the platinum helices to a temperature about 15 °C above the block temperature. Manganin resistors were used for the other two arms of the bridge.

Daynes worked with Shakespear at Birmingham University, as a research student, on the further development and application of the katharometer throughout the 1914–18 war and their work on hydrogen permeability through balloon fabrics was published in a series of reports to the Advisory Committee for Aeronautics.[22,23,24,25]

It appears that Shakespear did not become aware of the other work in this field, in particular that of the Germans, until he applied for

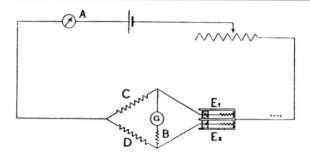

Figure 16.2 Circuit diagram for 2-spiral katharometer. A, milli-ammeter (bridge current normally set to 100 mA); B, calibration resistance; C, D fixed bridge resistors; E_1, E_2, platinum spirals in gas cells; G, galvanometer calibrated in gas concentration. (Diagram: Cambridge Monograph No. 3—The Thermal Conductivity Method of Gas Analysis, p. 2.)

patents. His application for a British patent was filed on 4 January, 1916, but because of the wartime conditions the patent was not granted until 3 April, 1919. In the meantime, on 15 October, 1918, Shakespear filed an application for a patent in the USA.[26] By this time, however, several other thermal conductivity analysers had been designed in the States, including one at the United States Bureau of Standards.

The Bureau had begun its own work on the thermal conductivity analysis technique early on during the war. After a year or so the project was abandoned, apparently because of the delicacy of the indicating instrument needed in order to achieve the particular objective at that time. During 1915 or 1916 the Sperry Gyroscope Company developed an analyser similar to the Siemens and Halske instrument. Also, in 1917 a group at the University of California designed a thermal conductivity analyser which was tested by the US Navy Department and successfully met a variety of applications. Early in 1918 work was started again at the Bureau of Standards by a team led by E. R. Weaver and P. E. Palmer and a multipurpose analyser was developed, although the armistice subsequently caused the cancellation of some of the major proposed applications for the equipment. (The analytical control of the synthetic ammonia plant at Sheffield, Alabama, was one such application. Work on the plant was cancelled at the end of the war when the pressing need for explosives was no longer extant.) The development team at the Bureau of Standards published a detailed account of its work in two articles in 1920 followed by a Bureau of Standards Paper in 1924.[27,28,29] The first article included a brief history of the method, followed by the note:

> *The history of this development is given in such detail in order to clear up a situation which might otherwise give rise to ill feeling.*

It is known that one of the recent experimenters believed himself the first to utilize heat conductivity measurements for making gas analyses until his apparatus was submitted to the Bureau of Standards for test, and a similar claim has been repeatedly made for another investigator, though not by the investigator himself.

The apparatus referred to in this note as having been submitted for test by the Bureau may well have been Shakespear's as he is reported to have sent the Bureau a katharometer and permeameter for experiments at about this time.

Shakespear was granted a US patent on 20 May, 1919. His design had one signal advantage over the American instruments: his was the only analyser which allowed the gas to enter the measuring cells by molecular diffusion. The calibration of the katharometer was thus independent of gas flow rate over the working range. With hindsight more might have been made of this feature in the patent specification.

Figure 16.3 Exploring katharometer for balloon fabrics and seams c. 1918. (Photo: C.S.I.Co., Neg. 2148.)

After the war Dr Daynes joined The Cambridge and Paul Instrument Company. Daynes was already an authority on the katharometer and he established this method of gas analysis on a firm commercial footing within the Company. At that time it was the only automatic, continuous analysis technique available. All other methods relied on the analysis of a discrete sample. When he left in 1926 his assistant, W. S. Griffiths, took over the responsibility for gas analysis development. Griffiths died at an early age in 1929 and the responsibility for the continuing development of the katharometer and ancillary equipment then passed to Dr Gilbert Jessop. Although a relatively young man, Dr

Jessop was an extremely talented chemist. In due course he became the Company's Chief Chemist and he retained overall responsibility for the development of katharometry until he retired in 1966.

One of the more unusual early demonstrations of the katharometer CO_2 analyser was that at the private exhibition organised by the Royal Society for their conversazione on 22 July, 1925. King George V and Queen Mary visited the exhibition and the Queen stopped to inspect The Cambridge Instrument Company exhibit. Next day, in the account in *The Daily Telegraph*, the incident was reported under the heading 'Fly's Death Warrant':[30]

> *Explaining another exhibit by The Cambridge Instrument Co., Mr R. S. Whipple pointed out that it was possible to measure the respiration of an insect. He had, he explained, a bluebottle in captivity, and an instrument measuring the gas given off by it. The Queen was concerned as to whether the fly was suffering in captivity, and was assured that it was quite happy. Mr Whipple said it would be liberated in the evening, but the Queen replied that she thought it ought to be killed, in case it had been suffering at all, and also because it was important to exterminate as many flies as possible, having regard to the damage they did.*
>   *'If your Majesty passes sentence of death it will be carried out,' was the assurance, and the Queen promptly replied, 'Yes, I think he ought to die.'*

List No. 144, published by the Company in June 1929, described the use of the katharometer in studying the respiration of insects. The level of carbon dioxide expired by a fly enclosed in a 5-cc tube reached about 10% after six hours. When the fly was quiet the carbon dioxide percentage remained constant but any movement immediately produced a sudden rise in the level of carbon dioxide.[31,32]

The construction of the Cambridge katharometer during the 1920s and '30s was very similar to Shakespear's original design. The block in which the two platinum helices were mounted was usually brass and the metal parts of the analysis cells were heavily gold plated to resist corrosion by any of the gases passing through the meter. Gas from the stream being analysed diffused into the measuring cell through three small holes at the end of the cell. The reference cell could either be left open to air or exposed in a similar way to a reference gas. In *Fig.* 16.4 the reference cell is shown connected to a cup (beneath the katharometer) which could be used to contain water or a drying agent, thus controlling the humidity of the air in the cell.

In this design of meter a reference gas could not be effectively sealed in. During 1931–2 the construction was changed, the platinum helices being mounted in glass tubes. Sealed reference cells were then possible.[33] At the same time meters containing two reference and two measuring cells (connected in opposite arms of a Wheatstone bridge) were

Figure 16.4 CO₂ katharometer c. 1921 showing pipe attachment.
(Photo: C.S.I.Co., Neg. 4246.)

introduced, increasing the sensitivity of the analyser. Fifty years later the process was reversed. Cheap solid state electronics eliminated the need for maximum sensitivity from the measuring device and the four-cell analyser was superseded by a two-cell instrument so that the relatively high production cost of two measuring cells might be saved.

About 1937–8 'all glass' systems, for the analysis of highly corrosive gases such as sulphur dioxide, began to be marketed. In these units the glass tube containing the platinum helix projected through the bottom of the katharometer block and all glass connections to the gas stream could be made.

During the war period which followed, the design of the much simpler 'hair-pin filament' cell was perfected by the Company, although it was not fully exploited until after the war, the two designs of cell running in parallel for some years. *Fig.* 16.5 is a sectional diagram showing the method of construction of the hair-pin cells. The design had many advantages over the helix design, being both more robust and simpler to make. 'Spirals' had been hand made but the hair-pin filaments were made in batches, jigs being used wherever possible to ensure repeatability and control of the production process. One end of a reel of $24\,\mu$ platinum filament wire was spot-welded to a platinum lead-in wire. The platinum filament was then laid over the second lead-in wire and the length adjusted whilst the resistance was compared to that of a standard filament. At balance the weld to the second lead-in wire was made and the

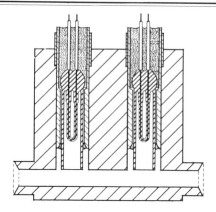

Figure 16.5 Construction of 'hair-pin' filament katharometer c. 1945.
(Diagram: Cambridge Monograph No. 3—The Thermal Conductivity
Method of Gas Analysis, p. 10.)

filament cut off from the reel. The assembly was then threaded into a fine
glass capillary, just longer than the 24 μ filament, and passed through a
small furnace to shrink the glass on to the wire. Next the glass-covered
filament was bent into a hairpin using a small gas flame and, finally, it
was sealed into a glass tube to form a measuring cell.

Since the thermal conductivity analysis technique is not specific
to the gas being analysed, each new application of the katharometer had
to be carefully assessed. In its simplest form, it was used to monitor the
variation of gases in a binary mixture when the thermal conductivities of
the two gases were significantly different, e.g. hydrogen in oxygen.

Figure 16.6 Differential katharometer with heater for combustion of one
gas component c. 1922. (Photo: C.S.I.Co., Neg. 3003.)

For successful use with anything other than a binary mixture the effective thermal conductivity of the background gases had to remain constant. The measurement of carbon dioxide in flue gases was just such a case and the advantage of the katharometer as an instrument for monitoring the efficiency of the combustion process in a boiler house was soon realised. The background gases consisted chiefly of nitrogen with a small amount of oxygen, water vapour, hydrogen, methane and carbon monoxide. Since carbon monoxide, oxygen and nitrogen all have nearly the same thermal conductivity, the small variations of these gases did not affect the measurement. The residual hydrogen and methane is very small and by keeping the gases in both reference and measuring cell saturated, the effect of water vapour could be ignored.

An alternative method of using the katharometer was as a differential meter (*Fig.* 16.6): one analysis cell was exposed to the original gas mixture and the second cell to the gas after an appropriate chemical reaction had been made to take place. The determination of the carbon monoxide content of flue gas was made in this way. After the first cell was exposed to the gas mixture the combustible gases were burnt in a small furnace and the gas stream then returned through the katharometer. Combined units for both carbon dioxide and carbon monoxide determination were frequently supplied (*Fig.* 16.7), a continuous gas sample being taken from the flue by means of a water aspirator.[34]

Figure 16.7 Combined CO and CO₂ analyser with aspirator, indicators and recorder for monitoring boiler flue gases etc. c. 1932. (Photo: C.S.I.Co., Neg. 5246.)

More complex analysis systems, in which the composition of the sample gas was chemically changed prior to analysis in order to make analysis possible, were also developed. Thus, what had started as an empirical technique, to meet specific and pressing wartime needs, became over the years, a predictable and definitive method of gas analysis, applicable to many different processes.

*   *   *   *   *

CHAPTER SEVENTEEN

The invention of the cloud chamber

1913 The Wilson expansion apparatus
1921 Ray-track apparatus (Shimizu's patent)
1927 Cambridge ray-track apparatus (School's version)

WHEN Charles Thomson Rees Wilson began his researches into cloud phenomena he had no idea that they would eventually lead to the design of an apparatus by which the tracks of ionising particles could be made visible. Born near Edinburgh, his love of the Scottish mountains was kindled when he visited the Island of Arran in the Clyde at the age of 15. He had always been interested in the natural sciences, although there was no science taught at the school which he attended. When he was given a microscope he proceeded to spend a great deal of time studying beetles and pond life. At the age of 18 he obtained his BSc degree at Owen's College and he went up to Sidney Sussex College at Cambridge in October 1888, sitting the Physics Tripos examination in 1892.

After graduating, Wilson stayed on in Cambridge, demonstrating in physics and chemistry and taking some private pupils. He had little time to spare in which to do research, but nevertheless began work on a project: a study of the distribution of a substance in solution in a hot liquid, comparing its behaviour with that of a gas. After two years he abandoned both his teaching and his research work in frustration, finding it impossible to devote sufficient time to the research. Almost in desperation he took a post as assistant master at Bradford Grammar School, hoping he would have more time to spend on research, and then immediately realised his mistake; he enjoyed teaching the boys geology but had even less time for research.

So Wilson determined to return to Cambridge before it was too late to change his career again, even though he had no post to return to.

Fortunately, he soon found work as a demonstrator in medical physics, which provided him with just sufficient income to allow him to return to research.

He now had a new project on which he was keen to start work. The previous September (1894) he had spent a fortnight or so working at the Observatory on Ben Nevis. During this time he had become enthralled with the beautiful coloured optical phenomena, the 'coronas and glories', produced when the sun shone on the clouds surrounding the hill top. Back in the Cavendish Laboratory Wilson began to try to reproduce these effects.

The technique of artifically producing clouds was not new. As early as 1660 Guericke had shown how to produce clouds in his own laboratory. Using two flasks with taps, he had evacuated one, joined them together and opened the taps. The equalisation of pressure caused the air in the un-evacuated flask to 'give up its surplus moisture' which then became visible.[1]

For the next two centuries it was assumed that this change of state occurred without any assistance. When it was established that air was cooled by its expansion it was postulated that water vapour condensed into cloud as soon as the air reached dew point. But in 1875 Coulier published some experimental results which caused considerable surprise. He had been experimenting with a glass flask containing some water, and connected by a tube to a hollow rubber ball. This was a completely closed system and the pressure in the flask could be repeatedly raised and lowered suddenly, as often as desired. Coulier found that when repeated experiments were made fog did not continue to form indefinitely. Also if the flask and water were shaken for a few minutes a cloud would not form when the pressure was lowered. However, if some of the air was replaced by air from the room, the fog would form again.[2]

Coulier suspected that something was entering the flask as well as air, and tried filtering the room air through a cotton-wool plug. It became inactive and he came to the conclusion that dust was needed if a cloud was to form. In 1881 John Aitken repeated these experiments, not knowing of Coulier's work. He did, however, go further than Coulier and he found that the fewer the number of dust particles, the coarser-grained the resulting fog, indicating that the water vapour present was being shared amongst the particles.[3] Wilson carried the work still farther, when he returned to Cambridge in 1895.

He began his attempts to reproduce the effects he had seen on Ben Nevis, by producing clouds by expansion in a closed chamber (*Fig 17.1*), in a similar manner to Coulier and Aitken. He soon found that once the dust particles had been removed from the air by several small cloud-producing expansions, it was still possible to produce condensation drops provided the expansion ratio exceeded 1·25. For expansion ratios

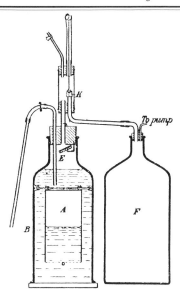

Figure 17.1 C. T. R. Wilson's first adiabatic expansion apparatus. A, gas to be expanded. Vessel F is evacuated with valve K closed. When K is opened, air in top of B is admitted to F and gas A expands until valve E is closed by rising water level. (Diagram: Philosophical Transactions of the Royal Society, A, Vol. 189, p 268.)

between 1·25 and 1·37 a few drops were always produced, no matter how many times the expansions were repeated. Wilson concluded that this rain-like condensation must therefore be due to some nuclei which were always present in small numbers, being replaced as fast as they were removed by condensation. He reported his results in a short paper to the Cambridge Philosophical Society in the spring of 1895.[4] This paper was to be the first of a steady stream of published work.

Wilson now started to construct a second smaller apparatus which would allow greater expansion speeds. The making of this cloud chamber was a long and tedious task. It involved quite difficult glass-blowing, followed by hours of patient glass grinding to get a good sliding fit between the glass piston and sleeve and a good conical seal when the piston reached the bottom of the sleeve. He did all of this work himself during the long vacation and autumn of 1895. Frequently the hours of patient grinding would be wasted when he attempted the final glass-blowing to complete the chamber.

His apparently endless grinding was the subject of a number of good-humoured comments. Lord Rutherford in later life recalled seeing Wilson in the workshop of the Cavendish Laboratory, patiently grinding away. Rutherford was then called away for some weeks and when he returned, there was Wilson in exactly the same position, doing precisely the same job, as though it was later the same day.

Eventually Wilson succeeded in making about three usable expansion chambers. With this new apparatus the expansion speed was much higher and he was able to obtain expansion ratios greater than 1·38. At these high ratios the condensation was no longer rain-like but instead became a fog, which would take a minute or more to clear. At still higher ratios, between 1·40 and 1·42, with the drops becoming smaller with increasing expansion, a series of very striking diffraction rings was produced, the chamber apparently being filled with a beautifully coloured liquid, the colours changing from blue to red as the ratio was raised to 1·42. When the ratio was increased still further to 1·44 the drops became so small that the colours were no longer produced. Wilson calculated the numbers of droplets produced in these fog-like condensations and came to the conclusion that they must be simple aggregations of water molecules.[5]

Roentgen's announcements of his discovery of X-rays were at this time attracting a great deal of interest. In the Cavendish J. J. Thomson and Rutherford were engaged in investigations of the electrical conductivity acquired by air exposed to X-rays. They were able to explain the complicated behaviour of such air by postulating the production of positive and negative 'ions' within it. Wilson had already speculated that the few nuclei which were always being produced in air might be charged atoms. He borrowed one of Thomson's X-ray tubes and carried out an expansion experiment whilst the air in the chamber was exposed to X-rays. The expansion which previously had produced but a few nuclei now produced a dense cloud.[6]

By 1897 Wilson had also experimented with the rays from uranium and had definitely identified the nuclei produced by both X-rays and the rays from uranium with the nuclei which were always present in small numbers in clean air and which produced the rain-like condensation.[7,8] Continuing his experiments, Wilson was soon able to show conclusively that these nuclei were ions and by 1899 he was investigating the relative efficiencies of positive and negative ions as condensation nuclei, using an appropriately polarised electric field across the expansion chamber to separate the positive and negative ions.[9,10]

In 1899 Wilson agreed to work for the Meteorological Council for a year, investigating atmospheric electricity and assessing the records at Kew and Greenwich with a view to suggesting improvements in the methods of measurement. The work on atmospheric electricity was to influence his researches for the next ten years and Wilson did not resume his work on condensation phenomena until 1910. During the intervening period the nature of radioactivity and X-rays had become better understood and in 1910 Wilson conceived the idea that it might be possible to make the track of an ionising particle visible by photographing the drops of water condensing on the ions in its track.

He constructed a small flat-topped cloud chamber, 7·5 cm in diameter, and in the spring of 1911 took the first photographs of α-ray tracks from a weak radium source and the short trails of electrons resulting from the passage of an X-ray beam. The following year Wilson was able to show many more photographs, taken this time using a larger cloud chamber.[11,12] This larger cloud chamber was Wilson's final design and he used it for experiments well into the 1920s. It was also the design that the Cambridge Scientific Instrument Company marketed in 1913 after receiving a number of enquiries from customers wishing to purchase cloud chambers.[13] The instrument is shown in *Figs*. 17.2 and 17.3.

The cylindrical cloud chamber A was about 16·5 cm in diameter and 3·4 cm high. The roof, walls and floor were of glass, coated inside with gelatine, that on the floor being blackened by adding a little ink. The plate-glass floor B was fixed on the top of a thin-walled cylindrical brass plunger, 10 cm high, open below, and sliding freely within an outer brass expansion cylinder C, of the same height and about 16 cm in internal diameter. The expansion cylinder supported the walls of the cloud chamber and rested on a thin sheet of indiarubber lying on a thick brass disc, which formed the bottom of a shallow dish D. This dish contained water to a depth of about 2 cm, to separate the air in the cloud chamber from that below the plunger.

The expansion was effected by opening the valve E. This connected the air space below the plunger with the evacuated flask F. The floor of the cloud chamber would then drop suddenly until the plunger struck the indiarubber-covered base plate, where it remained, held by the pressure of the air in the cloud chamber. In the air space below the plunger the metal cylinder G was filled with water as a means of reducing the volume of air passing through the connecting tubes at each expansion. The starting height of the plunger could be adjusted by the pinch clips H and J so as to give any desired expansion ratio during the operation of the cloud chamber.

The gelatine layer under the roof of the cloud chamber was connected with one terminal of a battery via a ring of tinfoil cemented between the cylindrical wall and the roof. The layer of blackened gelatine on the floor of the cloud chamber was connected to the other terminal of the battery through the brass expansion cylinder and plunger. By this means a vertical electrostatic field of any desired intensity could be maintained across the cloud chamber. This field removed all ions immediately after their liberation so that during an expansion the clouds formed consisted entirely of drops condensed on newly liberated ions. Under these conditions the tracks of ionising particles could be seen as lines of cloud and were especially sharply defined if the particles had traversed the air immediately after its expansion.

Figure 17.2 Commercial cloud chamber c. *1913. The apparatus is shown partially dismantled with the cloud chamber removed from its position on top of the expansion vessel. (Photo: C.S.I.Co., Neg. 1726.)*

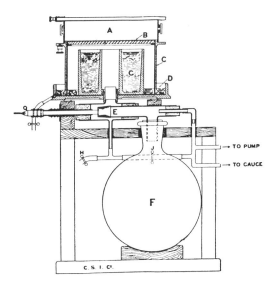

Figure 17.3 Constructional details of the cloud chamber manufactured by The Cambridge Scientific Instrument Company. A, cloud chamber; B, plate-glass floor of chamber; C, brass expansion cylinder; D, shallow dish containing water; E, valve; F, vacuum chamber; G, water ballast; H, J, pinch clips. (Diagram: C.S.I.Co. Catalogues 1912–15, List No. 217.)

After the 1914–18 War Takeo Shimizu designed a reciprocating cloud chamber whilst studying the continuous emission of alpha and beta particles at the Cavendish Laboratory. The instrument was capable of 50–200 expansions per minute and, having assisted Shimizu to patent his design, the Company subsequently manufactured it under a royalty agreement with him.[14,15]

Figure 17.4 Shimizu's reciprocating cloud chamber c. 1921. (Photo: C.S.I.Co., Neg. 2752.)

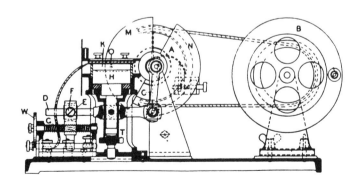

Figure 17.5 Constructional details of Shimizu's reciprocating cloud chamber. A, crank; B, handwheel; C, D, connecting rods; E, sleeve; F, supporting piece; G, screw; H, piston; K, expansion chamber; M, N, lead shutters; O, tube (to admit radio-active source); W, expansion ratio adjustment. (Diagram: C.S.I.Co. Catalogues 1921–26, List No. 106.)

The instrument (shown in *Figs.* 17.4 and 17.5) had a relatively small expansion chamber, only 5·5 cm in diameter and 1 cm high. The piston H, which formed the floor of the expansion chamber, was coupled to the horizontal connecting rod D near its centre point. This rod was driven by an upright connecting rod C and a crank A, the crank being operated either by a motor or the handwheel B. The far end of rod D slid in a sleeve E which was free to rock in the piece F. Screw G adjusted the position of F horizontally and thus the length of the vertical stroke given to the piston H, enabling the expansion ratio of the stroke to be adjusted while the instrument was in operation.

Various refinements were fitted including a commutator to cut off the electrostatic field during the period of cloud formation and rotating lead segments, M and N, to allow X-rays to be admitted in synchronism with the operation of the cloud chamber. A radio-active source could be inserted into the expansion chamber via a small tube O.

Figure 17.6 Schools' cloud chamber c. *1926. (Photo: C.S.I.Co., Neg. 3813.)*

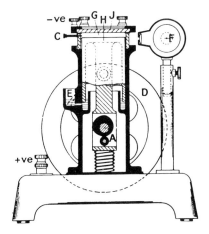

Figure 17.7 Constructional details of the schools' cloud chamber. A, crank; C, pin with radioactive source on tip; D, handwheel; E, water seal; F, lamp; G, expansion chamber; H, piston; J, cover plate. (Diagram: C.S.I.Co. Catalogues 1927–30, List No. 106.)

As the diameter of the chamber was so small, the velocity of the α-rays was reduced by passing them through a mica screen. Stereoscopic cinematograph photographs could also be taken using the apparatus and a stereoscopic camera was supplied as an optional accessory.

In 1926, in order to satisfy the needs of schools and colleges, the Company designed a simplified version of Shimizu's instrument, with a fixed expansion ratio (*Figs.* 17.6 and 17.7).[16]

Although it was only suitable for showing the tracks of α particles the instrument proved very popular and sold in considerable numbers. As mentioned in Chapter 3, two such instruments were exhibited at the Festival of Britain, in 1951, and operated by some 60 000 visitors during the five-month long exhibition. Comparison with Wilson's experimental apparatus provides an interesting illustration of the way a piece of laboratory apparatus may be refined into a relatively simple piece of equipment to demonstrate scientific phenomena in a manner which can be understood by those who have only a limited knowledge of science.

*　*　*　*　*

Notes & References

Archival material relating to the Company is preserved at several locations in Cambridge and the Whipple Museum of the History of Science also has a considerable collection of the early instruments of the Company.

Cambridge University Library (Manuscripts Room)

This archive contains the largest collection of material and generally comprises:

Some 10 000 photographic negatives, with album prints, covering the period from about 1900 to 1970.

Bound volumes of the Company's catalogues and early price lists from 1882 to 1953.

A large number of the manufacturing drawings (with many assembly drawings) for the Company's products from about 1890 to 1970. Some of the early drawings are of particular historical interest, e.g. Duddell's original drawings for his oscillograph.

A notebook belonging to Horace Darwin with entries dating from 1873 to 1890.

Two press-copy letter-books *c.* 1877–83, belonging to Horace Darwin and four of the Company's press-copy letter-books of the 1880s.

One Sales Order Book and two of the Company's Cash Books for the 1880s.

The 1895 Articles of Association of the Company together with the Directors' Agenda Book for the period 1895 to 1906.

Early Minute Books of the Social Club and Benefit Fund.

A large collection of miscellaneous documents including agreements, patents, memoranda and letters dating from *c.* 1890 to *c.* 1970.

Copies of the Board Minutes, accounts etc. for the American associate company.

A large collection of operating instructions and repair manuals for the Company's instruments.

Regettably, a potentially important source of information, the Board Room Minute Books from 1895 to the 1960s, was lost during the takeover period, prior to the accession of the archive by the University Library, but the archive does contain a copy of the comprehensive notes of important items in the minutes, compiled by A F Wolfe *c.* 1962.

Cambridgeshire County Record Office at Shire Hall

Apart from the Trade School Log Book for the period 1917–1921 this archive mainly relates to gas analysis instruments:

Operating instructions for various instruments for the period 1900 to 1970.

Catalogues of gas analysers from 1958 to 1980.

Various circuit/wiring diagrams of indicators, recorders and gas analysers *c.* 1935 to *c.* 1970.

Various laboratory notebooks *c.* 1922 to *c.* 1974.

Floor plans (*c.* 1979) of the Rosemary Lane factory.

Whipple Museum of the History of Science

A collection of the Company's instruments *c.* 1883 to *c.* 1966.

Serial number record books for the period 1907 to 1957.

Forty-two bound volumes of pamphlets on scientific/engineering topics collected by Horace Darwin and Robert Whipple as being relevant to the products of the Company.

*   *   *   *   *

In the captions to the figures and in the chapter notes and references which follow, 'C.S.I.Co.' indicates the archive in the University Library (located under the class heading 'Cambridge Scientific Instrument Company archive'), 'County Record Office' refers to the archive at the Shire Hall (known as 'Cambridge Scientific Instrument Company documents'), and 'Cambs. Collection' refers to material housed in the Cambridgeshire local history collection at the Cambridge Central Library in Lion Yard. 'Dar.' and 'Add.' are Cambridge University Library Manuscripts Room classifications for collections of Darwin and additional material respectively. CUL UA COMP is a classification for Cambridge University Archives, Computer material which is also available from the University Library Manuscripts Room.

References &
Further Reading

CHAPTER 1

1. C.S.I. Co., Box 3, MS, Anon. (L Darwin?): Horace Darwin, undated (12 June 1932?).
2. Darwin F (ed.) 1887 *Life and Letters of Charles Darwin*, vol. I (London: Murray) p 132.
3. Moore J R July 1977 On the education of Darwin's sons: the correspondence between Charles Darwin and the Reverend G V Reed 1857–1864. *Notes and Records of the Royal Society of London*, vol. 32, No. 1, pp 51–70.
4. Darwin F and Seward A C (ed.) 1903 *More Letters of Charles Darwin*, vol. I (New York: Appleton) p 204.
5. Dar. 185, Letter, C Darwin to H Darwin, 15 Dec. 1871.
6. C.S.I.Co., Box 38, Notebook: H Darwin, 1873–90.
7. Woodforde J 1970 *The Story of the Bicycle* (London: Routledge & Kegan Paul) pp 34–8.
8. Darwin H 1901 On the small vertical movements of a stone laid on the surface of the ground. *Proc. R. Soc.* **LXVIII** No. 446, pp. 253–61.
9. Dar. 219, Letter, H Darwin to E Darwin, Jan. 1878.
10. C.S.I.Co., Box 33, MS, R S Whipple: The Story of The Cambridge Scientific Instrument Company, undated.
11. Thomson J J 1936 *Recollections and Reflections* (London: Bell) pp 285–7.
12. Colvin S 1921 *Memories and Notes of Persons and Places, 1852–1912* (London: Arnold) pp 126–7.
13. Foster M and Dew-Smith A G 1875 On the behaviour of the hearts of mollusks under the influence of electric currents. *Proc. R. Soc.* **XXII** pp. 318–43.
14. Foster M and Dew-Smith A G 1876 The effects of the constant current on the heart. *J. Anat. Physiol.* **10** 735–71.
15. Sharpey-Schafer E Dec. 1927 History of the Physiological Society during its first fifty years, 1876–1926. *J. Physiol. (Lond.) Suppl.* p 26.
16. Thompson S P 1910 *The Life of William Thomson, Baron Kelvin of Largs* (London: Macmillan) p 563.
17. Add. 8118, Box 1, Letters (TS extracts), J Stuart to his mother, 1878.
18. Add. 8118, Box 1, Account Book: J Stuart, 1878–9.
19. C.S.I. Co., Box 3, Notebook: R S Whipple, undated.
20. Foster M 30 April 1903 Obituary Notice of A G Dew-Smith. *The Cambridge Review*, pp 261–2.
21. *Journal of Physiology* 1879 **I** No. 6, Advertisement inside back cover.

22. Dar. 219, Letter, H Darwin to G Darwin, 15 March 1879.
23. *Spalding's Street and General Directory of Cambridge: 1881* (Cambridge: Spalding) p 82.
24. Dar. 219, Letter, H Darwin to G Darwin, 17 Feb. 1879.
25. *See* ref. 22 above.
26. Guillemin A 1891 *Electricity and Magnetism* ed. S P Thompson (London) p 932.
27. Moore J W 1910 *Meteorology—Practical and Applied* (London: Rebman) p 93.
28. C.S.I. Co., Box 37, MS, A F Wolfe: Notes of Papers written by Horace Darwin, undated.
29. Raverat G 1952 *Period Piece* (London: Faber & Faber) pp 195–6.
30. C.S.I. Co., Box 1, Letter-book p 418, H Darwin to H E Roscoe, 10 May 1880.
31. C.S.I. Co., Box 1, Letter-book p 15, H Darwin to W de W Abney, 28 Dec. 1880.
32. Gaskell W H 1908 Obituary Notice—Sir Michael Foster *Proc. R. Soc.* B **LXXX** lxxviii.
33. C.S.I. Co., Box 1, Letter-book p 17, H Darwin to J H Poynting, 28 Dec. 1880.
34. Dar. 219, Letter, I Darwin to G Darwin, 13 Feb. 1881.
35. C.S.I. Co., Box 1, Letter-book p 37, A G Dew-Smith to C Dew, 26 Jan. 1881.

Further Reading

Bryden D J Dec. 1972 *Royal Scottish Museum Information Series: Technology 1; Scottish Scientific Instrument-Makers 1600–1900* (Edinburgh: Royal Scottish Museum).
Darwin L July–Dec. 1929 *The Nineteenth Century and After*, **CVI** pp 118–23. Memories of Down House
Dictionary of National Biography: 1912–21, Sir William de Wiveleslie Abney.
Dictionary of National Biography: 1912–21, John Henry Poynting.
Dictionary of National Biography: 1912–21, Sir Henry Enfield Roscoe.
Geison G L 1978 *Michael Foster and the Cambridge School of Physiology* (New Jersey: Princeton University Press).
Hilken T J N 1967 *Engineering at Cambridge University 1783–1965* (Cambridge: University Press)
Langley J N 1906–7 Sir Michael Foster in Memoriam. *J. Physiol. (Lond.)* **XXXV** pp 233–46.
Thomson J J 1915–16, Obituary Notice—John Henry Poynting. *Proc. R. Soc.* A **XCII**, pp i–ix.

CHAPTER 2

1. C.S.I. Co., Box 1, Letter-book p 499, A G Dew-Smith and H Darwin to W Pye, 16 Dec. 1880.
2. Thomson J J 1936 *Recollections and Reflections* (London: Bell) p 286.
3. Dar. 219, Letter, I Darwin to G Darwin, 13 Feb. 1881.
4. C.S.I. Co., Box 1, Letter-book p 211, A G Dew-Smith to R Solomon, 18 May 1881.
5. C.S.I. Co., Box 1, Letter-book p 58, A G Dew-Smith to I W Mills, 4 Feb. 1881.
6. C.S.I. Co., Box 1, Letter-book p 54, A G Dew-Smith to R Middleton, 4 Feb. 1881.
7. C.S.I. Co., Box 1, Letter-book p 287, A G Dew-Smith and H Darwin to C S Roy, 27 July 1881.
8. C.S.I. Co., Box 1, Letter-book pp 8–10, A G Dew-Smith to C S Roy, 31 Dec. 1881.
9. C.S.I. Co., Box 1, Letter-book p 31, A G Dew-Smith to C S Roy, 16 Jan. 1882.
10. C.S.I. Co., Box 1, Letter-book p 298, A G Dew-Smith to H P Bowditch, 15 Aug. 1881.

11.   C.S.I. Co., Box 1, Letter-book p 449, H Darwin to D P Anderson Stuart, 29 Nov. 1881.
12.   C.S.I. Co., Box 1, Letter-book p 28, H Darwin to R Thacker, 21 Jan. 1881.
13.   C.S.I. Co., Box 1, Letter-book p 103, A G Dew-Smith to Lord Rayleigh, 3 Mar. 1881.
14.   Dar. 219, Letter, I Darwin to G Darwin, 13 Feb. 1881.
15.   Strachey R E and Whipple G M 1891 Cloud photography conducted under the Meteorological Council at the Kew Observatory. *Proc. R. Soc.* **XLIX** pp 467–80.
16.   *Proceedings of the Royal Society* 1884 **37** p 467. Report of the Kew Committee for the year ending 31 October, 1884.
17.   Darwin H 1913 Scientific instruments, their design and use in aeronautics. *Aeronaut. J.*, **XVII** pp 181–2.
18.   *Nature* 1886 **XXXIII** pp 248–50. Distribution of driving-power in laboratories.
19.   Boys C V 1887 On the production, properties and some suggested uses of the finest fibres. *Phil. Mag.* **XXIII** pp 489–99.
20.   Boys C V 1887 Measuring the most feeble radiation. *Proc. R. Soc.* **XLII** pp 189–93.
21.   C.S.I. Co., Price Lists 1882–90.
22.   C.S.I. Co. Catalogues 1889–1901. A Descriptive List of Anthropometric Apparatus.
23.   C.S.I. Co., Box 5, Order Book, 11 July 1887.
24.   C.S.I. Co., Box 1, Letter-book p 165, A G Dew-Smith and H Darwin to W Pye, 6 April 1882.
25.   C.S.I. Co., Box 1, Letter-book p 218, A G Dew-Smith to G Hudson, 22 May 1882.
26.   *See* ref. 21 above.
27.   Archer-Hind R D 1905 *Translations into Greek Verse and Prose* (Cambridge: University Press) pp 146–7.
28.   C.S.I. Co., Box 34, Letter (TS Copy), T L Heath to C G (?) Darwin, 3 Feb. 1933.
29.   *See* ref. 21 above.
30.   *See* ref. 21 above.
31.   Symons G J (ed). 1888, *The Eruption of Krakatoa and Subsequent Phenomena* (London: The Royal Society) Frontispiece.
32.   Dar. 219, Letter (TS Copy), Emma Darwin to G Darwin, 2 April 1884.
33.   C.S.I. Co., Box 5, Order Book, 9 July 1887.
34.   C.S.I. Co., Box 2, Letter, A G Dew-Smith to H Darwin, 23 Nov. 1887.
35.   C.S.I. Co., Box 2, Letter, A G Dew-Smith to H Darwin, 14 June 1888.
36.   C.S.I. Co., Box 2, Letter, A G Dew-Smith to H Darwin, 16 May 1889.
37.   C.S.I. Co., Box 2, Letter, A G Dew-Smith to H Darwin, 20 May 1889.
38.   C.S.I. Co., Box 2, Letter, A G Dew-Smith to H Darwin, 6 Oct. 1889.

Further Reading

Brown W H 1940 *Co-operation in a University Town* (London: Co-operative Printing Society).

Dictionary of National Biography: 1941–50, Charles Vernon Boys.

Foster M 30 April 1903 Obituary Notice of A G Dew-Smith. *The Cambridge Review*, pp 261–2.

Geison G L 1978 *Michael Foster and the Cambridge School of Physiology* (New Jersey: Princeton University Press).

The Making of a Name .... Everett Edgcumbe, 1950 (London: Everett Edgcumbe).

Proceedings of the Royal Society 1905 **LXXV** pp 131–6. Obituary Notice—C S Roy.

Rayleigh Lord, 1944, *Obit. Not. Fell. R. Soc.* **4**, No. 13, pp 771–88. Charles Vernon Boys.

Wilson J Dover 1969 *Milestones on the Dover Road* (London: Faber & Faber).

CHAPTER 3

1. C.S.I. Co., Box 33, Circular, H Darwin, 1 Jan. 1891.
2. Thomson J J 1936 *Recollections and Reflections* (London: Bell) p 131.
3. *Report of the British Association for the Advancement of Science* 1874 pp 242–9. The new pyrometer of Mr Siemens.
4. Callendar H L 1887 On the practical measurement of temperature. *Phil. Trans. R. Soc.* A, **178** pp 161–230.
5. C.S.I. Co., Catalogues 1889–1901. Platinum Thermometers and Pyrometers, November 1893.
6. Carey Foster G 1894 Platinum-resistance thermometers. *Nature*, **L** p 399.
7. Litchfield H (Ed) 1915 *Emma Darwin: A Century of Family Letters 1792–1896*, **II** (London: Murray) p 309.
8. C.S.I. Co., Catalogues 1889–1901. Duddell Patent Oscillographs, 1899.
9. C.S.I. Co., Box 33, MS, R S Whipple: Discussion of early Balance Sheets undated.
10. C.S.I. Co., Box 2, Letter-book p 113, H Darwin to W F Barrett, 21 Feb. 1899.
11. C.S.I. Co., Box 2, Letter-book p 166, H Darwin to H Pye, 4 Mar. 1899.
12. C.S.I. Co., Box 3, Patents 5089 (1899); 12252 (1899), E H Griffiths and W C D Whetham. Patents 5743 (1900); 322 (1901), E H Griffiths, W C D Whetham and The Cambridge Sentinel Manufacturing Co. Ltd. All titled:*Improvements in or relating to Mechanisms for Controlling and Indicating Temperature Limits.*
13. C.S.I. Co., Box 30, *Cambridge Comment*, December 1963, No. 36. Those were the Days.
14. C.S.I. Co., Box 33, MS & TS, F Doggett: Notes, October 1966.
15. Gamgee A 1908 On methods for the continuous (photographic) and quasi-continuous registration of the diurnal curve of the temperature of the animal body. *Phil. Trans. R. Soc.* B, **200** pp 219–40.
16. Féry C 1902 La mesure des temperatures élevées et la loi de Stéfan. *C. R. Hebd. Séanc. Acad. Sci. Paris.* **CXXXIV**, pp 977–82.
17. Féry C 1904 Télescope Pyrométrique. *J. Phys. Théor. Appl.*, **3**, Series 4, Tome III pp 701–4.
18. Lucas K 22 June 1908, British Patent 13242/08: Improvements in or relating to Adjustment Mechanism for Microscopes and other Apparatus.
19. *Daily Mail*, 27 Dec. 1906. The Recent Earthquakes—Did they affect St Paul's?
20. *Daily Mail*, 28 Dec. 1906. Do Earthquakes affect St Paul's?—Tests being made in the Crypt.
21. C.S.I. Co., Box 2, Letter, E Darwin to H Darwin, 28 May 1907
22. C.S.I. Co., Box 2, Letter, E Darwin to H Darwin, 5 June 1907.
23. C.S.I. Co., Box 2, Letter, E Darwin to H Darwin, undated ('Thursday evening').
24. C.S.I. Co., Box 2, Letter, E Darwin to H Darwin, 11 June 1907.
25. Foster C E 9 April 1907, British Patent 8205/07: Improvements in Relay Mechanism for use in Indicating or Recording Instruments.
26. C.S.I. Co., Box 2, Letter, E Darwin to H Darwin, 9 Mar. 1908.
27. C.S.I. Co., Box 2, Letter, E Darwin to H Darwin, 10 Mar. 1908.
28. C.S.I. Co., Box 2, Letter, E Darwin to H Darwin, 30 Mar. 1908.
29. C.S.I. Co., Box 2, Letter, H Darwin to R S Whipple, 17 Feb. 1925.
30. C.S.I. Co., Box 2, Letter-book p 20, R S Whipple to W Hall, 31 Jan. 1899.
31. C.S.I. Co., Box 2, Letter-book p 33, R S Whipple to R H Chilton, 1 Feb. 1899.
32. C.S.I. Co., Catalogues 1912–15, List No. 207 (May 1913) Electrocardiographic Apparatus (Taylor-Cambridge).
33. Scott R F 1913 *Scott's Last Expedition* (London: Murray) p 217.

34.   Wilson C T R 1911 On a method of making visible the paths of ionising particles through a gas. *Proc. R. Soc.* A **LXXXV** pp 285–8.
35.   Wilson C T R 1912 On an expansion apparatus for making visible the tracks of ionising particles in gases and some results obtained by its use. *Proc. R. Soc.* A, **LXXXVII** pp 277–92.
36.   *The Electrician.* 15 Jan. 1915 **LXXIV** pp 488–91. The works of The Cambridge Scientific Instrument Co. Ltd.

Further Reading

Barron S L 1950 *The Development of the Duddell Oscillograph* (London: Cambridge Instrument Company—Cambridge Monograph No. 2).

Barron S L 1952 *The Development of the Electrocardiograph* (London: Cambridge Instrument Company—Cambridge Monograph No. 5).

Briggs G E 1948 *Obit. Not. Fell. R. Soc,* **5**, pp 651–8. Frederick Frost Blackman 1866–1947.

Cambridge Daily News, 12 Sept. 1958. Obituary: C C Mason.

Dictionary of National Biography: 1922–30, Hugh Longbourne Callendar.

Dictionary of National Biography: 1941–50, Sir William Napier Shaw.

Engineering 1953 **176** p 820. Obituary Notice—Robert S Whipple.

Gold E 1945–8, *Obit. Not. Fell. R. Soc. Lond.* **5** pp 203–30. William Napier Shaw 1854–1945.

Keith-Lucas A (ed.) 1934 *Keith Lucas* (Cambridge: Heffer).

Milne E A 1944 *Obit. Not. Fell. R. Soc.* **4** No. 13, pp 717–32. Hugh Frank Newall.

The Old Persean Society Chronicle, Oct. 1974, p 19. Obituary: Alderman F Doggett.

Proceedings of the Royal Society A 1918 **XCIV** pp. xxxiv–v. Obituary Notice —William du Bois Duddell 1872–1917.

The Story of Pye, 1962 (Cambridge: Pye Ltd).

Venn J A 1951 *Alumni Cantabrigienses Part II 1752–1900* (Cambridge: University Press). Mason, Cecil Charles.

CHAPTER 4

1.   C.S.I. Co., Box 33, MS, A F Wolfe: Extracts from Board Minutes, undated.
2.   *See* ref. 1 above (Report to Shareholders: March 1917).
3.   *See* ref. 1 above.
4.   Dar. 219, Corrected proof copy for entry in *The Roll of Honour* (London: Standard Art Book Company), 13 May 1916. Erasmus Darwin: Second Lieutenant, 4th Battalion, Alaxendra, Princess of Wales, Own Yorkshire Regiment.
5.   Thomson J J 1936 *Recollections and Reflections* (London: Bell) pp 206–7.
6.   *Engineering* 1945 **159** p 402. 50 Years of Scientific Instrument Manufacture.
7.   Public Record Office, BT/55/22, Engineering Industries Enquiry, R S Whipple: Evidence, 7 September 1916.
8.   Shakespear G A 1923 *PSI (Birmingham University Archives),* **II**, p 46. The Katharometer.
9.   Ministry of Home Security Air Raid Precautions Department, 1939, *The Detection and Identification of War Gases* (London: HMSO).
10.   Hunt I F Letter to M J G Cattermole, 31 July 1984.
11.   Moon P B and Ibbs T L July 1980 *Physics at Birmingham 1880–1980* (Birmingham: University of Birmingham Department of Physics) p 13.
12.   *Cambridge Independent Press and Cambridgeshire Weekly News Express* 28 Mar. 1919. How Cambridge helped to win the war—Mr R S Whipple's Address to the Chamber of Commerce.
13.   C.S.I. Co., Box 34, Invitation Card, 4 Nov. 1918, and Concert Programme, undated.

14. Bragg W L, Dowson A H and Hemming H H 1971 *Artillery Survey in the First World War* (London: Field Survey Association) p 36.
15. Moon P B and Ibbs T L *loc. cit.* pp 13–14.
16. C.S.I. Co., Box 16, Letter, R S Whipple to Mrs S A Bolton, 16 Oct. 1917.
17. *Engineering* 1945 **159** p 501. 50 Years of Scientific Instrument Manufacture.
18. *75 Years of Successful Endeavour 1881–1956*, 1956 (London: Cambridge Instrument Company) p 12.
19. Jellicoe Earl 1934 *The Submarine Peril* (London: Cassell & Co.) p 12.
20. Wood A B July 1965 *J. R. Nav. Scient. Serv.* **20** No. 4, p 32. From the Board of Invention and Research to the Royal Naval Scientific Service.
21. Bacon R H 1929 *The Life of Lord Fisher of Kilverstone* (London: Hodder & Stoughton) **II**, p 286.
22. *See* ref. 18 above, pp 12 and 19.
23. Wood A B *loc. cit.* pp 35–6.
24. Wood A B *loc. cit.* p 25.
25. Wood A B *loc. cit.* p 55.
26. Cambs. Collection, pam C76.9, TS, C S Manning: *The Cinemas of Cambridge*, 11 April 1983.
27. *See* ref. 1 above.
28. County Record Office, C.S.I. Co. Trade School Log Book, 1917–21.

Further Reading

Barron S L 1951 *The Thermal Conductivity Method of Gas Analysis* (London: Cambridge Instrument Company—Cambridge Monograph No. 3).
Darwin H and Bayliss W M 1917–19 *Proc. R. Soc.* B **XC**, xxxi–xlii. Obituary Notice: Keith Lucas 1879–1916.
Dewar G A B 1921 *The Great Munition Feat; 1914–18* (London: Constable).
Dictionary of National Biography: 1931–40, Sir John Cunningham McLennan.
Dictionary of National Biography: 1961–70. Sir Charles Galton Darwin.
Goodeve C F 1972 *Biogr. Mem. Fellows R. Soc.* **18** pp 525–48. Frank Edward Smith.
Innes J R 1935 *Flash Spotters and Sound Rangers* (London: George Allen & Unwin).
Keith-Lucas A (ed.) 1934 *Keith Lucas* (Cambridge: Heffer).
Langton H H 1939 *Sir John Cunningham McLennan—A Memoir* (Toronto: University of Toronto Press).
Nature 1935 **CXXXVI** pp 633–4. Obituary: Sir John McLennan, KBE, FRS.
Nature 1951 **CLXVIII** p 496. Obituary Notice: Dr G A Shakespear.
Newnham College Roll: Letter, January 1947, pp 47–9 and Frontispiece. Obituary Notice: Dame Ethel Shakespear.
13. Ordway F I and Sharpe M R 1979 *The Rocket Team* (London: Heinemann).
14. Venn J A 1953 *Alumni Cantabrigienses Part II 1752–1900* (Cambridge: University Press). Shakespear, Gilbert Arden.

CHAPTER 5

1. C.S.I. Co., Box 33, MS, A F Wolfe: Extracts from Board Minutes, undated.
2. *English Mechanics and World of Science* 1896 **63** p 11—Scientific News; pp 51/2—The Theatrograph.
3. *Strand Magazine* 1896 **XII,** pp 134–40. The Prince's Derby.
4. Eccles W H 1943 *Electronic Engineering* **XVI** pp 99–102. Obituary: Robert W Paul.
5. *The Electrical Review* 1914 **75** pp 495–8. Mr Robert W Paul's Electrical Instrument Works at New Southgate.
6. C.S.I. Co., Box 33, Pamphlet, R W Paul: Address to Employees, 10 Aug. 1914.
7. Whipple R S 1943 *Proc. Phys. Soc.* **LV** pp 502–5. Obituary Notice: Robert William Paul.

8.   *See* ref. 4 above.

9.   Wood A B July 1965 *J. R. Nav. Scient. Serv.* **20** No. 4, p 31. From the Board of Invention and Research to the Royal Naval Scientific Service.

10.   Tookey Kerridge P M 1934 Artificial respiration for two years. *Lancet* **CCXXVI** pp 786–8.

11.   Collins W G and The Cambridge and Paul Instrument Co. Ltd, 12 March 1923, British Patent 195,116: Improvements in and relating to the Recording of Movements.

12.   *Journal of Scientific Instruments* 1925 **II** No. 4, pp 131–5. Cambridge Stress Recorder (Collins' Patent).

13.   *Engineering* 1925 **119** p 271. The Cambridge Vibrograph.

14.   Sorenson S P L 1909 Etudes enzymatiques; II: Sur la mesure et l'importance de la concentration des ions hydrogène dans les réactions enzymatiques. *C. R. Trav. Lab. Carlsberg* **8** p 1.

15.   Barron S L *c.* 1944, *The Export Review* (of the British Drug and Chemical Industries). The Development of pH Apparatus in Great Britain.

16.   Orchard J L and Cambridge Instrument Co. Ltd, 4 March 1926, British Patent 248,301: Improvements in and relating to Temperature-measuring Devices.

17.   *Engineering* 1936 **141** pp 445–7, 557 and 597. Total-heat Measuring Equipment at Orgreave By-product Plant.

18.   C.S.I. Co., Box 39, TS, Minutes of C.I.Co. Inc. Directors' Annual Meeting, 1 Dec. 1926.

19.   *Engineering* 1923 **115** pp 474–7. The Galitzin Seismographs.

Further Reading

Coe B 1981 *The History of Movie Photography* (London: Ash & Grant).

Dictionary of National Biography: 1961–70, Sir James Alan Noel Barlow.

Dictionary of National Biography: 1961–70, Sir Charles Galton Darwin.

Eccles W H 1930 *The Influence of Physical Research on the Development of Wireless* (London: Institute of Physics—Presidential Address).

The Times, 29 March 1943. Obituary Notice—Robert William Paul.

CHAPTER 6

1.   Raverat G 1952 *Period Piece* (London: Faber & Faber) pp 205–6.

2.   Dar. 166, Letters, W Hacon to C Darwin, 13 Oct. 1879, 4 Nov. 1879, 7 Nov. 1879, 10 Nov. 1879, 31 Dec. 1879.

3.   Raverat G *loc. cit.* pp 206–8.

4.   Raverat G *loc. cit.* pp 204–5.

5.   Raverat G *loc. cit.* p 203.

6.   *Cambridge University Reporter*, 29 Jan. 1924, **LIV** No. 23, pp 562–3. Gift to the University.

7.   *Cambridge Daily News*, 9 Nov. 1896. Cambridge Town Council—Election of Mayor.

8.   Dar. 219, Letter, H Darwin to G Darwin, 18 July 1877.

9.   Dar. 219, Letter, I Darwin to G and M Darwin, 5 Sept. 1884.

10.   C.S.I. Co., Box 1, Letter-book pp 362–9 H Darwin to C I Parkin, 3 Feb. 1880.

11.   Muggleton D J 1970 *A Postal History of Cambridge* (Cambridge: Cambridge Philatelic Society) p 97.

12.   C.S.I. Co., Box 1, Letter-book p 78, H Darwin to T H Farrer, 18 April 1883.

13.   C.S.I. Co., Box 3, Pamphlet, H Darwin: Engineering Laboratories, 22 Feb. 1890.

14.   Ewing J A 1933 *An Engineer's Outlook* (London: Methuen) p xi.

15.   Dar 219, Letters, J A Ewing to H Darwin, 14 Oct. 1890, 29 Oct. 1890, 5 Nov. 1890, 14 Nov. 1890.

16. Ewing A W 1939 *The Man of Room 40* (London: Hutchinson) p 100.
17. *Cambridge Independent Press*, 13 Nov. 1896. The Ex-Mayor of Cambridge-
     —Complimentary Dinner.
18. C.S.I. Co., Box 2, Letter (MS Copy), J A Ewing to I Darwin, 27 Sept. 1928.
19. Darwin H and Burton C V. 1904 *Engineering* **78** pp 352–4, Side-slip in
     Motor-Cars.
20. Darwin H 1913 *Aeronaut. J.* **XVII** pp 170–85. Scientific instruments, their
     design and use in aeronautics.
21. Darwin H Nov. 1913 *Nature* **XCII** pp 370–1. Migration routes.
22. C.S.I. Co., Box 2, Letter, M O'Gorman to R S Whipple, 8 Jan. 1943.
23. *The London Gazette*, 7 June 1918, p 6686. ('Horace Darwin Esq. FRS.
     Chairman of the Cambridge Scientific Instrument Co. Ltd. Member of the
     Munitions Inventions Department Panel.')
24. *The Times*, 24 Sept. 1928. Obituary Notice—Sir H Darwin.

Further Reading

The Carrow Works Magazine, Jan. 1914, **VII** No. 2, p 42. Obituary Notice
—James Stuart.
Colman H C 1905 *Jeremiah James Colman* (London: Privately Printed).
Dictionary of National Biography: 1931–40, Sir James Alfred Ewing.
Glazebrook R T 1935 James Alfred Ewing 1855–1935. *Obit. Not. Fell. R. Soc.*
1, No. 4, pp 475–92.
Hilken T J N 1967 *Engineering at Cambridge University 1783–1965* (Cambridge:
University Press).
Whipple R S Oct. 1928 Obituary—Sir Horace Darwin. *The Cambridge Review*
L, No. 1221, pp 48–50.
Woodcock J 1983, *75 Years of Voluntary Endeavour* (Cambridge: Cambridge-
shire Mental Welfare Association).

CHAPTER 7

1.   C.S.I. Co., Box 33, MS, A F Wolfe: Extracts from Board Minutes, undated.
2.   *Engineering* 1931 **132** pp 1–5. The Works of the Cambridge Instrument
     Company Ltd.
3.   Mallock R R M 1933 An electrical calculating machine. *Proc. R. Soc.* A **CXL**,
     pp 457–83.
4.   Mallock R R M 1933 British Patent 389,524.
5.   *Engineering* 1934 **137** pp 698–700. The Mallock Electrical Calculating
     Machine.
6.   Shute N 1954 *Slide Rule* (London: Heinemann) pp 72–3.
7.   *Nature* 1934 **CXXXIV** p 877. An electrical calculating machine.
8.   *Nature* 1935 **CXXXV** p 63. Electrical calculating machine for simultaneous
     equations.
9.   *Nature* 1937 **CXXXIX** pp 851–2. Calculating machines in scientific comput-
     ing.
10. Wilkes M V 1940 A Method of solving second order simultaneous linear
     differential equations using the Mallock machine. *Proc. Camb. Phil. Soc.* **36** pp
     204–8.
11. CUL UA COMP F1 1, TS Notes, M V Wilkes: The Functions of the
     Mathematical Laboratory, February 1946.
12. CUL UA COMP F1 2, TS, Report of the Mathematical Laboratory
     Committee to the Faculty Board of Mathematics, July 1947.
13. Besterman T, Gatty O 1934 Report of an investigation into the mediumship
     of Rudi Schneider. *Proc. Soc. Psych. Res.* **XLII** Part 137, pp 251–85.
14. *Engineering* 1934 **137** pp 55–8, 165–7 and 311–3. The Mersey Road Tunnel.
15. *Engineering* 1935 **140** pp 700–2. The control of the Mersey Tunnel ventilating
     system.

16.   *Measurement and Control* 1962 **1** No. 12, pp 537–9. Control of road tunnel atmosphere.

17.   C.S.I. Co., Box 31, *Cambridge Bulletin,* October 1938, **II** No. 31, p 1. Adam Hilger Ltd.

18.   C.S.I. Co., Box 50, Letter, R W Paul to R S Whipple, 21 July 1941.

19.   C.S.I. Co., Box 50, Letter, R S Whipple to R W Paul, 28 July 1941.

20.   C.S.I. Co., Box 50, Letter, R W Paul to R S Whipple, 25 Dec. 1941.

21.   *Daily Express,* 15 October 1959. The Cyclist.

22.   *Cambridge Daily News,* 15 October 1959. Symbol of faith in future.

23.   C.S.I. Co., Box 31, *Cambridge Bulletin.* January 1950, **III**, No. 52, p 2. Electronically Speaking.

24.   Castaing R and Guinier A 1949 *Proc. Int. Conf. Electron Microsc. Delft.* Application des sondes electroniques à l'analyse metallographie.

25.   Oatley C W 1982 The early history of the scanning electron microscope. *J. Appl. Phys.* **53**(2), pp R1–R13.

Further Reading

Biogr. Mem. Fellows R. Soc. 1976 **22** pp 381–413. Eric Keightley Rideal.

Dictionary of National Biography: 1961–70, Sir Frank Edward Smith.

Jervis P 1971/2, Innovation in electron optical instruments: two British case histories. *Res. Pol.* **I** No. 2.

Management Today, January 1967, pp 50–53 and 96. New Readings at Cambridge Instrument.

Menzies A C 1959 Frank Twyman. *Biogr. Mem. Fellows R. Soc.* **5** pp 269–70.

The Times, 21 June 1968. Lessons of the Cambridge Fight.

Who was who: 1971–80, Percy Dunsheath.

CHAPTER 8

1.   Hill J 1770 *The Construction of Timber* (London: Hill) pp 4–10.

2.   Adams G 1787 *Essays on the Microscope* (1st edition) (London: Adams) pp 21 and 124–5; Plate IX.

3.   Adams G 1798 *Essays on the Microscope* (2nd edition) (London: Jones) pp 21 and 127–8; Plate IX, Figs. 1 and 2.

4.   Thornton R 1799 Account of the new machine invented by the late Mr. Custance for making vegetable cuttings for the microscope. *Phil. Mag.* **III** pp 302–9; Plate VII.

5.   Raspail F V 1825 Développement de la fécule dans les organes de la fructification des céréales, et analyse microscopique de la fécule, suivie d'expériences propres à en expliquer la conversion en gomme. *Annls Sci. Nat.* **6** pp 224–39.

6.   Stilling B 1859 *Neue Untersuchungen über den Bau des Rückenmarks* (Cassel: Hotop).

7.   Rutherford W 1871 On some improvements in the mode of making sections of tissues for microscopical observation. *J. Anat. Physiol.* **V** pp 324–8.

8.   Rutherford W 1873 A new freezing microtome. *Trans R. Microsc. Soc.* **X** pp 185–9.

9.   Roy C S 1879–80 A new microtome. *J. Physiol. (Lond.)* **II** pp 19–23.

10.   Roy C S 1881 Neues Schnellgefrier-Microtom. *Arch. Mikrosk. Anat.* Band XIX, Heft 1, pp 137–43; Taf VI.

11.   Rivet G 1868 Sur un nouveau microtome. *Bull. Soc. Bot. Fr.* **15** pp 31–2.

12.   Gronland J 1878 Rivet's microtome and its use. *Am. J. Microsc.* **3** pp 25–9.

13.   Brandt A 1871 Ueber ein Mikrotom. *Arch. Mikrosk Anat.* Band VII, pp 175–9.

14.   Thoma R F K 1881 Ueber ein Mikrotom. *Virchows Arch. Path. Anal. Physiol.* **84**, pp 189–91.

15.   *Journal of the Royal Microscopical Society* 1883 pp 298–307. Thoma's sliding microtome.

16. C.S.I. Co., Box 34, Various photographs.
17. C.S.I. Co., Box 1, Letter-book pp 1–4, A G Dew-Smith to J D Munsen, 17 Feb. 1881.
18. Bidder G P 1941 Obituary: W H Caldwell. *Nature* **CXLVIII** pp 557–9.
19. C.S.I. Co., Box 34: TS, R S Whipple: Notes of a Conversation with Mr. W H Caldwell, October 1928; MS, R S Whipple: Preliminary notes of conversation, unsigned and undated.
20. Threlfall R 1930 The origin of the automatic microtome. *Biol. Rev.* **V** No. 4, pp 357–61.
21. C.S.I. Co., Box 34; Letter R S Whipple to R Threlfall, 13 March 1929; TS Copies, R Threlfall: Reports: A Substance for Imbedding; Imbedding Material (16 January 1884), 18 March 1929.
22. C.S.I. Co., Price Lists 1882–90. Caldwell's Automatic Microtome.
23. C.S.I. Co., Price Lists 1882–90. Rocking Microtome.

Further Reading
Bracegirdle B 1978 *A History of Microtechnique* (London: Heinemann).

CHAPTER 9

1. Richter C F 1958 *Elementary Seismology* (San Francisco: Freeman) p 210.
2. Mallett R 1858 On the facts and theory of earthquake phenomena. *Rep. Br. Ass. Advmt Sci.*, pp 73 and 78–9.
3. Mallett R *loc. cit.* pp 74–5.
4. Mallett R 1846 On the objects, construction and use of certain new instruments for self-registration of the passage of earthquake shocks. *Trans. R. Ir. Acad.*, **XXI** pp 107–13.
5. *Report of the British Association for the Advancement of Science* 1847 p xxi. Synopsis of grants of money appropriated to scientific objects in June 1847.
6. Mallett R 1853 Provisional report on earthquake wave transits; and on seismometrical instruments. *Rep. Br. Ass. Advmt Sci.* pp 86–7.
7. Ewing J A 1933 *An Engineer's Outlook* (London: Methuen) p xiv.
8. Ewing J A 1883 Earthquake measurement. *Memoirs of the Science Department, University of Tokio*, No. 9
9. Milne D 1842 On earthquakes in Great Britain. *Rep. Br. Ass. Advmt Sci.* pp 92–8.
10. Gray T 1881 On instruments for measuring and recording earthquake motion. *Phil. Mag.* **XII** pp 199–212.
11. C.S.I. Co., Price Lists 1882–90. Ewing's Seismographs (March 1889).
12. *See* ref. 11 above.

Further Reading
Glazebrook R T (ed) 1923 Seismometry. *A Dictionary of Applied Physics* (London: Macmillan & Co.) Vol. III, pp 735–41.

CHAPTER 10

1. Wedgwood J 1782 An attempt to make a thermometer for measuring the higher degrees of heat, from a red heat up to the strongest that vessels made of clay can support. *Phil. Trans. R. Soc.* **LXXII** pp 305–26.
2. Seebeck T J 1826 Ueber die magnetische Polarisation der Metalle und Erze durch Temperatur-Differenz. *Annln. Phys. Chem. (Poggendorff)*, **6** pp 130–60 and 253–86.
3. Becquerel A C 1826 Recherches sur les effets électriques de contact produits dans les changements de température, et application qu'on peut en faire à la détermination des hautes températures. *Annls Chim. Phys.* **31** pp 371–92.
4. Pouillet 1836 Recherches sur les hautes températures et sur plusieurs phénomènes qui en dépendent. *C. R. Hebd. Séanc. Acad. Sci. Paris* **III** pp 782–90.

5.   Pouillet 1837 Détermination des basses températures au moyen du pyromètre à air, du pyromètre magnétique et du thermomètre à alcool. *C. R. Hebd. Séanc. Acad. Sci. Paris* **IV** pp 513–9.

6.   Le Châtelier H 1886 Sur la variation produite par une élévation de température, dans la force électromotrice des couples thermo-électriques. *C. R. Hebd. Séanc. Acad. Sci. Paris* **CII** pp 819–22.

7.   Le Châtelier H 1887 De la mesure des températures élevées par les couples thermo-électriques. *J. Phys. Théor. Appl.* Series 2, **6** 23–31.

8.   Siemens W 1871 On the increase of electrical resistance in conductors with rise of temperature, and its application to the measure of ordinary and furnace temperatures; also on a simple method of measuring electrical resistances. *Proc. R. Soc.* **XIX** pp 443–5.

9.   *Report of the British Association for the Advancement of Science* 1874 pp 242–9. The new pyrometer of Mr Siemens.

10. Callendar H L 1887 On the practical measurement of temperature. *Phil. Trans. R. Soc.* A **178** pp 161–230.

11. Callendar H L 1891 On the construction of platinum thermometers. *Phil. Mag.* **XXXII** pp 104–13.

12. Callendar H L 1892 On platinum pyrometers. *J. Iron Steel Inst.* **1** pp 164–82.

13. C.S.I. Co., Catalogues 1889–1901, List No. 12 (June 1892), p 29. Callendar's Platinum Thermometer.

14. C.S.I. Co., Catalogues 1889–1901. Platinum Thermometers and Pyrometers, November 1893.

15. Callendar H L 1891 British Patents: 5342, Improvements in Electrical Thermometers or Pyrometers; 22326, Improvements in Wheatstone Bridge Apparatus and in the Adaptation of the same to the Measurement of Temperatures, Electric Potential and Current.

16. C.S.I. Co., Catalogues 1889–1901. Callendar Electric Recorders, Platinum Thermometers and Apparatus for the Measurement of Small Resistances (1901) p 29. Temperature Indicator.

17. C.S.I. Co., Catalogues 1902–5, List No. 25 (1904), Technical Thermometry, p 15.

18. C.S.I. Co., Catalogues 1905–11, Leaflet 76a (July 1910), Thermo-electric Pyrometers, p 2. Peake's Patent Compensating Leads.

19. Peake W S and C.S.I. Co., 7 Jan. 1909, British Patent 370/09: Thermo-electric Pyrometers.

20. Peake W S and C.S.I. Co., 21 Oct. 1910, British Patent 24457/10: Determination of Low Voltages.

21. C.S.I. Co., Catalogues 1905–11, List No. 94 (November 1911)—Scale Control Board (Peake's Patent).

22. Becquerel A E 1862 Recherches sur la détermination des hautes températures au moyen de l'intensité de la lumière émise par les corps incandescents. *C. R. Hebd. Séanc. Acad. Sci. Paris* **LV** pp 826–9.

23. Becquerel A E 1863 Recherches sur la détermination des hautes températures et l'irradiation des corps incandescents. *Annls. Chim. Phys.* **68** pp 49–143.

24. Le Châtelier H 1892 Sur la mesure optique des températures élevées. *C. R. Hebd. Séanc. Acad. Sci. Paris* **CXIV** pp 214–16.

25. Le Châtelier H 1892 Sur la mesure optique des températures élevées. *J. Phys. Théor. Appl.* Series 3, **1** pp 185–205.

26. Féry C 1902 La mesure des températures élevées et la loi de Stéfan. *C. R. Hebd. Séanc. Acad. Sci. Paris* **CXXXIV** pp 977–82.

27. Féry C 1904 Télescope pyrométrique. *J. Phys. Théor. Appl.* Series 4, **3**, pp 701–4.

28. C.S.I. Co., Catalogues 1902–5; List No. 30 (April 1905) and List No. 36 (October 1905)—The Féry Radiation Pyrometer.

Further Reading

The British Clayworker, 15 March 1906. The Féry Patent Radiation Pyrometer.

Burgess G K and Le Châtelier H 1912 *The Measurement of High Temperatures* (New York: Wiley).
Darling C R 1920 *Pyrometry* (London: Spon).
Iron and Coal Trades Review, 27 Oct. 1905. The Féry Radiation Pyrometer.

CHAPTER 11

1. Benoit J.-René 1881 Études sur l'appareil de M. Fizeau pour la mesure des dilations. *Trav. Mém. Bur. Int. Poids Mes.* **1**, p C.10–15.
2. C.S.I. Co., Box 3, Pamphlet, C.S.I. Co.: An Improved Form of Temperature Regulator, December 1885.
3. C.S.I. Co., Robert Paul's Catalogue 1914, p 254. Unipivot Relay Device or Alarm.
4. C.S.I. Co., Catalogues 1905–11, List No. 39 (1906), Technical Thermometry, p 6. Temperature Alarms.
5. Apthorpe W H and The Cambridge and Paul Instrument Co. Ltd, 15 March 1923, British Patent 194,597: An Adjustable Sensitive Electrical Regulating Device.
6. C.S.I. Co., Catalogues 1921–6, List No. 150 (December 1926), Cambridge Automatic Temperature Regulators, pp 4–5. Control Units: Electrical Type.

CHAPTER 12

1. Callendar H L 1897 British Patent 16718; 1898, German Patent 104299; 1898, French Patent 276968.
2. C.S.I. Co., Catalogues 1905–11, List No. 39 (1906), Technical Thermometry, pp 3–4. Annealing Furnaces.
3. *Engineering* 1899 **67** pp 675–6. Callendar's Recorder and Platinum Thermometer.
4. C.S.I. Co., Catalogues 1889–1901. Callendar Electric Recorders, Platinum Thermometers and Apparatus for the Measurement of Small Resistances, 1901. p 15. Temperature or Pressure Regulators.
5. C.S.I. Co., Catalogues 1905–11, List No. 39 (1906), Technical Thermometry, p 25. Recording.

CHAPTER 13

1. Fahie J J 1931 Electricity and electromagnetism up to the time of the crowning work of Michael Faraday in 1831: A Retrospect. *J. Inst. Elect. Engrs* **69** II, pp 1351–3.
2. Oersted H C 1876 Experiments on the effect of electric action on the magnetic needle. (Translated from the Latin by Rev. J E Kempe.) *J. Soc. Telegr. Engrs* **V** pp 459–69.
3. De Launay L 1936 *Correspondance du Grand Ampère*, **2** (Paris: Librairie—Imprimerie Gauthier-Villars) pp 804–16. Bibliography of Ampère's publications.
4. Sturgeon W 1836 *Ann. Electricity, Magnetism and Chemistry*, **1** pp 3–5. The Galvanometer.
5. Pouillet 1837 Mémoire sur la pile de Volta et sur la loi générale de l'intensité que prennent les courants, soit qu'ils proviennent d'un seul élément, soit qu'ils proviennent d'une pile à grande ou à petite tension. *C. R. Hebd. Séanc. Acad. Sci. Paris* **IV** pp 267–79.
6. Sturgeon W 1838 *Ann. Electricity, Magnetism and Chemistry*, **2** pp 144–5 and Plate IV, Figs 31 and 32—Description of an electro-magnetic apparatus; pp 286–9 and Plate VIII, Fig 63—Dr Page's Rotary Multiplier or Astatic Galvanometer.
7. Ewing J A 1876 Thomson's Siphon Recorder. *J. Soc. Telegr. Engrs* **V** pp 185–212.
8. *Comptes Rendus hebdomadaires des séances de l'Académie des Sciences* 1882 **XCIV** pp 1347–50. Galvanomètre apériodique de MM Deprez et d'Arsonval.

9. *Journal of the Society of Telegraph Engineers* 1883 **XII** p 448. Deprez and d'Arsonval—Dead-Beat Galvanometer.
10. Kohlrausch F 1894 *An Introduction to Physical Measurements* (London: Churchill) p 287. (Translation of 7th German edition by T Hutchinson Waller and H Richardson Proctor.)
11. Paul R W 1903 British Patents 6113 and 28234.
12. C.S.I. Co., Robert Paul's Catalogue 1914, pp 207–8. The Unipivot Principle.
13. Whipple R S 1943 Obituary Notice—Robert William Paul. *Proc. Phys. Soc.* **LV** pp 502–5.

Further Reading

Drysdale C V, Jolley A C and Tagg G F 1952 *Electrical Measuring Instruments* Pt 1 (London: Chapman & Hall).
Dunsheath P., 1962, *A History of Electrical Engineering* (London: Faber & Faber).

CHAPTER 14

1. Faraday M 1832 Experimental researches in electricity. *Phil. Trans. R. Soc.* Part I, pp 125–62.
2. Joubert J 1880 Sur les courants alternatifs et la force électromotrice de l'arc électrique. *J. Phys. Théor. Appl.* **IX** pp 297–303.
3. Duddell W du B 1897 Oscillographs. *Electrician* **39** pp 636–8.
4. Blondel A 1891 The photographic record of alternate-current curves. *Electrician* **27** pp 603–4.
5. Blondel A 1893 Oscillographs: nouveaux appareils pour l'étude des oscillations électriques lentes. *C. R. Hebd. Séanc. Acad. Sci. Paris* **CXVI** pp 502–6.
6. Blondel A 1893 Conditions générales que doivent remplir les instruments enregistreurs ou indicateurs; problème de la synchronisation intégrale. *C. R. Hebd. Séanc. Acad. Sci. Paris* **CXVI** pp 748–52.
7. Ewing J A 1892 A magnetic curve tracer. *Rep. Br. Assoc. Advmt Sci.* pp 653–4.
8. Ewing J A and Klaasen H G 1893 Experiments made with the magnetic curve tracer. *Phil. Trans. R. Soc.* A **184** p 1025.
9. Barron S L 1950 *The Development of the Duddell Oscillograph* (London: Cambridge Instrument Company—Cambridge Monograph No. 2) Foreword.
10. *Report of the British Association for the Advancement of Science* 1897, p 575. An instrument for recording rapidly varying potential differences by W Duddell.
11. C.S.I. Co., Catalogues 1902–5, List No. 20—Duddell Patent Oscillographs.
12. C.S.I. Co., Catalogues 1902–5. Physical and Electrical Instruments (1902) pp 89–95. Duddell Patent Oscillographs
13. C.S.I. Co., Drawings Box 1, Duddell's drawings.

Further Reading

Bowers B 1982 *A History of Electric Light and Power* (London: Peter Peregrinus).
Derry T K and Williams T I 1960 *A Short History of Technology* (Oxford: The Clarendon Press).
Dunsheath P 1962 *A History of Electrical Engineering* (London: Faber & Faber).
Engineering 1900 **69** pp 582–4. The Duddell oscillograph.

CHAPTER 15

1. Kölliker A and Müller H 1855 Nachweis der negativen Schwankung des Muskelstroms am natürlich sich contrahirenden Muskel. *Verh. phys.-med. Ges. Würzt.* **VI** pp 528–33.
2. Sanderson J B and Page F J M 1879–80 On the time-relations of the excitatory process in the ventricle of the heart of the frog. *J. Physiol. (Lond.)* **II** pp 384–435.

3.   Sanderson J B and Page F J M 1883–4 On the electrical phenomena of the excitatory process in the heart of the frog and of the tortoise as investigated photographically. *J. Physiol. (Lond.)* **IV** pp 327–38.

4.   Waller A D 1887 A demonstration on man of electromotive changes accompanying the heart's beat. *J. Physiol. (Lond.)* **VIII** pp 229–34.

5.   Waller A D and Waymouth Reid E 1887 On the action of the excised mammalian heart. *Phil. Trans. R. Soc.* B **178** pp 215–56.

6.   Waller A D 1890 On the electromotive changes connected with the beat of the mammalian heart, and of the human heart in particular. *Phil. Trans. R. Soc.* B **180** pp 169–94.

7.   Bayliss W M and Starling E H 1892 On the electromotive phenomena of the mammalian heart. *Int. Mschr. Anat. Physiol.* **IX** pp 256–81.

8.   Ader C 1897 Sur un nouvel appareil enregistreur pour cables sous-marins. *C. R. Hebd. Séanc. Acad. Sci. Paris* **CXXIV** pp 1440–2.

9.   Einthoven W 1903 Ein neues galvanometer. *Annln Phys.* Series IV, **12** pp 1059–71.

10. Einthoven W 1904 Enregistrement galvanométrique de l'électrocardiogramme humain et contrôle des résultats obtenus par l'emploi de l'électromètre capillaire en physiologie. *Archs néerl. Sci.* Année 11 **9** pp 202–10.

11. Einthoven W 1908 Weiteres über das Elektrokardiogramm. *Pflügers Arch. ges. Physiol.* **122** pp 517–84.

12. C.S.I. Co., Box 16, Letters (TS copied extracts), R S Whipple to W Duddell, 15 June 1904 and W Duddell to R S Whipple.

13. C.S.I. Co., Catalogues 1905–11, List No. 53 (1908), Electrical Instruments, pp v and 14–21. The Einthoven String Galvanometer.

14. C.S.I. Co., Catalogues 1912–15, List No. 107 (May 1913)—Electrocardiographic Apparatus.

15. Boys C V 1887 On the production, properties and some suggested uses of the finest threads. *Proc. Phys. Soc.* **IX** pp 8–19.

16. *See* ref. 14 above, pp 15–16. Time Markers.

17. C.S.I. Co., Catalogues 1915–21, List No. 180 (1920), Cambridge Electrocardiographs, p 14. Time Marker.

18. *See* ref 17 above, p 17. Electrodes.

19. C.S.I. Co., Catalogues 1927–30, List No. 980 (1929), Cambridge Portable Electrocardiograph.

20. C.S.I. Co., Catalogues 1944–52, Sheet No. 263 (1944)—Cambridge Portable Cardiograph in leather case.

21. C.S.I. Co., Catalogues 1944–52, Sheets No. 296 and 296A (1952)—Cambridge Electrite Cardiograph.

22. C.S.I. Co., Catalogues, Box 66, Temporary List 341 (June 1960)—Cambridge Transrite Cardiograph.

23. C.S.I. Co., Catalogues, Box 66, List 341/1 (March 1963)—Transrite III Cardiograph.

24. C.S.I. Co., Catalogues, Box 66, List 341/2 (April 1967)—Transrite IIIA Cardiograph.

Further Reading

Barron S L 1952 *The Development of the Electrocardiograph* (London: Cambridge Instrument Company—Cambridge Monograph No. 5).

CHAPTER 16

1.   Leslie J 1804 *An Experimental Inquiry into the nature and Propagation of Heat* (London: J. Mawman, No. 22 Poultry) pp vii and x.

2.   Dalton J 1799 On the power of fluids to conduct heat. *Memoirs of the Literary and Philosophical Society of Manchester* **V** Part II pp 373–97.

3.   Thompson B (Count Rumford) 1792 Experiments on heat. *Phil. Trans. R. Soc.* Part I pp 48–80.

4.   Leslie J *loc. cit.* p 483.
5.   Davy H 1817 Some researches on flame. *Phil. Trans. R. Soc.* Part I, pp 45–76.
6.   Andrews T 1840 On the cooling power of gases. *Proc. R. Ir. Acad.* **I** pp 465–9.
7.   Grove W R 1845 On the application of voltaic ignition to lighting mines. *Phil. Mag.* **XXVII** pp 442–6.
8.   Magnus G 1861 *Phil. Mag.* Series IV **22** Part 1, pp 1–12; 85–106.
9.   Magnus G 1861 Über die Verbreitung der Wärme in den gasen. *Annln Phys. Chem. (Poggendorff)* **112** pp 497–548.
10.   Bottomley J T 1884 On the permanent temperatures of conductors through which an electric current is passing. *Proc. R. Soc.* **37** pp 177–89.
11.   Bottomley J T 1887 On radiation from dull and bright surfaces. *Proc. R. Soc.* **XLII** pp 433–7.
12.   Schleiermacher A 1888 Über die Wärmeleitung der Gase. *Annln Phys. Chem. (Wiedemann)* **34** pp 623–46.
13.   Schleiermacher A 1889 Über die Wärmeleitungsfähigkeit des Quecksilberdampfes. *Annln Phys. Chem. (Wiedemann)*, **36** pp 346–57.
14.   Goldschmidt R 1902 Thesis, Brussels University.
15.   Goldschmidt R 1911 *Phys. Z.* **12** p 417.
16.   Weaver E R, Palmer P E, Frantz H W, Ledig P G and Pickering S F 1920 Automatic methods of gas analysis depending upon thermal conductivity. *J. Ind. Engng Chem.* **12** p 359.
17.   Vereinigte Maschinenfabrik Augsburg und Maschinenbaugesellschaft Nürnberg, A-G 1904 Deutsches Republik Patent 165,349; British Patent 15,706.
18.   Koepsel A 1908 Über eine neue Methode zur fortlaufenden Analyse von Gasgemischen auf elektrischem Wege mit Anwendung auf die Bestimmung der Strömungsgeschwindigkeit von Gasen. *Ber. Dt. Phys. Ges.* pp 814–27.
19.   Koepsel A 1909 Bemerkungen und Nachträge zu dem Aufsatz: Über eine neue Methode zur fortlaufenden Analyse von Gasgemischen auf elektrischem Wege mit Anwendung auf die Bestimmung der Strömungsgeschwindigkeit von Gasen. *Ber. Dt. Phys. Ges.* pp 237–42.
20.   Siemens und Halske A-G 1913 Deutsches Republik Patent 283,677.
21.   Daynes H A and Shakespear G A 1920 The theory of the katharometer. *Proc. R. Soc. A* **XCVII** pp 273–86.
22.   Shakespear G A *Tech. Rep. Adv. Comm. Aeronaut.*
      1916–17, **2**, p 579 (Report No. 317); A New Permeability Tester for Balloon Fabrics.
      1917–18, **3**, pp 1080–6 (Reports and Memoranda No. 516); Further Notes on the Hydrogen Permeameter.
      1917–18, **3**, pp 1113–15 (Reports and Memoranda No. 517); Some Notes on Balloon Seams.
      1917–18, **3**, p 1116 (Reports and Memoranda No. 518); Results of some Experiments on the Permeability of Clear Delta Dope.
      1918–19, pp 1386–8 (Reports and Memoranda No. 447); On the Permeability of Films and Proofed Fabrics.
23.   Shakespear G A and Daynes H A *Tech. Rep. Adv. Comm. Aeronaut.*
      1917–18, **3**, pp 1087–99 (Reports and Memoranda No. 435); Further Applications of the Katharometer with an Investigation of some Sources of Error in the testing of Fabrics.
      1917–18, **3**, pp 1103–12 (New Series Reports and Memoranda No. 367); On the Diffusion of Hydrogen along the Textile of Balloon Fabrics with Special Reference to the Effect of Lateral Leakage at Seams.
24.   Barr G 1918–19 *Tech. Rep. Adv. Comm. Aeronaut.* p 1300 (Report No. 504). Evaluation of a Shakespear Permeameter.
25.   Shakespear G A, Daynes H A and Lambourn L J 1918–19 *Tech. Rep. Adv. Comm. Aeronaut.* pp 1380–5 (Reports and Memoranda No. 622). A Brief Account of some Experiments on the Permeability of Balloon Fabrics to Air.
26.   Shakespear G A 1919 British Patent 124,453; USA Patent 1,304,208.
27.   *See* ref. 16 above pp 359–65.

28. Weaver E R and Palmer P E 1920 The application of the thermal conductivity method to the automatic analysis of complex mixtures of gases. *J. Ind. Engng Chem.* **12** pp 894–9.

29. Palmer P E and Weaver E R 1924 *Technologic. Pap. Bur. Stand.* No. 249, **18** pp 35–100. Thermal conductivity method for the analysis of gases.

30. *The Daily Telegraph*, 23 July 1925. King and Queen at Royal Society.

31. C.S.I. Co., Catalogues 1927–30, List No. 144 (June 1929), Cambridge Gas Analysers (Electrical Type), p 18.

32. Daynes H A 1925 Demonstration of some experiments to illustrate the applications of the Shakespear katharometer. *Proc. Phys. Soc.* **XXXVII** p 349.

33. C.S.I. Co., Box 31, *Cambridge Bulletin*, October 1932, **I** No. 7, p 4. Sealed Type Katharometers.

34. C.S.I. Co., Catalogues 1936–43, List No 157 (March 1940), Cambridge Electrical CO_2 and CO Instruments, p 11.

Further Reading

Barron S L 1951 *The Thermal Conductivity Method of Gas Analysis* (London: Cambridge Instrument Company—Cambridge Monograph No. 3)

Daynes H A 1933 *Gas Analysis by Measurement of Thermal Conductivity* (Cambridge: University Press).

CHAPTER 17

1. Middleton W E Knowles 1965 *A History of the Theories of Rain* (London: Oldbourne Book Co. Ltd.) p 45.

2. Coulier P J 1875 Note sur une nouvelle propriété de l'air. *J. Pharm. Chim. Paris* **22** pp 165–73 and 254–5.

3. Aitken J 1881 On dust, fogs and clouds. *Trans. R. Soc. Edinb.* **30** pp 337–68.

4. Wilson C T R 1895 On the formation of a cloud in the absence of dust. *Proc. Camb. Phil. Soc.* **8** p 306.

5. Wilson C T R 1897 Condensation of water vapour in the presence of dust-free air and other gases. *Phil. Trans. R. Soc.* A **189** pp 265–307.

6. Wilson C T R 1896 The effect of Röntgen's rays on cloudy condensation. *Proc. R. Soc.* **LIX** pp 338–9.

7. Wilson C T R 1897 On the action of uranium rays on the condensation of water vapour. *Proc. Camb. Phil. Soc.* **9** p 333.

8. Wilson C T R 1897 On the production of a cloud by the action of ultra-violet light on moist air. *Proc. Camb. Phil. Soc.* **9** p 392.

9. Wilson C T R 1899 On the condensation nuclei produced in gases by the action of Röntgen rays, uranium rays, ultra-violet light and other agents. *Phil. Trans. R. Soc.* A **192** pp 403–53.

10. Wilson C. T. R. 1899 On the comparative efficiency as condensation nuclei of positively and negatively charged ions. *Phil. Trans. R. Soc.* A **193** pp 289–308.

11. Wilson C T R 1911 On a method of making visible the paths of ionising particles through a gas. *Proc. R. Soc* A **LXXXV** pp 285–8.

12. Wilson C T R 1912 On an expansion apparatus for making visible the tracks of ionising particles in gases and some results obtained by its use. *Proc. R. Soc.* A **LXXXVII** pp 277–92.

13. C.S.I. Co., Catalogues 1912–15, List No. 217 (August 1913)—The Wilson Expansion Apparatus, pp 1–3.

14. Shimizu T 1922 British Patent 177,353: Improvements in and relating to expansion apparatus for rendering visible the paths of ionizing particles.

15. C.S.I. Co., Catalogues 1921–6, List No. 106 (1921)—Ray-track Apparatus.

16. C.S.I. Co., Catalogues 1927–30, List No. 106 (May 1927)—Cambridge Ray-track Apparatus.

Further Reading

Barron S L 1952 *C T R Wilson and the Cloud Chamber* (London: Cambridge Instrument Company—Cambridge Monograph No. 4).

Blackett P M S 1960 *Biogr. Mem. Fellows R. Soc.* **6** pp 269–70. Charles Thomson Rees Wilson.

Wilson C T R 1959 Reminiscences of my early years. *Notes Rec. R. Soc. Lond.* **14** No. 2, pp 163–73.

INDEX